"no other gods"

"*no other* gods"

An Interpretation of the Biblical Myth for a Transbiblical Age

Phyllis Boswell Moore

Chiron Publications • Wilmette, Illinois

The Chiron Monograph Series, Volume VI
General Editors: Nathan Schwartz-Salant and Murray Stein
Managing Editor: Siobhan Drummond

Library of Congress Catalog Card Number: 91-25041

Printed in the United States of America.
Editing and book design by Siobhan Drummond.
Cover design by Michael Barron.
Cover photograph by Siobhan Drummond.

Library of Congress Cataloging-in-Publication Data:

Moore, Phyllis B.
    "No other gods" : an interpretation of the Biblical myth for a
transbiblical age / Phyllis Boswell Moore.
        p. cm. — (The Chiron monograph series ; v. 6)
    Includes bibliographical references.
    ISBN 978-1-63051-076-3
    1. God—Biblical teaching—Psychology. 2. Monotheism—Psychology.
3. Ego (Psychology)—Religious aspects. 4. Psychoanalysis and
religion. 5. Jung, C. G. (Carl Gustav), 1875–1961. I. Title.
II. Series.
BS544.M66 1992
291.2'11'019—dc20
                                                    91–25041
                                                    CIP

ISBN 0-933029-46-2

CONTENTS

FOREWORD

Near the end of his life, Paul Tillich is supposed to have said that were he to start his career over, he would begin by reading all the works of Jung and Eliade. If this is true, it might be because he glimpsed in the distant future the possibility of a work like Phyllis Moore's "*No Other Gods.*"

The title, "*No Other Gods,*" is taken, of course, from the First Commandment: "Thou shalt have no other gods before me." (Exodus 20:3). Yahweh's demand for mythic supremacy in this Commandment eventually became a theological conviction that there were indeed no other real gods, *period*. An original polytheistic pantheon, with one god asserting supremacy, was turned into a monotheistic conviction. As a consequence, the "other gods" disappeared altogether, except as threatening temptations or temptors, and the biblical view held that Yahweh rules all: He is the creator, the sustainer, and the redeemer for the whole world. This is the biblical myth.

If the Hebrews did not originate the idea of monotheism (it was probably the Egyptians), they certainly did, by their fierce loyalty to Yahweh, carry it a long way. Their God and His covenant with them defined their existence and provided the source of meaning for their life on earth. They were His chosen people, or, looked at another way, Yahweh was their chosen God, and they would please no other Gods before Him. This single-minded devotion to a single diety created a singular people, from whom have derived three of the world's major religions: Judaism, Christianity, and Islam, all of them masculine and monotheistic. (Christianity's Trinity is simply a differentiation internal to the single Godhead, not a polytheistic notion.)

Hebrew monotheism joined forces with Greek philosophy (not with Greek religion, which was floridly polytheistic) to provide the religious, philosophical, and intellectual underpinnings for Western culture over the past two millenia. Until recently, the idea that monotheism is superior to polytheism was not seriously questioned in the West. It was generally considered to be a higher kind of religious awareness than the ignorance of a pagan mentality that had not yet groped its way to the enlightenment of the monotheist or been vouchsafed a revelation. There was little appreciation for the diversity of consciousness made available by polytheistic religions. The monotheistic consensus of biblical religion cast a long shadow on earlier or foreign religious perceptions, and in that darkness only something lesser and inferior could be discerned.

This cultural and religious parochialism has been shattered in the twentieth century. Through the work of anthropologists and other sensitive students of world cultures and religions, the vision of Westerners has been opened up to include much broader vistas of authentic religious experience and mentation, and much of the bias imposed by the "no other gods" ideology of ancient Hebrew culture has been removed. An early warning of this revolution in perception came from Nietzsche when he put into the mouth of his prophet Zarathustra the famous announcement, "God is dead!" A familiar God image has most certainly died recently in the West.

Among those who have been most influential in expanding the religious horizon of the West in our century have been Carl Jung and Mircea Eliade. Jung proposed that all mythologies have a common source, the human collective unconscious, and that all human beings are therefore heir to all religions. There is no god or goddess who is utterly alien to anyone, and, in fact, all dieties have a place in the psyche's pantheon. This notion runs exactly counter to the "no other gods" injunction; it embraces *all* the gods. There are no "other" gods. Each image of God—whether male or female, animal or human or superhuman, concrete or abstract—sheds some additional light on the Wholeness of the God image embedded in the human psyche. Eliade's research and many publications, too, have set off a veritable avalanche of comparative studies, which have now made it possible for us parochial Westerners, locked into our cultural and religious blinders, to begin to apprehend what the "other Gods" are saying, what those images have to offer.

Nietzsche was correct that the parochial God image of biblical culture is dead. Jung and Eliade helped to dig His grave and many others attended the funeral and have either mourned or celebrated His demise. In the 1960s this death and burial were even acknowledged and openly celebrated in some seminaries and divinity schools. *"No Other Gods"* may be its tombstone. It is a radical and convincing work.

"No Other Gods" is a wide-ranging analysis of the biblical myth of God and of its impact on culture and human consciousness, from the perspective of the evolution of consciousness that precedes and postdates it. Moore deeply appreciates biblical thought and practice and understands the psychological value of this patriarchal, monotheistic movement. It created a new and distinctive kind of individual ego consciousness. But it did so at a great price, and Moore is fully aware of this, too. Those who attend to Moore's insights will come away from a reading of this profound and provocative work with a keen grasp of what the biblical vision of God and of man/woman have contributed, and denied, to the development of human consciousness. She also hints broadly at what will come along to supersede the biblical myth.

It is most regrettable that Phyllis Moore died so shortly after having finished writing this manuscript. When I first read it, I was astonished at its brilliance and self-confidence. Who *is* this radical person? I wondered. I had the privilege of meeting Phyllis several times during her last year of life, and I came to appreciate even more her intellectual rigor and the sparkling clarity of her vision. At first, she seemed to be all Southern charm and gentility, but quickly she became razor keen and adamantine. She knew her thoughts well, she had formulated her insights over many years of study and reflection, and she was now prepared to present her work to the world. It is a gem.

Masterful, too, is the editing by Siobhan Drummond, who began the task while Phyllis was still alive and then had to finish it alone, though under the general purview of Thomas Moore, Phyllis's husband, and myself. To Siobhan goes the credit for selecting, arranging, and unifying the pages here from a much larger manuscript. We have chosen the passages that represent the core of Phyllis's argument and portray her vision with the greatest sharpness and clarity.

I try to imagine Phyllis today. She is in quite a different place. I am sure she is pleased with this book and thrilled to have it out and being read and discussed. I also imagine her to be busy with some other study, for at Phyllis's core there was a passionate scholar. She delighted in ideas and words, and if there is an opportunity for pursuing that type of work on the other side, she must be doing just that. Over here, we miss her and the further contributions she surely would have made.

Murray Stein

ACKNOWLEDGMENTS

*P*hyllis, my wife, finalized arrangements for editing and publishing this book only a few weeks prior to her death from cancer. It is a condensed version of her 1989 doctorial dissertation. In that manuscript, she acknowledged the help of many, and I quote below part of her statement.

"I am grateful to the authors of the formidable body of literature which inspired me, in particular to June Singer and Ken Wilber who spoke most cogently to the issues of the dissertation. I am grateful to my hardworking and patient dissertation committee: Jill Mellick and Dwight Judy, both of the Institute of Transpersonal Psychology; and Loy Witherspoon, Professor of Religious Studies, at the University of North Carolina at Charlotte.

"Along the way, many people, to whom I am deeply grateful, encouraged me. The many are too numerous to be mentioned here by name. Without implicating them in any way for the finished product, I would like, however, to acknowledge a few. Richard Underwood, Professor of Religious Studies at the University of North Carolina at Charlotte, offered valuable suggestions along theoretical and organizational lines. Sandra and Brewster Beach, of the C. G. Jung Foundation in New York, and Murray Stein, of the C. G. Jung Institute of Chicago, had the patience to read and evaluate sections of this study along both Jungian and theological lines. Emma Lou Benignus, retired as Professor of Pastoral Theology of the Episcopal Divinity School and former director of studies at the Interfaith Metropolitan Theological Education, Incorporated (seminary known as Intermet), encouraged and critiqued this work out of the rich experience of her own spiritual life."

I am appreciative to those who encouraged my daughters and me to continue with the book's publication and to those who participated in making it possible. In particular, I thank June Singer for her timely advice and counsel; Siobhan Drummond, managing editor of Chiron Publications, for her superb editing job; Murray Stein for supervising the project; and the members of the Charlotte Friends of Jung for their sincere concerns.

Thomas M. Moore

Part One

Chapter One

THE EVOLUTION
OF THE
BIBLICAL GOD

*A*s evolution speeds onward, carrying us willy-nilly beyond the familiar parameters of the biblical god, we are led to consider that the biblical story—fundamental to Western civilization and playing an essential role in human development—may not be the whole story of human development, and thus cannot be the sole myth of an evolving humanity. In the postbiblical world of the Christian era, we increasingly encounter evidence of the advent of transbiblical myth. Both ontogenetically and phylogenetically, evolution nudges us forward, toward a higher consciousness, a new centering, a rereading of the biblical myth—but in terms of a larger, encompassing myth that heals the primal split in human consciousness.

In exploring the possibilities of such a hypothesis, we seek to develop principles for a new hermeneutical point of view, both accepting of and yet transcending the biblical tradition. These principles are derived primarily from the concepts of Jungian psychology but will be augmented by related disciplines.

Heisig encourages a hermeneutical application of Jungian psychology and makes a persuasive case for placing Jung's work "among the human rather than among the natural sciences," for subjecting it "not to the verification procedures" of natural science, but "to the canons of hermeneutical critique" (1979, p. 144). Jung's own scientific methodology (in contrast to natural science) was not by any means divorced from the mythic, but rather, retained the mythic as an essential (and scientific) aspect of human psychology. Jung's own explorations (in contrast to natural science) were not confined to the linear paradigm of history, but investigated other paradigms of consciousness as well.

The time and space of history, however, is the time and space of the development of natural science. The milieu of history provided the paradigm in which the natural sciences could evolve. Capra makes a case for this point of view most succinctly:

> The view of man as dominating nature and woman, and the belief in the superior role of the rational mind, have been supported and encouraged by the Judeo-Christian tradition, which adheres to the image of a male god, personification of supreme reason and source of ultimate power, who rules the world from above by imposing his divine law on it. The laws of nature searched for by the scientists were seen as reflections of this divine law, originating in the mind of God. (1982, p. 41)

We need to recognize, however, that the "mind of God" is the mind of Yahweh, the Logos of the biblical god. Thus the "laws of nature" have been subtly transformed, through the biblical genesis, into the "laws of Yahweh." What the scientists discover, therefore, are not the laws of nature, but the laws of ego — an ego itself demythologized and internalized in the personal psyche, locked into a subjective/objective dichotomy. In the world of natural science (the modern world), the human personal psyche occupies center stage, shouldering its singular responsibility for the world's being—running like Alice in Wonderland, as fast as it can, through the linear time/space of history, to stay where it is.

The internalized ego of scientific humanity is not, at this stage of evolution, transpersonalized (in Jungian terminology, it is not recentered in the Self). Ego consciousness at the level of natural science is still being formed in human consciousness. Natural science, in its assumption of ego centrality, fulfills an essential requirement for translating Yahweh into human consciousness, but it by no means represents the paradigmatic transformation of Yahwistic consciousness.

Jung himself, seeking to develop a transpersonal psychology for which there was no paradigmatic container, sought to protect his psychology from the dogmatic attacks of the Judeo-Christian tradition by attempting to disguise his psychology in the canons of natural science. He was often hardpressed, for the paradigm of natural science provided no hiding place. Modern science in itself is essentially biblical, and Jung was as apt to chafe at the restrictions of Yahwistic science as he was to take umbrage at the assumptions of Yahwistic theology. He referred, for instance, to the blind positivism of Yahwistic science (its strict adherence to the quantitative, its denial of the qualitative, its one-sided ego epistemology) as scientistic. In positing the scientific right of the internalized ego to probe even the sacred, Jung sought to dichotomize the physical and the metaphysical, to separate an experiential archetypal reality (about which something could be said psychologically) from a "revealed" spiritual reality (about which psychology was incompetent to speak). Jung's psychology pulled these two realities together into an amalgamated archetypal spectrum of consciousness which included both matter and spirit, both the human and the divine. The Jungian spectrum of consciousness existentialized (or actualized) the archetypal elements of human consciousness in ways unacceptable to ego consciousness. Jung sought both to redeem the goddesses and gods of nature and to open ego to higher, still latent, reaches of consciousness. Ultimately, Jung made no unbridgeable distinction between carbon (i.e., matter) and god, both being developmental aspects of a single spectrum of consciousness. This could not sit well in a paradigm of consciousness that theologically devalued carbon and scientifically ruled out god.

However, as Jung probed the overall mythic story, he seemed at times to lose sight of the mythic dimensions of ego, not always recognizing that ego per se is not merely "human," but is in itself archetypal. He tells us that, early on, in his school years, he discovered the "egoic" dimensions of Yahweh, but rejected those dimensions as theologically inept and godless (1965, p. 57). In his later years, Jung only partially recovered from this early rejection of the egoic implications of the biblical god. He recognized the place and essential importance of ego emergence in the spectrum, but did not definitively tie it in with the emergence and work of the god called Yahweh, nor did he exegete the biblical myth in those specific terms.

Thus Jung was not always clear about the radical ramifications of his own psychology for biblical hermeneutics. Even in his later years, he demanded of the biblical god transegoic, or ultimate, qualifications that this god, in the thrust of the biblical story, does not possess. Jung's difficulty in accepting Yahweh as "archetypal ego" presents a major hurdle in Jungian scholarship; nevertheless, it seems clear that a hermeneutical potential is contained in Jungian psychology which cannot be hidden behind the canons of natural science, and that this potential has essentially to do with the "imago dei," the image of god (Heisig 1979).

The major premises in this book will be drawn from three disciplines: analytical (or Jungian) psychology, transpersonal psychology, and biblical theology. In addition, since each of these disciplines finds a hermeneutical challenge and response in the growing corpus of feminist theology, feminist perspectives provide a fourth strain of thought. The inclusion of feminist theology possesses a symbolic significance of its own, as we shall see when we explore Jung's delineation of trinitarian and quarternitarian consciousness, in which the feminine aspects of deity take the lead.

In the process, each discipline will find itself qualified by the others. This particular convergence of disciplines is becoming apparent today, although in certain ways their convergence is being misconstrued. Terrien, for instance, in the practice of biblical theology, deplores the impact of Jungian psychology on biblical interpretation (1985, p. 60). His objection may be based on a misunderstanding of Jung's work. Similarly, a trend toward distortion has surfaced in the field of feminist theology, wherein the "socially constructed world" of patriarchy is "deontologized" or deprived of archetypal reality (Wehr 1985, pp. 23–26). The feminist attempt to deontologize patriarchy resolves itself into a sociological positivism, which is as much at loggerheads with the Jungian psychology it seeks to uphold as it is with biblical theology it seeks to correct. Such a position dismisses the integrity of myth altogether. It represents an attempt to contrive myth rather than to read myth. It ignores the archetypal process of evolution for short-term social gain, but this policy, not rooted in archetypal reality, cannot be sustained.

In the face of such misappropriation, Terrien quite rightly points out that the archetypal evidence of the biblical myth sometimes receives short shrift in Jungian-related argument. The Great Mother myths, for instance, are not read against the urgency of the evolutionary requirements of Yahweh, and the regressive aspects of the Great Mother are glossed over. Goddess culture is romanticized as equalitarian (Eisler 1987), ignoring the fact that human development was not yet fully egoic (not yet fully invested with personal identity) in the goddess cultures. The threshold of personhood (the development of ego consciousness) is crossed in the biblical myth.

Westman (1983), following Jung, opens evolution to a move beyond the biblical myth, to a move beyond ego consciousness. Terrien, by contrast, proclaiming the ultimacy of Yahweh, fails to come to grips with the real challenge afforded by Jungian and transpersonal psychology, of a transpersonal view of the psyche which transcends Yahweh. Terrien struggles against transcendence of the biblical story in a feminist era confronted by the regressive tendencies of Yahweh. Such a struggle, it seems to me, is ultimately in vain. Feminist theology (wrong in its denial of the archetypal validity of Yahwism) quite rightly draws our attention to the reactionary pull, or "psychic inertia" (Whitmont 1983), of Yahwism. Fixation on the myth of Yahweh, as Robert Moore (1987) points out, can no longer be tolerated. Yahwism per se, except as it is seen in a larger-than-biblical context, is no longer with, but against, the direction of evolution.

The postbiblical world has outgrown the biblical myth and moves toward transbiblical consciousness. We might ask: If the biblical myth is outmoded, is it thus obsolete? The answer to be given here is "no." Its essential meaning remains developmentally significant in both the overall evolutionary process (phylogenesis) and in the individual personality system (ontogenesis). Transformation, paradoxically, does not devalue transcended myth, but rather enhances it. The microcosm of the personal psyche moves that much nearer to the ultimate, evolutionary fulfillment of the macrocosm of the transpersonal psyche.

We have reached a point in the development of biblical hermeneutics where a convergence of disciplines is necessary to provide a larger perspective from which to view the biblical myth. Both feminist theology and biblical theology need to be rooted in archetypal totality and consciously aligned with the overall story of evolution. Such a consciousness prevents the claim of biblical theology that the biblical myth is ultimate and corrects the positivistic trend within feminist theology toward a dismissal (or essential misreading) of the biblical myth altogether.

In the field of biblical criticism itself, a new hermeneutical urgency seems to be making itself felt. A leading biblical theologian of today expresses this urgency as he writes: "Biblical hermeneutics – the science of biblical interpretation – lies at the heart of the crisis that smothers Christian life and thought today" (Terrien 1985, p. 11). Terrien's statement refers exclusively to the biblical myth, which, from Terrien's point of view, is the ultimate and absolute myth, containing the ultimate, essential truth of the one true god. Nevertheless, by its note of urgency, Terrien's statement suggests that a certain paradigm (generally accepted and taken for granted as a way of life) is drawing toward its close, and that, therefore, a new mythic understanding is essential in order to bring humanity (Christian life and thought) beyond its current crisis (its smothering) and into a higher potential, a larger breathing space.

Despite its biblical exclusiveness, Terrien's plea for a more substantive biblical hermeneutic implies the view of Jungian and transpersonal psychology that myth per se (all myth) is of essential importance to human existence. From the Jungian transpersonal point of view, myth guides the development of human consciousness and possesses an essential integrity which, in the long run, does not permit misrepresentation. Myth delineates and instills in human consciousness that which Jung called the a priori archetypal essentials of human existence, the primal energies (imaged in human consciousness as goddesses and gods) which motivate and guide evolution.

In the Jungian view, these archetypal essentials, these a priori organizing principles, cannot be gainsaid. Humanity is required to actualize its myths, as, in an Aristotelian sense, it is required to understand its history. It is permitted neither to misread its history nor to contrive its myths. This point of view, although it expands considerably upon Terrien's view of mythic truth, also underscores his sense of urgency in regard to the biblical myth.

In fact, as we shall come to discover, in the biblical myth, myth and history converge. From the biblical point of view, history *is* myth. It is my contention that the biblical myth contributes this unique essential – the mythic proportions of history – to the overall mythic story of evolution of human consciousness. History is the mythic milieu – the fundamental dimension of consciousness – of the biblical god called Yahweh. The continuum of history emerges in its fullest proportions in the wake of Yahweh. History is established in the biblical story as a specific paradigm of consciousness, a paradigm that underlies genesis and has become the current norm of human consciousness and existence.

It is the biblical god who establishes in human consciousness the essential categories and parameters of historical time/space. The god who calls himself Yahweh (the great "I AM") draws human existence into linear time and into differentiated space, or into historical time/space. Historical time/space provides the continuum through which the personal psyche develops, through which each human being is separated from every other human being, through which the penultimate subjective/objective dichotomy prevails—between personal beings, between humanity and animality, between humanity and physicality, between the human and the divine.

Historical time/space provides the continuum through which the great realm of nature is objectified and demythologized. The goddesses and gods of nature (the earthy or chthonic deities) disappear from Yahwistic consciousness. In the terms of depth psychology, they are repressed and demonized, rendered subconscious or unconscious. Thus the paradigm of history imposes upon nature a "thingness" devoid of consciousness, devoid of its chthonic deities, devoid of its own spirituality. The paradigm of history represents the creation of a consciousness which places the personal, ego-centered psyche in the forefront of human personality and the human personality in the forefront of evolution.

Yahweh is the god who instills ego ("I AM") consciousness as central to the personal psyche, and who thus creates (and seeks to create) humanity in his own image. Yahweh is a god who decrees "no other gods" and who thus places a barrier called "sin" between human personality and the goddesses and gods who instill other modes of consciousness. Yahweh instills within human consciousness a distinction between good and evil, a distinction relative to his own decrees and designed to sustain his own paradigm.

The biblical myth makes clear that the centralizing of ego in human consciousness requires both a decree of "no other gods" and the containing, transcendent-to-nature continuum of the time and space of history. The centralizing of ego requires a god who, in himself, is transcendent to nature, a suprahistorical Lord of History.[1]

As Terrien rightly perceives, there is a grave danger for our time and culture in a distorted hermeneutical approach to the biblical myth. Beyond this, however, I maintain that the crisis smothering us is deeper than a mere rereading of the Bible can resolve. It is a crisis that threatens not only Christian life

---

[1]Suprahistoricity, however, is not to be confused with transhistoricity. Suprahistorical deity posits history and ego centrality. Transhistorical deity moves beyond history and the ego-centered personal psyche into transpersonal consciousness. It is the budding emergence of a transhistorical and transpersonal archetypal reality into the still-dominant paradigm of history that now challenges the paradigm of history and its self-sufficient hermeneutic of the biblical myth.

and thought, but the human whole. To fixate upon the biblical myth as ultimate myth is, paradoxically, to distort the truth of history; and to distort the truth of history is to oppose the process of evolution in its thrust beyond the paradigm of history. It is this opposition that brings about a crisis of evolutionary direction. At stake is the fulfillment of the paradigm of history. At risk is the formation of, or the transformation into, a higher dimension of consciousness — the passage from historical time/space (which transformed prehistory) into the nonlinear time and space of the eschaton.

The Greek word *eschaton* is a New Testament word meaning "end-time." The concept, however, derives from the Old Testament expectation of the establishment of the Kingdom of Yahweh. This expectation has varied shades of meaning, but essentially, in both Testaments, it indicates an anticipated end-time of history, in which the ambiguities of history are overcome and the goals of history are accomplished. Thus, in biblical parlance, the eschaton is both a completion and an eternalization of the paradigm of history. Temporality is not an opposite, but an aspect of the eternal (Tillich 1951, pp. 144–147, 274–276).

In its completion and eternalization — as yet mysterious to ego consciousness — the biblical eschaton includes both the quick and the dead. In other words, at its eschaton, the paradigm of history comprehends not only those living in the end-time of history, but, retroactively, it comprehends also the dead, those seemingly lost through physical death from the Yahwistic domain of history. The biblical concept of the eschaton is that it both motivates history and preserves its fruits: the blossoming of ego in human consciousness.

This mysterious eschatological landscape is vouchsafed to ego by faith in the biblical god. It is not as yet a property of being that can be defined. Eschatological existence takes on new overtones, however, as we look from a Jungian perspective. From this perspective, we recognize in the eschaton not only the biblical fulfillment of history, but also the precipitation of a new transformative transcendence, a transcendence not only of nature, but also of history. Humanity (both the quick and the dead) has the potential to discover a new consciousness, higher than that afforded by the biblical myth and its god. Thus, from a Jungian transpersonal point of view, the eternalization in the psyche of the egoic paradigm of history (defeating the physical death) is but one phase of the evolutionary story. The next phase conjoins Yahweh to his defeated enemy — physical death. As we shall explore, physical death is an aspect of the evolutionary story belonging to the chthonic domain of the Great Mother (as she is mythically recalled in human consciousness) and her consort, "the prince of demons," the lord of chthonic physicality with its cycle of life and death.

In this sense, the current hermeneutical crisis begs further definition of Yahweh, the biblical god. Granting the trinitarian aseity (or ultimate essence) of Yahweh, the questions become: Does "Father, Son, and Holy Ghost" comprise the Godhead? Does the biblical trinity convey, or fail to convey, archetypal totality? Does thge biblical myth encompass, or fail to encompass, ontological essence (the whole truth of being)? Does the biblical myth, standing alone, carry humanity, either ontogenetically (pertaining to the individual member of a species) or phylogenetically (pertaining to the species as a whole) toward its highest potential, to the ultimate goal of evolution?

What is the ultimate goal of evolution? In the Jungian transpersonal perspective, it is to differentiate each of the elemental aspects of being, to make them conscious, and to fuse them into a monistic wholeness. Archetypal totality is a concept brought into prominence through Jungian psychology and referring to the ontological wholeness of being, to the full complement of primal energies by which life evolves. These primal energies derive from a monistic polarity composed of an archetypal feminine and an archetypal masculine. These energies, through the process of evolution, must ultimately be actualized, both ontogenetically and phylogenetically, in human consciousness. Thus archetypal totality fosters an evolutionary process, which cannot, in the long run of evolution, be contained in an incomplete god image or in a partial myth.

In Jung's terms, the basic movement of evolution is from an undifferentiated oneness through the differentiation of ego consciousness (which creates the personal psyche), toward a differentiated oneness (the reconstituted wholeness of the differentiated self). An opposition between the feminine and masculine principles which develops in the advent of the second phase must be resolved in the third phase. The third phase serves a transcendent, or integrative, function.

Wilber, a leading theoretician of transpersonal psychology, provides a more precise terminology for this process. As Wilber expresses it, the evolutionary process functions through developmental, or "phase-specific," myths, which are essential but not, in themselves, ultimate (1983b, p. 76). Phase-specific myths (and their phase-specific goddesses and gods) are thus to be ultimately transcended in evolutionary process. Transcendence, however, does not mean dissolution or loss of deity. Rather it means the integration of all aspects of deity (Jung's archetypal totality) into higher consciousness.

Both Wilber and Jung, in depicting evolutionary process, emphasize both aspects of the eschaton—the fulfillment (or victory) of the paradigm of history and its transcendence (or transformation). In Wilber's view, each developmental phase, or basic structure, of the evolutionary process must be fulfilled, completed, or translated into human consciousness, as well as transcended or transformed. Only through adequate translation can a clean differentiation into the emerging structure occur. Lacking appropriate translation, dissociation (or repression) occurs. Dissociation refers to unactualized, unintegrated, and thus split-off, archetypal energies pertaining to either the prior paradigm or a latent, not-yet-emerged paradigm. These splinter energy formations cling to the psyche, forming pockets of unconsciousness within the emergent paradigm. These (as Freud discovered and brought into scientific prominence) continue to demand appropriate translation into consciousness. Their energy is not lost, but pathologized, through dissociation or repression.

Jung recognized that these dissociated (or latent) archetypal energies manifest themselves in human consciousness in personalized form, in the collective milieu, as goddesses and gods, and in the personal psyche as complexes. Complexes function in the personal psyche (albeit neurotically) to actualize the unactualized, to translate the frustrated archetypal demands. In a sense, Jung depathologized pathology, finding in pathological display a teleological guide to the healthy development of the personal psyche, connecting the personal psyche with the emerging transpersonal dimension of consciousness.

The biblical myth in itself represents a depathologized pathology. It represents a cosmic dissociation, an archetypal (or primal) split between the feminine and the masculine. The Bible, in bald terms, presents the mythic record of a holy war—a total and uncompromising repudiation (or repression) of the primal archetypal feminine by the emergent archetypal masculine. Furthermore, each of these two basic primal forces are syzygistic. This means that each, in its own essence, contains both a feminine and masculine element, the one of which is dominant.

The archetypal feminine, in her original chthonic manifestation as the Great Mother, contains an impersonal masculinity (often presented in Jungian psychology as the ithyphallic, fertility consort of the Great Mother). This masculinity, attached to the archetypal feminine, opposes the Logos masculinity (the discriminating Word, or mind masculinity) of the archetypal masculine. The archetypal masculine seeks to superimpose its own differentiating Logos consciousness upon a chthonic, prepersonal humanity. It seeks to organize human consciousness around the centralizing force of ego, thereby creating in the human milieu the phenomenon of the personal psyche. Furthermore, it seeks to preserve the phenomenon of ego consciousness against physical death. And contained within Logos masculinity is a femininity which opposes the chthonic, indiscriminate Great Mother manifestation of the archetypal feminine.

This unresolved holy war between the primal syzygies fosters an ineluctable primal split in the human psyche: a complex which is of cosmic as well as personal dimension, with ontogenetic as well as phylogenetic ramifications. Somewhat in contradistinction to prevalent Jungian and transpersonal theory, but accepting of the biblical necessity, we will look at the primal split—this kink in the tail of evolution—not as inherently pathological, but as essential and deriving from evolutionary requirement. In the spirit of Jung, we will depathologize the seemingly pathological primal split.

From this it follows that the primal split in itself—or, as it also may be expressed, the radical separation between matriarchal and patriarchal consciousness—requires its own healthy fulfillment, or translation, in human consciousness. Patriarchal consciousness (formed at the direction of the primal archetypal masculine) has become pathological today, insisting upon its own ultimacy and resisting the new paradigm emerging. This—not the primal formation of patriarchy (too often the misguided target of feminist ire)—is the collective pathology that challenges biblical hermeneutics today. Two things, it would seem, are required of the biblically formed world: an appropriate and culminating *translation* on the stage of history of the biblical myth, so that *transformation* beyond the paradigm of history into transbiblical consciousness may occur.

Chapter Two

THE PROCESS OF HUMAN CHOICE

*B*asic to Jungian psychology is the idea of process. In his clinical endeavors, Jung discovered a developmental process inherent in the personality system and discovered that there are certain stages, or phases, of development that are organically and psychically obligatory to the growing personality — obligatory because they are archetypal. The archetypes, each in its differentiated essence, or aseity, are the organizing principles of the process of human development, describing the larger schema of an overall evolutionary process containing an innate teleological imperative (a teleos). In their undifferentiated, latent (and sometimes repressed) form, they compose a layer of the psyche which Jung referred to as the collective unconscious, belonging impartially to the human whole. The unfolding of the archetypal energies out of the collective unconscious, their ordered differentiation in human consciousness, is basic to the developmental process.

These differentiating primal energies tend initially to manifest themselves in human consciousness in the guise of goddesses and gods. Therefore, the individuation-evolutionary process would seem to comprise an overall mythic story, the story of the developmental emergence out of the collective unconscious of the goddesses and gods. Human consciousness per se is the prime carrier of evolution, the developmental arena of this evolutionary procession of the differentiating archetypal energies. Human consciousness receives and explicates the innate, ontological elements of being emerging mythically from the collective unconscious.

In Jung's conceptualization of the individuation-evolutionary process, the Self (the archetypal totality) exists first in unconscious or undifferentiated (pre-egoic) fusion (Jung 1951, par. 418). Fordham (1985) has emphasized the importance in personality development of this phase of the Self, relating it to the personal psyche as the primal self. As the primal self develops (in Fordham's terms, deintegrates) out of the collective unconscious, it gradually delimits itself and centers itself in ego consciousness, from which follows a conscious development of the personal psyche. The development of ego consciousness initiates the necessity of human choice, and this choice essentially is between the dictates of ego and the dictates of the pre-egoic, prepersonal instinctuality of the primal self inherent in the human constitution. As we shall see, this becomes an important point in the development of a Jungian hermeneutic of the biblical story. The primal self or pre-egoic instinctuality (very much a reality, as Jung consistently asserted) shows up in the biblical myth as "original sin." The biblical choice between the one true god of the biblical genesis, who is noncarnal and "good," and the allegedly false deities of the primal Self, who are carnal and "evil," was fraught from the very beginning with the ambivalence of psychological repression.

Despite this, however, in the perspective of Jungian psychology, the centering of ego is an essential requirement of evolution, a phase of the overall process that cannot be avoided. It is the midpoint, however, not the endpoint of personality development. The personal, egoic psyche must evolve into the transpersonal, transegoic psyche, and in this phase of evolution (both ontogenetically and phylogenetically) the primal self is reclaimed from repression and integrated into the total personality. Thus the centering of ego as an evolutionary phase is to be transcended, and ego consciousness per se is to be recentered (not decentered, or disintegrated) in the self. Under the aegis of ego, the personality is centered in a differentiated or conscious self, rather than the prior undifferentiated, preconscious primal self. The differentiated self is inclusive of ego, but also inclusive of the archetypal totality larger than ego. The pre-egoic energies are reactivated and legitimized, thus emerging from their period of egoic repression; concomitantly, latent energies are brought into play—the transegoic, or transpersonal. The personality, in its transpersonal formation, is both androgynous and microcosmic, a replication of the macrocosmic totality. It is this teleos, this evolutionary imperative, toward which human choice, the capacity initiated by ego, must ultimately move us.

Ontogenesis/phylogenesis and microcosm/macrocosm: these two sets of terms, working together, are basic to both Jungian and transpersonal psychology. Jung called his process of personality development the individuation process, and he recognized that the personal process of individuation echoes the overall process of evolution. Also, he recognized that the personal psyche, formed by the centering of ego, is intended finally to replicate the transpersonal psyche, which includes the totality of the Self. In Jung's estimation, the developmental process is both ontogenetic and phylogenetic, and also both microcosmic and macrocosmic. Simply put, these two sets of terms inform us that human consciousness ultimately reflects consciousness of all being.

By ontogenetic and phylogenetic, Jung indicated that the process of individuation-evolution occurs reciprocally within the individual and within humanity as a whole. Ontogeny (the development of the individual personality system) modifies and recapitulates phylogeny (the development of the species as a whole). Ontogeny, however, also carries the phylogenetic process forward. Archetypal innovation in the evolutionary process expresses itself initially through the individual: through "the epochal man" (Edinger 1984, p. 12) or "the Great Individual" (Neumann 1954, p. 424). Through this inherent reciprocity the phylogenetic advancement of humanity accrues to the individual, but also, in the long run of evolution, the advancement of the individual accrues to humanity as a whole.

This concept finds recent and unexpected confirmation in the biological discoveries of Rupert Sheldrake (1987). Sheldrake extends the evolutionary influence of the "Great Individual" to the formation of a "critical mass," a statistically significant number of individual members within a species (Grof 1985, p. 63). In Sheldrake's view, as critical mass forms around a new archetypal emergence, or new consciousness, a morphic resonance is set in motion, a resonance that permeates the morphogenetic (or phylogenetic) field of the species, and the new consciousness thus becomes the phylogenetic heritage of the species as a whole. This concept (which challenges the prevailing views of science) affords us a new and potentially clarifying way to examine biblical hermenutics. How does critical mass relate to archetypal demand (Yahweh's demand on human consciousness, for instance)? How does human choice relate to morphic resonance (the choice for or against Yahweh, for instance)? There is perhaps an inverse correlation between archetypal demand and the formation of critical mass—as the latter forms, the former recedes. Perhaps there is an inverse correlation between human choice and the phylogenetic effect of morphic resonance—as the latter is set in motion, the former is less critical.[1]

The next set of terms, also basic to Jung's thought, lift us out of our Newtonian-Cartesian heritage altogether and propel us into the esoteric atmosphere of transpersonal consciousness. *Microcosm* and *macrocosm* were rescued by Jung from the obscure alchemical depths of Hermetic philosophy (in Jung's opinion, an ancient precedent of "new science") and pressed into scientific service as empirical realities. Jung utilized these terms and the whole of the alchemical (or gnostic) tradition to indicate that the total ontology of all being—the macrocosm—is reflected in the microcosm of the individual personality system (or the personal psyche). The individual personality system develops, or individuates, both ontogenetically and phylogenetically, in response to the archetypal energies of the overall process of evolution.

---

[1]Sheldrake's version of this concept will be elaborated more fully in Chapter Nine, concerning the theoretical refinements of transpersonal psychology and its connection with the so-called "new sciences."

The Numinous God

The process of evolution can be discerned in an overall mythic story, a story anticipating the outworking of evolution in human consciousness. It is a story writ large on the human psyche by the mythological and religious systems of the world, and by the innate teleology of the macrocosm. Through the numinous activities of its goddesses and gods, mythology (including the biblical myth) conveys the archetypal energies of the macrocosm into the microcosm of the human milieu.

The word *numinous* (a term coined by the theologian, Rudolph Otto, and favored by Jung) conveys the immediate experience of a "living mythologem" (Jung 1952b, par. 450), an encounter with a living deity, one as yet unassimilated in ego consciousness and through whom the ego-centered personality is pulled beyond its current status. The term also applies to the encounter of a still pre-egoic humanity with the god, Yahweh, a numinous image of the ego archetype—a god who pulls humanity into ego consciousness (the "mental ego").

One sees Yahwistic numinosity in the biblical myth, in its most primal manifestation, as Abram is pulled out of Ur—a matriarchal culture, embedded in nature—to become Abraham, the "father" of a new culture—a patriarchal culture, embedded in history (Genesis 11–25). The distinction between these two cultures forms a paradigm, involving different worldviews deriving from different dimensions of consciousness. Primitive patriarchy, initially at great disadvantage in the face of a long-established matriarchal culture, required great numinosity in order to form its own critical mass in human consciousness. The "mighty acts" of Yahweh, as they are biblically termed, provided that numinous energy.

Jung also applied the term *enantiodromia* to the archetypal changes which are demanded of the evolving psyche. It is a Heraclitian term, familiar in ancient Greek philosophy, which captures the constancy of change. In the view of Heraclitus, nothing was absolute but change. As Jung saw it, whenever an aspect of the archetypal totality is unrecognized in consciousness, it generates a change factor in the psyche. Unactualized aspects of the archetypal totality accumulate a certain numinosity, a certain libido or psychic energy. As these gain strength enough to enter consciousness, they tend to upset the psyche, to disorient, but also to reorient. Thus, in Jungian terms, change is constant until the archetypal totality is fully expressed, until the microcosm fully reflects the macrocosm.

The terms *numinosity* and *enantiodromia* are connected with the term *liminality*, employed in Jungian literature by Robert Moore (1987, p. 153). In

Moore's usage, periods of transition in human consciousness are periods of liminality, of disorientation, of change from one form of consciousness into another. Periods of numinosity, enantiodromia, liminality, and discontinuity connect, both ontogenetically and phylogenetically, with the movement of consciousness from undifferentiated Self to ego consciousness to differentiated Self (or from prepersonal to personal to transpersonal modes of consciousness; or from matriarchal to patriarchal to androgynous being).

Paradoxically, Yahwistic numinosity is now at risk in its own historical milieu of ego consciousness, and his diminishing numinosity can be recovered only at a higher level of consciousness, as ego finds its higher centering in the Self. Biblical theologians have recognized a strange tension in the biblical myth between completion and incompletion. They speak of the "mighty acts of Yahweh" as proleptic, indicating that something outside the human milieu has intersected it or that something has happened archetypally within the human milieu, but yet it has not quite happened. In Sheldrake's terms, a morphic resonance has been set in motion, but it has not yet permeated the phylogenetic field of humanity in toto. The mighty acts of Yahweh (including the New Testament theology of the incarnation) have seeded human consciousness. They have set up a new morphic resonance. They have happened in history, yet await the eschaton of history for their fulfillment. Their full meaning, still in process, eludes us. Humanity veers between a fundamentalistic idolatry of the monotheistic god and the false independence of egoic secularity. The promise, or numinosity, of the beginning of history can be conclusive only at the end of history, only as a new period of numinosity (the biblical eschaton) emerges. Human consciousness is incomplete until the macrocosm brings forth the microcosm.

For Jung, *macrocosm* and *microcosm* were more encompassing terms than *phylogenesis* and *ontogenesis*. The latter refer to the evolutionary development of a specific species and its members (human or otherwise). The former terms refer exclusively to humanity, but they expand to include the whole individuation-evolutionary process. They indicate that potentially included within the human psyche is the whole evolutionary process, its archetypal entirety (its subhuman, pre-egoic human, egoic human, and transegoic human aspects). Microcosmic personality, reflecting the entirety of the macrocosm, designates the ultimate personality system, centered in Self, not ego. Nevertheless, it is clear in the Jungian perspective that microcosmic personality (with the potential of a microcosmic culture) cannot develop prior to the development of the personal, ego-centered psyche. Microcosmic personality requires the existence of an individual personality system secure in the stability of the mental ego. If the biblical god is to be taken as the god of ego formation, the god who insures (even in the face of physical death) the archetypal stability of the mental ego in human consciousness, this point becomes extremely important in biblical hermeneutics. The work of the biblical god must be "eternal-ized," but not "ultimatized," in the evolutionary process. The distinction between these two words, usually taken as synonymous, is important. The work of the biblical god is an essential aspect of human development (and therefore eternal), but, nevertheless, the work of Yahweh is developmentally penultimate, not ultimate.

The microcosmic/macrocosmic process, in Jung's view, is to be discerned in the complexes of the individual, and his psychology sought to develop clinical means by which this process could be facilitated. The complexes of the personal psyche were seen by Jung as subliminal structures in the nature of subpersonalities. They are not integrated into the mental ego structure of the personality, and thus, seen in the light of ego consciousness, they seem less than the mental ego. Nevertheless, complexes possess an unconscious auton-omy, a quasi-egoic structure of their own, which conflicts with the mental ego, but, in Jung's view, also compensates and complements the mental ego. Com-plexes reflect the archetypal energies of the Self, not merely as the person is indoctrinated in the ego world, but with an openness to the entirety of the macrocosm, its total consciousness, not merely its ego consciousness. Thus the Self in both of its aspects – the primal, undifferentiated (repressed) Self and the differentiated (latent) Self – is alive in the complexes.

This is, of course, a challenge to Judeo-Christian theology and remains an unsolved problem in the field of Judeo-Christian education, which perforce must focus exclusively on the biblical myth. It is difficult to indoctrinate a psyche with unconscious complexes and educationally impossible (although the effort has been made) to produce a psyche devoid of biblical "sin." The psycho-logical solution to ultimate psychological health is, of course, as Jung makes clear, not indoctrination, but transformation. The thrust of the complexes of the individual personality system toward transformation depathologizes the seemingly pathological, making regression into the primal self a pathway toward transformation, but making teleology, not etiology, the ultimate focus of Jungian psychology.

Complexes, in Jung's view, reveal the emotionally significant issues of the personality, the emotional deficits of archetypal expectations, the singular insufficiency of the biblical god. Despite biblical prohibition (and egoic repres-sion), complexes retain the hidden "other gods." At the core, complexes are always archetypal and thus, in the long run, irrepressible. They accumulate numinosity and generate enantiodromia in the personal psyche. Complexes manifest in various ways, but, in Jung's view, primarily through dreams, projec-tion, and synchronistic phenomena. These dynamics of the psyche challenge theological dogmatics.

The Manifestation of Yahweh

Dreams

In Jungian perspective, dreams present the psychic landscape, the archetypal drama, the emotional issues, which challenge the life process of the dreamer. They present the complexes in personalized, and sometimes in situational, form. Dreams speak symbolically, not in an effort to disguise their content, but in order to lead the personality beyond itself, into unknown territory, where the mental ego has not yet found its rational way (although, as we know from the biblical myth, dreams, along with the mighty acts of Yahweh, once led the psyche into mental ego). Dreams, in Jung's view, are not signs of the consciously known, but symbols leading toward the unknown, the unactualized aspects of the self. In Jung's view, it is not primarily the repressed and, therefore, disguised wishes of the dreamer that dreams present (as Freud had concluded), but the archetypal purposes of the macrocosm. Archetypes, whether emerging from the collective or the personal unconscious, do not seek to disguise themselves through the images of dreams, but to actualize themselves, to make the unconscious conscious to the ego personality. The image or symbol expresses precisely the essence of the archetype, not a disguise of it.

Dreams initiate a dialogue through which ego and the unconscious can communicate and debate, each complementing and supplementing the other. Dreams are compensatory to the conscious life of the dreamer and often hyperbolic in their attempt to communicate to the ego-delimited world. As the parables of Jesus functioned hyperbolically to correct egoic distortions of its own god (Yahweh), so dreams function to present the self (the archetypal totality) in its fullness. Dreams move the dreamer toward microcosmic personality, and sometimes toward epochal responsibility in the evolutionary process. Dreams are usually personal, directing the personal quest toward microcosmic wholeness. At times, however, dreams are transpersonal, directing not merely the personal process of the dreamer, but reaching through the individual personality system to the phylogenetic process of humanity as a whole. These general attributes of the unconscious manifested in dreams hold true also of the dynamics of projection and synchronicity.

Projection

Projection is the process of seeing in others those unconscious emotional contents (the complexes) which are unacknowledged within the psyche of the projector. Projection hangs, or hooks, the unconscious content onto others — another person or perhaps a situation. Edinger emphasizes that projection aims at personalizing archetypal energies, at bringing their essence into life within the personal psyche through the interpersonal and situational life of the individual. He prefers to think not of a "unilateral projection," but of "an archetypal field" in which persons (in particular patient and analyst) "share jointly" (1988, p. 279). As it often occurs, the image of a goddess or a god (the core of the complex) emerges into consciousness through projection. Such images may seem positive or negative, threatening or fulfilling, according to the cultural and interpersonal milieu, and according to the developmental experiences of the persons involved, but they are always numinous, carrying a tremendous sum of energy, a pull on the psyche that moves it in the direction of the conscious distillation of the projected archetype.

At times, as for dreams, the emergence is an isolated, ontogenetic phenomenon, effective for a particular individual. Other times, the archetypal emergence is epochal, a latent aspect of the collective unconscious. It spreads, forms a critical mass, and moves into the phylogenetic field of human development. This observation of Jung (affirmed by the experimental work of Sheldrake) addresses the Yahwistic emergence in the phylogenetic field of human consciousness through the avenues of Israel and the Church, and still later through the Umma of Islam. Israel, Church, and Umma seem to present a biblical (and koranic) illustration of the dynamics of morphic resonance and critical mass, related to the exclusive, monotheistic god of ego consciousness.

It would seem also, however, that Israel, Church, and Umma can represent Whitmont's "psychic inertia," seeking to curtail an epochal move beyond Yahweh. Moore (1987) speaks in terms of "pseudospeciation," the fixation of critical mass in its own phasic form, thereby obstructing new archetypal emergence. As such, Israel, Church, and Umma become theological obstacles to evolutionary process, stuck in a passing phase of the individuation-evolutionary process, not seeing their mythic particularity in the light of the overall mythic story.

The destructive or constructive effects of critical mass are thus somewhat uncertain. However, in the dynamics of Jungian psychology, dreams, projections, and synchronicity certainly seek to overleap theological dogma and religio-cultural rigidities. Projections must be withdrawn from the old images as critical mass forms anew in the collective psyche, seeking evolutionary redirection (an impetus beyond psychic inertia) in the light of new archetypal emergence.

Von Franz (1980) writes of the importance of projection, and of the withdrawal of projection, for the task of religious hermeneutics. She asks if, in the withdrawal of projection, we should deny the archetypal energies which manifest in human consciousness as goddesses and gods, or if we are to accept their archetypal reality and consciously assimilate their energies into the individuation-evolutionary process. She makes clear that Jung (in contrast to Freud) would say the latter, because he draws a basic distinction between archetypal image and archetypal essence. In Jung's thought, the images of deity are existential, not (in the parlance of existential philosophy) essential. The existential images of deity are the bearers of consciousness and culture in the human milieu. The archetypal essence, however, although symbolized or expressed through image, is independent of the image. The symbolic image, ultimately, is expendable; the essence is not. Essence is a priori and beyond the existential particularities of any deity or any projection. The essential archetypal energies are present, both ontogenetically and phylogenetically, both macrocosmically and microcosmically, even as the cultural projections onto specific symbols or images are withdrawn.

It is in this sense that we now seek the essence of Yahweh, even as the image of Yahweh loses its numinosity, even as ego capacity in the human milieu displaces the symbolic image of the god who conferred it, even as projection onto the great Word (and Word-Made-Flesh) god of the biblical story is withdrawn, even as the great god of the Bible — who refused any "graven" images of himself — dies. The two tablets of stone, the god-man named Jesus, the Koran — all from his heaven — which have conveyed his Word into the human arena, seem to have life now largely in the backwaters, the fixated or "fundamentalistic" areas of human consciousness. This is not to say that the fixated areas lack majority (to wit, the "moral majority"), but it is to say that they lack, to use Toynbee's term, the impetus of a "creative minority." In Sheldrake's words, they lack the thrust of a new "critical mass." In Wilber's words, they are in the nature of a backlash, estranged from the "growing tip" of evolution.[2] Nevertheless, the creative minority, and those who compose the growing tip of evolution, must comprehend the essence of the god called Yahweh/Christ/Allah.

Archetypal essence, in Jung's thought, is unknowable to the ego. Ego, it would seem, requires the image, an interpersonal dialogic "knowing" (in the sense of Buber's "I/Thou") or the objective knowledge of a subject (in the sense of modern science). Archetypal essence, however, seems to be knowable in a

---

[2]More on these thinkers and their terminology will be discussed in Chapters Four, Eight, and Nine.

gnostic sense. Admittedly, this is not altogether clear in Jung's thought, but the weight comes down in favor of immediate, epistemological participation in archetypal essence at the gnostic level. It is a knowing which goes beyond the image or, in effect, transcends the image. In Jung's view, this constituted in large degree the crisis of Job—that Job, unwittingly, transcended the current image of Yahweh and saw beyond the current archetypal distillation of Yahweh and thus precipitated the trinitarian unfolding and incarnation of Yahweh.[3] Distinctly clear in Jung's thought is that the egoic and gnostic modes of consciousness constitute contrasting epistemological avenues and that the inclusion of both in Jungian psychology presents a controversial aspect.[4]

Jung, in effect, revived the ancient feud between the exoteric and esoteric traditions of Yahwistic consciousness. He brought into the forefront of modern psychology, for reexamination, the symbolic meaning of Yahwistic consciousness, upon which both the Judeo-Christian tradition and modern science were built, the inner conflict of the Christian era of history. It was indeed a shaking of the paradigmatic foundations. The battle which Christian (and Judaic and Islamic) orthodoxy had thought decisively put to rest was again to be resumed, but at a higher level of consciousness. Moreover, it was now to be waged, not in the established and sacrosanct field of theology, but in the dubious and secular context of a hybrid brand of psychology.

Jung's protestations of theological and metaphysical innocence fell on deaf ears. His claim of psychological empiricism did little to assuage the injured feelings of both the scientifically and biblically astute. The latter worshipped a god who spoke Ego to ego, Person to person, and shut out of the human soul all other gods. To proclaim empirically, as science tended to proclaim, "no god" was bad enough (an intraparadigmatic conflict). To proclaim empirically, as Jung proclaimed, "many gods and goddesses" (often defining them as the "dark side of the biblical god") was worse (an interparadigmatic conflict).

---

[3]We will return to Jung's view of the drama of Job in Chapter Ten.

[4]Jung's interest in and openness to gnosticism brought him into conflict with the theological/scientific climate of the biblical world and, brought about a certain defensiveness, at times, a certain unclarity in his thought. Jung was vigorously attacked, by both Buber and Fromm in this regard, and, in the long run, his gnostic affinity (underscored in *Answer to Job*) cost him his friendship with the Dominican, Victor White. From the very beginning of Jung's fruitful association with Freud, it was a thorn in the flesh of Freud, who sought to maintain his own budding and highly problematic science within the classical context of science.

Introjection

Paralleling the dynamic of projection is the dynamic of introjection. Just as projection is an unconscious putting out of psychic content, so introjection is an unconscious taking in of psychic content. Introjection designates a psychological dynamic which accepts uncritically the indoctrination of religious and cultural mores, usually the parental worldview, but most certainly the prevalent paradigm, or god-view. Even a conscious rejection of these contents does not necessarily remove their unconscious power, but simply cathects the personality to their unconscious ("shadow") influence.

Introjection works in concert with repression. Introjection accepts indoctrination, while repression removes from consciousness those contents not compatible with indoctrination. Freud, discovering this dynamic, associated it in particular with his concept of the superego, which constitutes the psychic mainspring of repression in the ego personality. The ego personality thus is "programmed" with introjected contents, which tutor the intellect (the "mind") but seem often, although not always, to miss the affective center of the personal psyche (the "heart"). Introjection is thus a contributing factor in complex formation. It functions to hide the "other gods," those not accommodated in the conventional theological scheme of things. In Western, biblically formed culture, it has tended, on the one hand, to obey uncritically the biblical injunction: "You shall have no other gods [not to mention goddesses] before me" (Exodus 20:3). On the other hand, in the humanistic/scientific enterprise, deriving from Yahwistic consciousness, it has tended by logical extention to shrink even its one god into paradigmatic secularity.

For Freud (lacking Jung's distinction between archetypal essence and image), the Yahwistic essence was scientifically jettisoned with the Yahwistic image. The Yahwistic image had become a superegoic negative for Freud, the obverse of the Abrahamic experience, generating a negative image of the father/son relationship, throwing into dire relief the oedipal castration themes of Greek mythology. Circumcision, the sign and seal of Yahwistic humanity, branding the generative male organ with Yahwistic ownership (and dire consequences otherwise), underscored the patriarchal castration threat to chthonic masculinity. The incestuous specter of the mother/son relationship blinded Freud to a consideration of the positive aspects of matriarchal consciousness and convinced him that the need to divert (or "sublimate") raw, chthonic libido from the mother was the single motivating force for human development, and thus the sole source of civilization. Freud did not see that the primal energy of the Word-god, actualizing itself in human consciousness, had an archetypal and purposeful reality of its own and emerged of its own volition to establish its particular paradigm (the paradigm of Western civilization).

The validity in some cases of the Freudian "sublimation" point of view is not to be questioned, but its exclusivity and universal application, in Jung's opinion, was questionable. For Jung, Freud had merely negativized the exclusivity of the biblical god. He had reduced the archetypal energy (or libido) of Yahweh, and the libidinal entirety of the archetypal totality, to sublimated (actually desublimated) sexuality, but he had not moved beyond Yahweh, to whom he was held in negative cathexis. The founding father of depth psychology in actuality, it would seem, had stumbled into a mythic reality larger than the patriarchal worldview—into the "idian," impersonal, chthonic depths of sexuality—but his grasp of the mythic features of psychological development did not allow him to proceed through the muddy "occultism" of those depths, as he made clear to Jung (1965, p. 150). It was to Jung's dismay that Freud could not see Eros (chthonic sexuality) as a god. Freud's rejection of the Yahwistic image, which in effect was a rejection of all deity (and all libidinal energy except the libidinal conversion of sexuality), exposed him, in Jung's opinion, both to the repression and to the possession of Eros, rather than to the conscious assimilation of the sublimity of sexuality. Castration of an incestuous (oedipal) son by a superegoic (Yawistic) father was the obvious outcome of such a point of view. It produced the vicious cycle of constant fear between outraged superegoic fathers and patricidal sons, and this, in turn, for Freud, produced a sublimated (actually desublimated), civilized restraint, ironically divorced from the divine and teeming with complexes.

Introjection, it needs to be stressed, is not what Jung meant by withdrawal of projection. Withdrawal of projection means a conscious assimilation of the projected contents. It means a transcendence of mere introjection in favor of conscious (and critical) interaction with the archetypal energies. The personality recognizes that the essence of archetypal energy is not contained in the archetypal image itself (or in another person or situation), but is eternally active and energetically available apart from the image (person, or situation) and must be integrated into the overall developmental process of individuation-evolution. Thus the conscious assimilation of both Yahweh and Eros was the Jungian prescription. Neither phallic sublimation nor chthonic desublimation, which, in a sense, was the archetypal work of Yahweh, offered a final solution. Nevertheless, it must be noted for further discussion, that there is some question as to whether ego could form in human consciousness without the preliminary dynamic of introjection, without some "programming" of the mind, without some repression of the "other gods," without some resistance to the incestuous numinosity of the Great Mother. The question is important for biblical hermeneutics, since the biblical myth in its entirety is written against the incestuous numinosity of the Great Mother. Mature ego, developed in Torah and Eucharist (and including Muslim submission), derives from the superegoic base established in human consciousness through the emergence of Yahweh.

Synchronicity

The archetypal images of the goddesses and gods (hiding in the core of the personal complexes) would seem to manifest themselves initially through dreams and through projection, but, as these images emerge in human consciousness, they further activate the archetypal energies of the macrocosm in the human milieu. Jung coined the term *synchronicity* to designate this evolutionary dynamic and conceded, that it is perhaps a constant, although usually unnoted, occurrence, rather than the somewhat charismatic, unusual occurrence he originally depicted (Meier 1988, p. 321). Synchronicity denotes a correspondence between the microcosm and the macrocosm (a correspondence directed through the personal psyche by the complexes). Synchronistic phenomena involve connecting or corresponding events that are independent of the cause-and-effect syndrome of linear time. These meaningful coincidences bridge the different dimensions of time and space, aligning the prepersonal and transpersonal with the personal, or the nonhistorical with the historical.

Synchronicity becomes significant in the field of biblical hermeneutics, since the god of history, the suprahistorical source of the paradigm of history (in contradistinction to a transhistorical source), must move into and out of the human milieu synchronistically. The biblical concept of *kairos* (from the *koine*, or vernacular, Greek of the New Testament) is akin to Jung's concept of synchronicity. *Kairos* denotes "the fullness of time," or "the ripeness of time," as distinct from chronos, or linear time, which marches to a predictable past-present-future drumbeat. *Kairos*, in effect, denotes the numinous activity of Yahweh in the human milieu and, aligned with the concept of synchronicity, comprehends perhaps the whole of linear time.

The concepts of synchronicity and *kairos* also express the liminal response of the human psyche to a transitional condition induced by new archetypal activity. In the biblical myth, the emergence of the biblical patriarchs out of matriarchal culture, the exodus of the enslaved *bene Yisra'el* (the children of Israel) out of Egypt, the incarnational transition from Old to New Testament were kairotic (or synchronistic) events, involving an innovative approach of Yahweh himself to the human milieu. This multidimensional, synchronistic dynamic – confounding biblical "history" and biblical "myth" – has baffled biblical critics through generations of painstaking scholarship.

Jung saw and articulated, in the concept of synchronicity, the importance for human development of "meaningful coincidence," coincidence not determined by linear cause and effect (or the chronology of history). He recognized that correlative events could be multidimensional and that a certain numinosity, which led the personality forward, accompanied synchronicity. He discerned and utilized in his psychology the archetypal connections between all dimensions of consciousness. These dimensions—the matriarchal, partriarchal, and androgynous, or the prepersonal, personal, and transpersonal—contain within themselves many fine gradations and cultural gaps. No one mode of consciousness is immediately present, nor purely explicated, in the human milieu. Nevertheless, in the long view of evolutionary process, one mode seems to predominate (currently the personal) and to delineate the phylogenetic standard of human evolution, against which the developing personality (and culture) is measured.

The concept of synchronicity, as Jung developed it, carries with it the implication that archetypal energy is psychoid; that is, it is not purely psychic. It bridges matter and spirit. It encompasses, even in differentiation, both matter and spirit. Archetypal energy, in Jung's thought, is the expression of a dynamic spectrum of the elemental aspects of being—moving from matter to body to mind to higher soul/spirit (Jung 1954a, pars. 413–420). Each elemental aspect of the spectrum carried its own brand of consciousness (or soul). Ego consciousness, central to the archetypal energy of mind, was thus not to be considered as the only form and source of consciousness per se. Nor could physicality be considered as the sole property of the archetypal energies of the body. Mind can and, as the biblical myth implies, has produced its own distinct *prima materia* (its manna, its incarnation). The spectrum of consciousness, as Jung presented it, is analogous to the spectrum of light, stretching from the carbonic infrared of the earth to the spiritual ultraviolet of the heavens (heavens beyond Yahweh's heaven), and human consciousness ultimately encompasses the entire differentiated spectrum. The spectrum of consciousness and the elemental aspects of being are further refined in Wilber's thought and, as we shall explore in Chapter Eight, constitute the basic features of the transpersonal theory of the evolution of consciousness.

Thus the task of individuation-evolution, in order to encompass the entire macrocosmic spectrum of consciousness, is to open a synchronistic dialogue between the conscious ego structure of the personal psyche and the unconscious complexes of the personal psyche (including the superego). The complexes of the personal psyche connect it with the archetypal aspirations of the transpersonal psyche, so that gradually, as conscious integration occurs (and projections are withdrawn), microcosm comes to reflect macrocosm. The human personality system is recognized as the arena through which the macrocosm differentiates itself out of unconscious fusion. Through the personal psyche, centered in ego (or the differentiating capacity of mind), the macrocosm initially, but not finally, comes to actualize and "know" itself. This "knowing" is inclusive of both egoic and gnostic epistemologies. Thus microcosmic personality, both centered in ego and centering ego in the Self, is not only the planetary carrier of evolution, but also the ultimate goal of evolution.

In summary, from the perspective of Jungian psychology the dynamics of individuation-evolution occur by archetypal design. The function of myth and religion (including the biblical) is to energize and channel the ontogenetic/phylogenetic process of the evolution of human consciousness. The archetypal design is developmental, and each developmental phase or structure demands actualization (or translation) in the human milieu. The archetypal structures are enfolded as eternal potentialities in the macrocosm. They emerge as goddesses and gods in human consciousness, synchronistically, or as their time is ripe to eternalize themselves in human consciousness, so that microcosm comes gradually to reflect the macrocosm.

Chapter Three

PSYCHIC ANATOMY: EGO AND SELF

A natomy, both physical and psychical, in Jung's view, is archetypal. Each physical form, or species, develops according to an archetypal pattern, and each archetypal pattern carries within itself the blueprint (or teleos) for its further evolution in the realm of consciousness. The psychic anatomy, as Jung conceives it, is analogous to physical anatomy. It develops a skeletal structure distinctly germane to the species.

This does not mean, however, that the psychic anatomy is to be considered as an appendage to, or an epiphenomenon of, the physical anatomy, as it is scientifically (Jung would say scientistically) conceived. The psychic anatomy is potentially present in the collective unconscious and emerges as its time is ripe. The primal principles are a priori and provide the directive of all development. In Jung's view, archetypal energy is psychoid, meaning that the archetypal patterning is both physical and psychic, encompassing the total spectrum of consciousness. The psychoid nature of the archetypal organizing principles, which seek to actualize themselves in human consciousness, determines both the physical and the psychic aspects of humanity, and each is developmentally necessary to the other.

The two dominant structures of the human psychic anatomy, as set forth in Jungian psychology, are known as ego and self. These structures determine the basic dynamics of Jungian psychology; correlated with the archetypal feminine and the archetypal masculine, they also define the basic hermeneutical principle of the biblical story. We have discussed these two structures as the basic elements of a process (Chapter Two), but we must look at them now in terms of their unique structural capacities and their intrinsic hermeneutical connection with the whole mythic story, including the biblical myth. For purposes of this discussion, Ego and Self refer to the archetypal qualities as properties of the

FIGURE 3.1   **Taichitu**

Yin (dark): feminine principle
  with germ of Yang
Yang (light): masculine principle
  with germ of Yin

macrocosm, whereas ego and self refer to these same qualities as replicated in the personal psyche or, ultimately, the microcosmic personality.

The term *Self*, used in the Jungian sense, represents the archetypal totality of all being. It is a structure that organizes and contains the full complement of primal energies by which the individuation-evolutionary process occurs. The Self excludes no aspect of being; it includes the physical, mental, psychical, and spiritual elements of being and the mythic, or archetypal, energies that determine these elements. Thus the Self, in Jungian psychology, is synonymous with the ontology of the macrocosm. At its core, it consists of what Jung saw as the basic polarity of the macrocosm—the archetypal feminine and the archetypal masculine.

A significant model of the macrocosmic Self is provided by the Taoist symbol of the taichitu, depicting Yin and Yang as the feminine and masculine principles of all being (see Figure 3.1).

The taichitu, akin to the Sanskrit mandala, or circle of wholeness, indicates simultaneously the wholeness of the macrocosm and its basic polarity, its double-sexed, inherently androgynous nature. The taichitu, in other words, depicts a primal syzygy, a oneness composed of feminine and masculine principles.

Two features of the taichitu are of specific importance in developing a biblical hermeneutic from Jungian principles. First, the taichitu shows a peer (coequal) relationship between the two basic primal principles of being. They constitute a complementary, monistic polarity, not an antithetical, unequal duality – even though, from the egoic point of view, within the paradigm of history, they are experienced as such. A second feature of the taichitu (and one not clearly recognized in the Jungian literature) is its depiction of the syzygistic character of the archetypal feminine and the archetypal masculine per se, each in its own aseity, or essence. This archetypal situation is depicted by the germ of Yang within the feminine principle and the germ of Yin within the masculine principle. Each of the differentiated primal principles, the archetypal feminine and the archetypal masculine, is dominant, not one over the other, but each over its inner contrasexual opposite. Each represents a lesser syzygy that reflects the primal syzygy contrasexually, rather than coequally. Contrasexuality is indicative not of a peer relationship, but of a dominant/recessive relationship.

The important point for now, however, is that Self refers to the ontological totality and that ultimately the ontological totality constitutes a coequal monistic polarity. The Self, in other words, is not monotheistic, but monistic. It has a centering quality that pulls the disparate energies of a polarity into oneness. Monotheism prefigures the monistic centering quality of the Self: it organizes the human psyche at a centering point beyond identification with the polytheistic forces of nature, bringing these forces under its transcendent dominance. Monotheistic deity, in contrast to monistic deity, organizes by exclusion rather than inclusion. It seeks to differentiate, not to integrate.

Yahweh as Ego

According to our hypothesis, ego derives from an archetypal quality which is the psychological correlate of theological monotheism. We need, therefore, to look at the concept of ego in terms of the biblical myth as well as in terms of Jung's psychology. The question to be asked admittedly seems outrageous. To put it in its simplest terms, is Ego Yahweh and is Yahweh Ego? What are the connecting links between the Yahweh and ego consciousness? Does Yahweh fulfill mythologically the same function that ego fulfills psychologically? Does ego consciousness, in other words, derive from Yahweh? Here, we will examine the suggestion that without Yahweh (or the canonical experience of Yahweh) there would be no ego in the anatomy of the human psyche, and that, therefore, the biblical god is to be directly associated with ego and only indirectly with the Self.

In terms of Jungian psychology, ego refers to a specific, developmental aspect of self. Psychologically, ego prefigures self as monotheism prefigures monism. Ego relates to the mental aspect of human consciousness and is thus sometimes specified in psychological terms as the "mental ego."

Two structural characteristics of Ego/ego stand out. First of all, Ego/ego stands alone, in the archetypal heights and in the human milieu. Thus, the second characteristic of Ego/ego is that it is separate from the chthonic energies. It separates out from the realm of nature and from the chthonic energies of that realm. It moves in a different dimension of time and space, a paradigm of history as opposed to nature. It is separate from the body, which retains the chthonic energies of the natural realm and maintains the biorhythms of the natural realm. To borrow from Buber (1970), the relationship of Ego/ego to the world of nature, inclusive of the human body, is that of an "I" to an "it." Ego is transcendent to nature and does not participate in nature as one of nature's own. Ego creates the personal psyche, the ego-centered psyche, and thus is centered in itself, its own realm, the realm of personal mode consciousness, the "kingdom" of a personal god.

Ego, then, imparts a sense of I-ness (or I AM-ness) to the personality. Its relationship to other ego-centered personal psyches, including the Ego archetype, ideally is that of an "I" to a "Thou." In such a relationship, each person (including the personal god) remains centered in ego. Relatedness is from an exclusive center to an exclusive center, not from a joining within the encompassing center of the Self. Thus ego switches between two points of view – the I/it world of thingness (which includes the domain of nature) and the I/Thou world of interpersonal relationship. Both egoic points of view belong within the domain of personal mode consciousness.

Epistemologically and ethically, ego gets no higher than this. Nevertheless, in the exclusive centering of the personal psyche the evolutionary task of Ego is accomplished. It is an accomplishment not to be lightly dismissed. As Jung puts its, in the overall process of evolution, ego development is "the most difficult of all" (1940, par. 23). And, as he consistently maintained, ego development and maturation are to be considered as an essential and mandatory requirement of the overall evolutionary process.

There are, however, modes and degrees of consciousness other than ego, and thus there are archetypal references for consciousness other than the Ego archetype. Such a conclusion becomes obvious in the acceptance of a triphasic process of evolution, which derives from three distinct modes of consciousness: the matriarchal, which is both subpersonal (prehuman) and prepersonal; the patriarchal, which is personal and monotheistic; and the androgynous, which is transpersonal and monistic. The spectrum of consciousness, as we need always to remind ourselves, is subegoic, pre-egoic, egoic, and transegoic.

The Spectrum of Consciousness in the Myth

To look at the spectrum mythically, nature itself (the Great Mother of us all) would seem to carry a self-regulating, subpersonal form of consciousness.[1] Beyond the subpersonal, however, the redoubtable Great Mother and her chthonic consort initiated the prepersonal psyche. They left it sitting for aeons, however, within the subpersonal forces of nature. The prepersonal psyche refers to the early, primordial stages of human consciousness and corresponds to the nature of a budding personal psyche. The prepersonal psyche, although pre-egoic, is, nevertheless, not without egoic nuance, or rudimentary personality. It aligns with Fordham's definition of the primal self, indicating that the personal psyche is not yet formed and stabilized (deintegrated or differentiated) within the phylogenetic field of human consciousness. Humanity, at this point, has not yet transcended nature and thus orients itself within the chthonic and matriarchal forces of nature.

The complexes of the personal psyche provide psychological evidence of personalized chthonic energies within the monistic self. As Jung recognized, these complexes often (though not always) derive from the matriarchal substrate – split off and repressed in ego consciousness – and retain its archetypal energies. As Jung saw it, they connect "the living individual" with this substrate "by the bridge of emotion" (1965, p. 96).

We are predisposed to consider the matriarchal substrate – which, both ontogenetically and phylogenetically, is below the threshold of ego consciousness – as thus inferior to the egoic substrate. We are prone to forget that, although lower on the evolutionary scale, it is as essential as ego in the overall evolutionary scheme. Feminists, however, rediscovering this substrate, occasionally make the opposite error. They tend to erase the patriarchy from the mythic story and to romanticize the era of matriarchy. Jung's psychology reminds us that the Great Mother had her foibles also. She could be as wrathful and demanding as her archetypal opposite. She could be devouring. Many an aging king found out the hard way. Matriarchal culture had a way of resolving things through human sacrifice. Nevertheless, although it was probably a good idea to grow beyond it, we cannot overlook the fact that in its day matriarchal civilization reached a high point of complexity. Wilber (1981) describes this high point of matriarchal culture as "mythic membership."

---

[1]Research into such consciousness has been recently put forth as the Gaia theory (Lovelock 1979), which hypothesizes that the planet is a living organism. The theory finds support in both Jungian and transpersonal psychology.

Mythic membership culture constituted a kind of pre-egoic collective which failed to distinguish ego from ego, but which, nevertheless, brought the forces of nature more closely under human control and into agricultural commerce — creating, according to biblical description, a bountiful land of milk and honey. Such a culture, as we see from the biblical myth, had been created on Yahweh's land, which was all to the good, except that, of course, Yahweh expected to take over. This was not easy.

Fertility gods, consorts of the Great Mother, were prominent in mythic membership culture. They set up shop everywhere, fostering a kind of impersonal, ithyphallic sexualty, which was fine for agriculture and animal husbandry, but not so desirable for humanity, according to Yahweh. These fertility deities were exceedingly difficult to dislodge later on, when the psyche moved into the personal and attempted to focus itself on the ego god. Their names, in fact, were legion, as they informed a young man named Jesus, who was busy dislodging them from among the *bene Yisra'el* (Luke 8:30). But that was much later, when the *bene Yisra'el* were close to the zenith of ego development, close to the turning point of history and a long exile from the land of milk and honey, moving toward an almost global diaspora.

The biblical myth itself describes with grimness, but not without humor, the early Yahwistic takeover of the land of milk and honey. His primitive, nomadic Hebrews (which etymologically denotes "nobodies") swept through the matriarchal city-states of mythic membership culture and unexpectedly, against overwelming odds, conquered these gleaming, self-contained citadels of earthly abundance — seemingly impregnable to the likes of Yahweh, a god none too popular among goddesses and their devotees. By a rather staggering display of raw primitive power in the emerging continuum of history, the Hebrews began the long evolutionary struggle of displacing chthonic (or prepersonal) consciousness with Logos (or mental ego) consciousness.

In this displacement, chthonic consciousness is rendered unconscious to ego. Ego takes the center stage of evolution, spotlighting its own paradigm, the paradigm of history. On either side of the paradigm of history, the stage is darkened. Prepersonal and transpersonal modes of consciousness remain in shadow, defined only in reference to the mental ego. Through archaeology and related sciences, we can see the prehistorical, but just barely. Nevertheless, we can surmise, as Jung surmised, that the chthonic is there, a specific quality of consciousness alive in the archetypal totality of the monistic Self. And, inchoately, in the experience of a few, the teleological impetus of transpersonal consciousness pulls at the personal psyche, bespeaking a "knowing," an epistemologial pecularity, a *gnosis*, a cognitive intelligibility beyond ego, of which the mental ego is but a pale precursor.

For the moment, we want to return to the formation of the mental ego in itself, in its own aseity, as an essential constitutive element of human con-

sciousness. Although Jung's psychology emphasizes the evolutionary significance of the Self, it yields a great deal of evidence concerning the central
importance of the development and durability of ego in the evolution of consciousness. Where did it come from? Who formed it? Who sustains it?

Chapter Four

EGO AND THE ARCHETYPAL MASCULINE

A lthough occasionally disputed, it is generally conceded in Jungian psychology that the mental ego is the work of, and is thus dominated by, the archetypal masculine (the Yang element of the taichitu). The mental ego emerges gradually in the developmental process, in the wake of the previously dominant feminine (the Yin) and dominates (or represses) from human consciousness all other aspects of being. In particular, from the mythic point of view, the development of ego excludes the chthonic syzygy of the archetypal feminine and her inner masculine. Moreover, the emerging ego not only *displaces* the archetypal feminine, but also (albeit with extreme and somewhat esoteric caution) replaces it with the inner feminine (the germ of Yin) in the psychic economy, thus comprising a Logos syzygy.[1] The outcome of this archetypal situation (in which we now exist) is the creation of a patriarchal society dominated by a masculine deity, with a secondary positioning of the feminine and a repressed contrasexuality residing in each sex.

This Jungian position finds affirmation (although with a slightly different slant) in Toynbee's monumental *Study of History*. Toynbee speaks, for instance, of the "mythological clue" to civilization, by which he means that evolution moves and humanity develops in response to myth and not as a result of genetics or environment (1946, pp. 569–570). In effect, he bases his comprehensive analysis of the paradigm of history on the "mythological clue" which he finds provided by the elementary mythic factors of Yin and Yang. Although Toynbee does not speak of archetypes, or of archetypal feminine and masculine principles, the parallel is obvious. He traces the development of Western civilization (patriarchal society) to the activation of the Yang element in the

---

[1]This germ of Yin (this elusive "she" of Yahweh) is something of a biblical secret, and, until recently, she was something of a cultural secret as well. Feminist theology, however, has brought her to the fore of biblical exegesis.

soul, and he speaks of a "schism in the soul" comparable to the primal split. In response to this schism, there are two alternatives—the Yin response and the Yang response. The Yin alternative is that the soul "lets itself go" in the belief that, by giving free rein to its own spontaneous appetites and aversions, it will be living "according to nature" and will automatically receive back from that *mysterious goddess* the precious gift of creativity (Toynbee 1946, p. 429; italics added). We should not be surprised that the Yang response of the soul is to "'take itself in hand' and seek to discipline its "natural passions" in the belief that nature is the bane of creativity and not its source and that "to gain mastery over nature" is the only way of recovering the lost creative faculty (ibid., p. 429). The response of Yang sounds familiar because it is indeed the response of ego as it moves beyond the pre-egoic.

The "mysterious goddess," underscored above, is obscured in the main outlines of Toynbee's treatment of the paradigm of history; she is never brought fully into consciousness. But it is remarkable that she and the mythic element are there at all. It was certainly out of fashion: at the time when Toynbee used myth in a secular interpretation of secular history, biblical criticism was engaged in demythologizing the biblical myth. It is a strange twist of irony that two secular thinkers (a historian and a depth psychologist) picked up the importance of myth to history, while the custodians of the one and only myth of history were attempting to drop the mythic.

Toynbee goes on to struggle with the evolutionary elevation of the irascible, not very appealing, Jewish Lord of History above more genial, more appealing gods. He concludes that the god's personality was the key to his success. Yahweh, the great I AM, was intensely personal; he related Person to person—one might say Ego to ego—in the human milieu, and he took a very personal interest (both loving and wrathful) in his people and in humanity as a whole. On the strength of his forceful (even jealous) personality, Yahweh ruled out the mysterious goddess and her chthonic consorts. He in effect ruled out the Yin response to the schism of the soul or to the primal split. Creativity, the creativity of the soul, as Toynbee puts it, went in the other direction (ibid., pp. 502–505). The Yang phase of evolution had begun, and in its beginning was the Word, an irascible, superegoic word god, who made himself flesh.

Toynbee's history and Jung's psychology both find a basic orientation in the taichitu. Both systems recognize that the mental ego derives from the Yang principle of Logos masculinity. Logos masculinity (the archetypal masculine itself) constitutes a contrasexual singularity within the human psyche, a monotheistic entity which differentiates out of and denies monistic polarity, or the archetypal wholeness of the Self. The emergence of the mental ego engenders a primal split (a schism of the soul) between the archetypal feminine (Toynbee's mysterious goddess, known primally as the Great Mother) and the archetypal masculine (Toynbee's irascible Yahweh, known primally as the Great Father).

The evolution of human consciousness reflects this archetypal conflict, still raging in a patriarchal world, between the primal principles of being.

The main hermeneutical point to be gathered here is that ego is brought into prominence by the Great Father (or Word) energy of the archetypal masculine and a concomitant repression of the Great Mother (matter/body) energy of the archetypal feminine. From this perspective, one can see the beginning of the patriarchal world in Genesis and its envisioned ending (spanning both canons) in Revelation. In the parlance of biblical theology, "the one story of the Bible" (its Old and New Testaments) are alive in the psychological depths of depth psychology. In between Genesis and Revelation lies the biblical thrust toward the development of a masculine dominance and a recessive femininity in human consciousness.

The establishment of Logos masculinity in human consciousness is the overriding theme of the biblical myth. The creation of the personal psyche, or the establishment of Logos capacity in human personality, is the overriding task of the Great Father. As Toynbee recognizes, in all of the annals of mythology, among all of the other gods brought forth in human consciousness, this overriding task is nowhere more radically and more definitively undertaken than by the god called Yahweh. It is a task that brings the biblical god—the god of egoic mentality, the disincarnate "ungraven" Word god—into the time and space of history, into the throes of his own creation, through "incarnation."

This incarnation, this Torah or Logos-made-flesh (this unique substantiality of the trinitarian god), even in eucharistic presence, is substantially unique. It is concrete in history (Yahweh's own creative continuum), but transcendent to nature (the continuum of the mysterious goddess, or the Great Mother). Thus the incarnation of Yahweh radicalizes. It does not heal the primal split between the Yin and the Yang, the archetypal feminine and the archetypal masculine—on the contrary, it sharpens their opposition. The chthonic energy of the repressed Great Mother comes to the fore of evolution in the form of her own Yang energy. These two antithetical extremes of evolution are biblically symbolized by the figures of the Christ and the Antichrist—the Antichrist representing a potent concentration of the Legion globally exorcised (repressed) by the Christ. It would seem that the healing of the primal split can come only at the conclusion of patriarchal culture as it crosses the border between patriarchal and androgynous being. The transcendent function (or integrative mythic energy) can begin to function, or dominate collective consciousness, only at the eschaton of history.

The biblical myth makes clear, however, that transcendence of the paradigm of history is not to be construed, either biblically or transbiblically, as an escape from the conflicting throes of history. Fulfillment of history there must be. But it is doubtful that an ultimate resolution, or a clean translation, of patriachal culture can occur within the paradigm of history. The paradigm itself demands repression, and thus it cannot resolve the issues of the primal split. A center-point is established, however, on the stage of history, which makes an eschato-logical resolution possible.

In terms of New Testament theology, we might refer to this as the Christic point, but, as a viable symbol with global implications, this term must be detached from its institutional ties and recognized in its mythic setting as a phylogenetic requirement of evolution, for everyone and inherent in everyone. Granted this liberation, the Christic ego provides the prime example on the plane of history of the maturation of ego, and it supplies the ongoing mythic energy within the throes of history for the phylogenetic maturation of ego. In the Christic ego, differentiation (or dissociation) from the chthonic and total faith in the enterprise of Yahweh are complete. Through the Christic ego, humanity recognizes that ego is secure. Ego capacity survives. The achieve-ment of personal psyche will not be swallowed up in chthonic death. This then is the vindication of Abraham as he differentiates from the matriarchal world and moves at the behest of Yahweh into the continuum of history, into the paradigm of personal mode consciousness where death is a terrible threat to be faced, to be overcome.

Based on the Christic ego, translation of the paradigm of history (or victory for the great Lord of History) must leave ego phylogenetically secure in the human milieu. Ego must be the heritage of everyone, an archetypal property into which all of humanity is born, a part of the psychic anatomy of everyone. Translation must also leave ego sociologically secure: socially, politically, and culturally each ego, each person, must find egoic fulfillment within the paradigm of history.

Logos and Phallos

Logos masculinity (including the Christic), functioning at a mental level and inculcating ego in the human milieu, is to be distinguished from chthonic mascu-linity, which functions at a biological, pre-egoic level and is held in thrall to the archetypal feminine. Chthonic masculinity represents the inner masculine (the germ of Yang) of the archetypal feminine.

This archetype, often referred to mythologically as the consort of the Great Mother, constitutes a "nature god," a fertility god, the ithyphallic, fecundating element of the chthonic cosmogony. Prior to the mythic differentiation of chthonic masculinity, the Great Mother herself was considered ithyphallic, or hermaphroditic, illustrating, at that point, uroboric consciousness. The uroborus is depicted almost without exception throughout the primitive mythologies of the world.

The chthonic masculine represents the first dim glimmerings of otherness on the part of the incipient ego, contained within the primal Self of Fordham. In Fordham's terms, we can conclude that chthonic masculinity is the first deintegrate out of the primal Self. In the personal psyche, for the female, it is the first animus; for the male, the first inkling of the masculine aspect of the primal Self. In itself, chthonic masculinity represents a substantive step in consciousness while ego, the child of Logos masculinity, comes much later in the developmental scheme of things. Several millennia pass between chthonic and Logos masculinity in evolutionary timing—a blink, however, in the evolutionary eye of the monistic Self.

Note should be taken here of the work of Monick (1987), who seeks to free chthonic masculinity (Phallos) from the Great Mother (and from Neumann's schema in this respect). Neumann (1954, 1955) associates ithyphallic or chthonic masculinity with the Great Mother and ego consciousness with the Logos principle that supersedes the mother world. Monick feels that Phallos has thereby been repressed not authentically by evolution, but largely by Neumann's incorrect interpretation and seeks a more acceptable interpretation. His aim is to restore the potency of Phallos (chthonic masculinity) into human consciousness, and, although I am in sympathy with this aim, I take exception to his approach. It seems to me that the weight of the mythic records favors Neumann's schema which correctly interprets Jung's psychology and more cogently describes the overall mythic story of evolution that Jungian psychology, in its larger schema, begins to piece together.[2]

Jung's psychology is highly sensitive to the issues raised by archetypal gendering and engendering, but avoids the overreactive reflexes of feminism and what seems to be an emerging masculinism represented by Monick. Monick fails to recognize that the larger schema of Jungian psychology, although validating a developmental repression of Phallos, does not lose the energy of Phallos in the psychic economy.

It is not necessary to obscure the chthonic contrasexuality of the Great Mother, or to conflate Logos and Phallos, in order to restore the potency of Phallos. What is necessary is to see Phallos in its essential context and to recognize the eternal significance of the chthonic syzygy. This recognition not only puts the matriarchal order in clearer perspective, but gives us ground for transcending the patriarchal order and its necessary primal split, its schism of the soul. It sets the eschatological stage for the primal and numinous event of the *mysterium coniunctionis* and for the recovery of the mysterious goddess

---

[2]An explication of two perspectives on Jung's writing as they pertain to religion—a larger schema and a smaller one—is found in Chapter Ten.

which Toynbee glimpsed but could find no real place for in the history of civilization.

Yahweh and Zeus

We need to understand, as we examine the archetypal antecedents of ego, that the Yahwistic articulation of Logos masculinity and the creation of a patriarchal world was, of course, not the sole expression of patriarchy. A case can be made, perhaps, that all mythologies repeat, in rudimentary form, the triphasic process.

Two primary patriarchal mythologies thrust themselves forward on the stage of history. The Greek Olympians (contemporary to, but less radically transcendent-to-nature than Yahweh) were Yahweh's closest competitors in the critical establishment of patriarchy. Counterpoised against Yahweh at the dawning of the patriarchal era was Zeus, and with him a large panoply of pagan deities. Zeus conducted his patriarchal enterprise very differently from Yahweh. Here was no homoousia, no trinitarian three-in-one, revealing the inner essence of a god who entered the concretism of history, but not of nature. In the kingdom of Zeus, there was no real transcendence of nature and no firm sense of history. Zeus believed in superseding the Great Earth Mother, but he had extremely un-Yahwistic ways of doing it.

If, by means of active imagination, we read Yahweh's thoughts about the matter, a kind of ruminative exegesis occurs, a kind of reading between the lines of the biblical story at the point where these two gods meet on the stage of history.

Exegesis I

The trouble with Zeus was that he was still a part of the Great Mother. He had never really cut the apron strings. No two ways about it, he has descended from the great chthonic feminine (he doesn't bother to deny it) and, despite those lightning-bolt assertions of superiority, he has not transcended far. The tip of Olympus is as high as Zeus will ever get, and even there, even in his cabinet of twelve, he still maintains a bevy of feminine deities, goddesses in their own right — not aspects of Zeus himself.

Self-contained is not the word for Zeus. He has never bothered to center things in himself. He doesn't worry about other gods. Jealous of them? No. He doesn't care enough to be jealous. The outcome of history is not a high priority for Zeus. It suits him to shift responsibility for the wranglings of history to anyone who will take it and to remain entangled, in an adolescent sort of way, in nature.

But it seems to work. The human response to Zeus takes a jovial turn. No acrid "Thou shalt nots." No prophetic harangues. Judah hangs by a slender thread from the rafters of my unfulfilled heaven of history in the midst of a spreading Graeco-Roman world. A brilliant compromise. Half-history, half-nature.

Humanity, after all, understands nature. It was born in nature. Not even the Garden of Eden can erase that. Despite my best efforts, human psyches can still see and feel the energies of nature. Their lives are directly, instinctually affected. They have a difficult time understanding heaven and me — a god of heaven with no real ties to the earth, no earthly antecedents, no mother, no father that anyone can discover.

What good is heaven and the god of heaven to human persons? They themselves can never go there. They live and die on the earth. Dust they are and to dust they will inevitably return. Heaven, and a potential life in heaven, stretches their brains. A great deal of work still has to be done on their brains. At this point, humanity (even the chosen few) continue to pick up the resonance of matriarchy.

Zeus, of course, would never put a stop to that, not with his laxity. His proclivity toward the gods of nature is bad enough, but those goddesses of his carry the depths of the chthonic right up to the top of Olympus. Zeus can't see the error of his ways, how short of the mark he falls, how different his goddesses are from my own inner feminine. She keeps herself subservient to me and hidden most of the time. She wouldn't dream of bringing the chthonic into heaven. No more than I would dream of entering the realm of chthonic flesh and blood.

But Zeus is actually quite at home in that realm. He whizzes in and out of chthonic flesh with no compunction and as impersonally as a fly. His relationships, with divinity and humanity alike, are short and sweet and to the point. Zeus is an "I" all right — an adolescent "I." But he fails to comprehend the "Thou." The Zeusian world has never really produced a "Thou" — merely a Caesaristic playground.

So, there it is, laid out in archetypal black and white. A Yahwistic heaven opposing an Olympic pantheon composed of the gods and goddesses essentially of nature, not history. Zeus knows a little something about history, but not much. History is long-term commitment. Zeus wants short-term commitment. He's all for an adolescent macho. He likes armies and he wants his armies to win. He wants his people to conquer the earth and to rule the world. Of course, he's had to get rid of the matriarchal monstrosities — the cyclops, the typhons, the minatours (the levithans and behomoths of the chthonic creation). But as far as Zeus is concerned, it is not at all necessary to split off in any thoroughgoing way from the chthonic. That would take a great deal of fun out of living for Zeus. For sure, there on the tip of Olympus presides no contrasexual monotheistic singularity. And, with Zeus around, the will of Yahweh can never ever be done on earth as it is in heaven—my heaven.

This calls for a radical strategy. History seems certain to go the way of this short-term, playboy god. The whole world already belongs to Zeus, thanks to a young upstart of a world conqueror named Alexander. "Alexander the Great," they called him. What a travesty. That was worse than calling the Great Mother "Great." It is even more of an insult to the great Lord of History, the great I AM, who, after all, if there were any evolutionary justice, should be the world conqueror. My task is more profound than the Zeusian and, therefore, incomparably more difficult.

It is dismal to look down the corridors of time—historical time—and into the long years ahead containing the sweep of patriarchy. Alexander the Great (that young Grecian upstart, the product of Zeus and yet the product of an Aristotelian transcendence of Zeus) will evolve into the Caesars of Rome, still under the aegis of Zeus, however, and still the conqueror of Yahweh. The small worldly/unwordly nation of mine languishes under their rule, shriveling into the future, its own historical future, not actualizing heaven on earth, not encompassing both life and death. The bene Yisra'el *have been pared down to Judah now, a tiny remnant of a tiny, seemingly inconsequential nation in the scheme of things.*

And my Word—have they caught it? Not quite. Even after years of intensive inculcation and stringent purification through the ins and outs of history, the Word is still too difficult for Judah. The turning point of history looms into view, the radical strategy to defeat Zeus. A slim, but tightly packed drama, featuring a tragicomedian named Job will pick up the archetypal struggle of history.

It is often suggested, most notably by Whitmont (1983), that the pagan, polytheistic, but nevertheless patriarchal order of the Greeks resolved the chthonic consort into the ecstasized, hermaphroditic Dionysus—the god (Dio) of paradise (Nysos). This god, in essence, would seem to represent a semidifferentiation of (rather than a primal split between) the archetypal masculine and feminine elements. The word "hermaphrodite," for instance, is a glutinous word, suggesting a differentiated amalgamation of Hermes and Aphrodite.[3]

---

[3]Worth noting in this connection is the fact that the word *hermeneutic* also finds its etymological derivation in the Greek god, Hermes, indicating perhaps an approximate timing of the felt need in human consciousness for a conscious, egoic interpretation of the gods.

The point is that the Greeks did not, as in the biblical enterprise, separate from nature. Not only did they not repress the chthonic consort, they brought him into the Olympic council, and that by the generosity of the goddess, Hestia, who surrendered her own seat on the Council of Twelve to the strange new god. Qualls-Corbett (1988) adds hermeneutical insight to this maneuver as she informs us that Hestia was the ancient goddess of ritual marriage between the sacred prostitute – the vestal virgin – and the king as surrogate god (p. 36). Quoting Harding, Qualls-Corbett goes on to say of Hestia's virgins that "their feminine nature 'was dedicated to a higher purpose, that of bringing the fertilizing power of the goddess into effective contact with the lives of human beings'" (ibid.). Thus Dionysus could serve in Hestia's place as the chthonic consort – the fertilizing power of the goddess.

The patriarchal Romans, however, inheriting Dionysus from the more flexible Greeks, found him disruptive of their own more zealous way of life. He was an unproductive cog in the political/military machine of a Caesaristic world, a god whose main function seemed to be that of inducing women into maniacal unruliness devoid of domesticity and of seducing men into unmanly wantonness. The Romans thereby retrieved and domesticated Hestia (Vesta) and excommunicated Dionysus, depriving him of his place of honor in the pantheon and abolishing his orgiastic numinosity from the streets. Thus Dionysus, the last god to attain Olympic status, was also the first to lose it.

The Roman repression of Dionysus and the radical Christic repression of the great chthonic goat-god Pan (inclusive of all the archaic, ithyphallic gods of nature) became mythic hallmarks of matriarchal defeat in the arena of history – marking the midpoint of history, as history itself marked the midpoint of the overall story of the evolution of consciousness. The Romans themselves contributed a great deal to this midpoint – a cross and a crucifixion, among other things. But tiny Judah contributed a great deal more – its own god.

Exegesis II

As a matter of fact, this Aphrodite provided – if anyone had cared to ask Yahweh – an outstanding example of where the Greek patriarchy had gone wrong. The proper translation of Logos, as Yahweh consistently emphasized, was agape. His relationship with his own inner feminine was agapaic, not erotic, and his own begotten son was extremely mature in that regard. He walked among Aphrodite women without fear of them and with compassion. He hoped to bring them into higher mentality and into the fullness of Yahwistic consciousness. But agape provided eros with weak competition in the world at large. It often appeared that Aphrodite/Eros would win the day, and Zeus would have proved the wiser for putting up with her. His policy of lax repres-

sion won devotees, but could it carry evolution? Yahweh thought not. His own problems in that regard were manifold. There was this thing with Job. Job called for Wisdom, his own inner feminine which Yahweh had repressed in himself. Job made it impossible to repress her any longer. She must come to the fore and combat the wisdom of Zeus. This staying in touch with the erotic energies of the chthonic world was not the solution. There was a higher way. His own inner hieros gamos *must articulate in the world at large that higher way. It was terrible to repress the chthonic and the erotic—a cross to bear. The question was, could humanity bear the terrible split in the psyche. Yahweh did not know, but he knew that he would throw himself into it, his total Being, his total Word, the Logos clothed in his own unique flesh and blood.*

It is an important feature of our hypothesis that nothing less than a coming together (a *mysterium coniunctionis*) of the two extremes of matriarchal and patriarchal energy (represented by the archaic Great Mother and Yahweh) will actualize transhistorical consciousness in the human milieu. But their differentiation, as Yahweh recognized, must be extreme. The return of the Olympians to consciousness in our day is possibly a significant part of the process of reconciliation. The pagan deities, one step beyond the chthonic, inhabit a border area of the psyche between patriarchy and matriarchy. As one moves beyond ego, or beyond Yahwistic consciousness, one encounters again the pagan milieu. The pagan layer of the psyche comes alive again; its presence is a harbinger of *hieros gamos*, not the inner *hieros gamos* of Ego/ego, but the larger *hieros gamos* of the Self/self. The Olympians in themselves cannot provide that *hieros gamos*. They cannot provide a basis for the transcendence of history, since they never fully transcended nature.

The Turning Point: Satan and Job

The name of the Great Mother consort (the prince of the chthonic realm) became familiarized (and negativized) in the biblical world as Satan (or, more impersonally, as the devil). His name was legion, but throughout most of the biblical story the consort of the Great Mother was known indigenously by the Canaanite name of Baal. A highpoint in the archetypal contest between Yahweh and Satan/Baal comes in the biblical accounts of Elijah (an Old Testament forerunner of prophecy) and his dealings with a high priestess of the ancient Great Mother, known as Jezebel. The accounts of Elijah and Jezebel, chronicled largely in Kings I and II, provide an implicit background and reference for both Testaments of the biblical myth. As Jung recognized, however, the biblical contest between Yahweh and Satan reached an acute and decisive level in the Jobian drama. It precipitated the Yahwistic transition from Old to New Testament and a canonical split, still unresolved, on the plane of history. Again, active imagination provides an exegesis.

Exegesis III

It was not Yahweh's finest hour. No one could keep Yahweh's covenant, not even Yahweh, the Book of Job slyly insinuated. And if anyone could, the great god of the covenant would never be satisfied. The covenant was based on a slight deception, to put it mildly. I AM the only god, the only real god, in effect, he had told them. I AM the god to obey. These others are silly ersatz gods. But Yahweh himself knew better—so the drama of Job revealed. When the curtain drew back, there, center stage, sat Yahweh and his chthonic antagonist Satan making wagers. "Suppose someone does keep your covenant," said Satan. " Would he do it because he wants to, or because he wants your reward?" That was indeed the sixty-four-dollar question of the whole evolutionary enterprise. Could he actually separate humanity from the chthonic energies?

The drama of Job hooked into his own doubt, his own deception. He strongly suspected that Satan was right—the chosen few were only in it for reward. If he didn't reward them, they would all go running after Satan, or mongrel Zeus, or whoever.

Then the drama thrust further into the depths of his own humiliation. With this dreadful suspicion in his mind, even Yahweh could not keep Yahweh's covenant. This was Job's startling discovery. That hapless ashheap protagonist, who nevertheless had a way of looking Yahweh right in the eye, precipitated an archetypal upheaval in the mind of Yahweh. He withdrew for a few centuries of time (his own time) from the stage of history. He held long, earnest consultations in heaven (his own heaven) about it. What to do? If Yahweh himself couldn't keep covenant, then who could? How could one tiny nation in the midst of a pagan world keep it? How could the pagan world ever be brought into a nonfunctioning covenant? How could he, Yahweh, at one stroke, uphold his creation, uphold his covenant, enable the whole world to enter his covenant, and claim the continuum of history as his own? More to the point, how could Yahweh become a world conqueror and defeat the indefatigable Zeus? The archetypal solution became gradually clear (fed by an all too easily set-aside omniscience) and it soon trickled down to the stage of history. He, Yahweh, would begin anew with humanity. He would reenter the milieu of humanity a different way. He would rewrite the covenant. He would revise the terms of the covenant. He would make a new covenant, inscribing it not just on the mind of man, but on the heart of humanity. And through the new covenant, he would take Rome.

The contest, which Yahweh both won and lost, instigated the trinitarian unfolding of Yahweh. It issued in the Christic incarnation which radically repelled Satan from Yahweh's heaven, and, gradually, during the Middle Ages of the Christian (or common) era, in a battle drastically fought against witchcraft, it demythologized (or de-demonized) the earth and delivered the earth over to egoic science. The negative energy of the displaced demon has been accumulating during the years of patriarchy, and the expectation, both biblical and psychological, is that it will reemerge in the form of the Antichrist. In the minds of some, there would seem to be little doubt that it already has reemerged.

Satan, however (as Jung emphasized in his seminal treatment in *Answer to Job*), was known also as Lucifer, the "light-bringer." This appellation would seem to point toward a higher, gnostic, transpersonal conception of the Satanic element (the larger light), which Jung found implicit in the Jobian drama. The Luciferian potential indicated for Jung a biblical "seeding" from the great reservoir of the collective unconscious and a final "answer to Job," beyond the Christic, which has yet to be given.

The Trinitarian Unfolding of Logos Syzygy

We have looked at ego consciousness in terms of its correlation with Yahweh, the biblical god, and at the biblical god in terms of his correlation with the Logos principle of masculinity. Logos is the primal manifestation of the archetypal masculine in human consciousness, and Yahweh radically surpasses his analogues in his manifestation of the Logos principle.

As Jung tells it in *Answer to Job*, Yahweh glimpsed himself in the eyes of his servant Job. In that glimpse, he had seen his own shortcomings, his own partiality, the partiality of his covenant creation, of relationship by Word. It was one thing to be transcendent to nature, another thing to remain unembodied in the continuum of history, the dimension he had set for humanity, his own creation. It was a troublesome issue to say the least, an issue on which all history, not merely Judah's history, turned. Thus Yahweh, according to Jung, consulted his omniscience (or, perhaps, we might read *the* Omniscience, the

Self). And concurrently, as Jung informs us, after years of neglect, Yahweh also remembered and brought into consciousness his own feminine.

Exegesis IV

She had been there (he remembered now) when he first created. She had brooded over the chaos of the Great Earth Mother—the tohu wa-bohu, *the unformed void. She was the* ruach, *the breath he had breathed into Adam, and the breath of Eve. She was his Spirit, imparting his own unique essence into the stuff of creation, transforming the chthonic cosmogony into his own. But he had thrust her into the background of creation, assigned her an underground role.*

Nevertheless, despite his somewhat paranoid reluctance, Israel knew her. The seemingly motherless bene Yisra'el *sensed their own mother. They called her the Shekhinah, meaning the feminine soul of Yahweh's creation, of Israel herself. They had taken the name somewhat ingeniously from their own* shaken, *the tent of meeting between Yahweh and Moses in the desert crossing—indicating thereby Israel's containment of Yahweh. The imagery, a less-tolerant god might suggest, was all too obvious—Israel/Shekhinah as the bride, Yahweh as the bridegroom.*

He tried to ignore the imagery. He wouldn't sanctify it. It would never enter his canon. But, as long as they kept it muted, he didn't really mind. It was even true in a way. Israel was his bride—his bride, his child, his family. Of all the nations of the earth, Israel belonged to him. He had formed her in the wilderness of an alien cosmogony. He had snatched her from the clutches of the chthonic pair.

Still that hybrid Zeus owned her officially, no way around that—although he found her a bit prickly. And Satan wanted her. Satan was out to recover the whole patriarchal world for the Great Mother. Satan bided his time, positive that he would get the bene Yisra'el *in the end. He could easily strike deals with Zeus. And the two of them could easily confound the great Yahweh. It would take a lot of wisdom—more wisdom than Yahweh cared to call upon, a Shekhinah wisdom—to defeat those two archtypal miscreants. Yahweh could write a book—was writing a book—about that.*

Sometimes Israel called the Shekhinah his wisdom, his Hokmah or— translated into Greek—his Sophia. He wasn't fond of Greek. You could say almost anything in Greek, a very careless language, a word for everything. There was even a word for goddess in the Greek, which, thanks to his heaven, you wouldn't find in Hebrew—the sacred language of the sacred people, the language of the "nobodies" (the apiru, or hebrews) of the world. It was a joke, of course, calling them the "hebrews," but a joke with some truth to it. They were *nobodies, and that was not all bad. In the first place, it had set both him and his people apart from the accumulated wealth of the Great Earth Mother and her chthonic minions. It had distinguished his people, his Israel, his Hebrews, from the chthonic humanity of the earth. In the second place, it had insured that the Hebrews would learn to use their minds, not just their brawn. Well, the earth people were clever in their way. They could do wonders with swords and plowshares, but just wait until they saw what he could do, the civilization that he would build someday out of the new brain that he would establish in the human cranium.*

In the meantime, being the heavenly god of the so-called nobodies of the earth had certainly set his Wisdom apart from the so-called wisdom of the earth. His Sophia of the mind was nothing like the earth Sophia. She knew her place. He was first and she was secondary. She wouldn't think of putting herself before him.

Still, his avoidance of the feminine had gone perhaps too far. The Hebrew vocabulary was perhaps too subtle in this regard. Despite masculine and feminine forms in it, no one really caught on to the fact (or perhaps no one would say) that the feminine words spelled out the feminine of him. "Ruach," "shaken," "hokhmah," all feminine, but only a few seemed to recognize what that meant. His own inner feminine for the most part had been left in anonymity in a heaven concerned mostly with males.

It was not easy to know what to do with the Eves. Eves, of course, there must be, but obviously they had to be kept in their place, and that place was secondary. Anything more was sheer apostasy to the Great Mother. The Eves of his world had to be loyal to the Holy Spirit. They had been created in her image, but all too easily defected to the goddess world. They succumbed too quickly to the chthonic.

There was no doubt in Yahweh's mind that Zeus got along better with women than he did, but that after all was not a criterion of history. It would not help Zeus in the long term of history. The short term perhaps. Zeus had that ithyphallic magic, that chthonic carelessness which Yahweh avoided like the plague. Thus Zeus did not store up enmity in the chthonic gut as Yahweh did.

In the long run, of course, Zeus, and the people of Zeus, would be bound to collapse into the chthonic. They were hellbent and there were no two ways about it. They were patriarchal frauds, you might say. Zeus and his Olympic cohorts were not defeating the chthonic. They were merely playing at creation. They were like children in the marketplace, playing hero, pretending to conquer dragons, but really only kidnapping the daughters of dragons. Evolution was prodigious with its wares, but tricky. It always weeded out the inauthentic, the fake, the pseudo-gods. It had a winnowing fork which sifted out the chaff. It was true, of course, that anyone who wanted to buy a god in the veritable marketplace of gods would pick Zeus over Yahweh. Zeus was much easier for humanity to digest. Communion with Yahweh was infinitely more demanding. Yahweh had set for himself, and for his people, the harder course. And he must get on with it. He must now take upon himself the burdens of that course. He would heed Job, and Job's call for Hokhmah — his Wisdom — his Sophia — his Shekhinah — his Holy spirit — his inner feminine. No more wagers with Satan. No more covert deals with the Great Mother. When the curtain reopened on the archetypal drama of Yahweh, humanity would find Hokhmah on center stage.

Through his own inner feminine, he would recreate his own cosmogony. He would embody himself in his own unique flesh and blood, enter his own history, live in his own history, implant himself in the inner core of the human soul. He would keep his own covenant and die in the keeping of his covenant, and he would rise again from the chthonic jaws of death. His own flesh and blood, as the nefarious Great Mother/Satan would soon discover, would not decay. It would be heavenly, a new kind of substance, impervious to moth and rust. Through his own inner feminine, he would give himself in covenant to the world at large, even to chthonic humanity. It would change things. It would put Israel down temporarily. But it would defeat Satan. It would challenge the chthonic prince on his own turf. It would usurp his power and dislodge him from the archetypal heights. Satan would no longer have the run of the earth, nor the run of heaven. He would thrust Satan (and the analogues of Satan everywhere) into an underground for pre-egoic souls, those who refused the egoic way, his way.

And without Satan, the Great Mother could not create. Creativity, the thrust of evolution, would belong now not to nature, but to history — to Yahweh, to his begotten Son, and to his Holy Spirit. The thrust of evolution would belong to the Holy Trinity. It would be a true Oneness, a true centeredness of the mind, tying heaven and earth together in a concrete way. Thus it completely excluded, as Zeus could not exclude, the chthonic. Zeus, the world conqueror, would wither in the aftermath of the great incarnational victory of Yahweh, For he, the great Yahweh, would have then not only the world, but heaven, to offer humanity — a heaven they now, through his amazing new covenant, could enter.

Thus, the Logos principle constitutes a syzygy, carrying within itself its own inner feminine (a germ of Yin). This feminine is as radically differentiated from the archetypal feminine as Logos masculinity is differentiated from chthonic masculinity. In the primal split, the inner feminine of Yahweh goes with Yahweh. She is a fragment of the archetypal feminine (as chthonic masculinity is a fragment of the archetypal masculine), but she is split off from the archetypal feminine. Aligned with Logos masculinity, she is nonchthonic or, in other words, noncarnal.

Chapter Five

THE REST OF
THE MYTHIC
PERSONALITY

*T*he Logos syzygy, which was not thoroughly differentiated in the Old
Testament, connects with the New Testament trinitarian unfolding in a
surprising and canonically ambivalent way. Jung's recognition of trinitarian oneness and his later recognition of the femininity of the Holy Spirit shed new light
on the New Testament event of the Yahwistic incarnation.[1]

The unfolding of the biblical story into "Father, Son, and Holy Spirit" offers a
trinitarian basis of ego consciousness, which opposes the quarternitarian consciousness of the Self. "The Trinity," Jung writes, "is undoubtedly a higher form
of God-concept than mere unity, since it corresponds to a level of reflection on
which man [humanity] has become more conscious" (1948, par. 205). A feature
of the hermeneutic presented here, however, will be to stress both the evolutionary necessity of trinitarian (ego) consciousness in its move beyond primal
unity and its thrust toward a higher unity, which involves the ultimate comple-
mentarity of trinitarian and quarternitarian consciousness in the Self (see Jung
1948, pars. 283–284).

In order to explore the developmental distinction between trinity and quarternity, however, we need a more complete picture of Jung's delineation of the
psyche. Correlative to ego development, and conducive to the gradual evolution of the Self, Jung discovered three additional basic structural elements in
the anatomy of the psyche: the *persona*, the *shadow*, and the *anima/animus*.
Along with *ego* and *self*, they constitute the primary elements of a psychic unit,
functioning as structural containers of whatever archetypal contents reside
there. Complexes, for instance, are filed within these basic containers, some-

---

[1]Jung tried unsuccessfully to avoid the scandal of the self-contained *hieros gamos*
between Yahweh and his Holy Spirit. It is a notion that points in the direction of a
higher *hieros gamos* and, although Jung does not clearly differentiate the two
feminines, he moves in this direction in *Mysterium Coniunctionis*.

times associated with only one of them, sometimes overlapping.[2] As with all psychic contents, Jung treated these basic structural elements in a personalized way, and he looked for their personalized appearance in dreams or in any manifestation of archetypal energies.

These elements of the psyche are important in biblical hermeneutics in that they clarify the intrapsychic dynamics of Yahwistic consciousness, its trinitarian completion. The Jungian structure both recognizes the partiality of the trinitarian unfolding of the mental ego and functions to supplement that partiality.

1. *Father/Persona* Law-giver; creator of the ego world in the continuum of history; transcendent to nature; incurring a primal split between the archetypal feminine and the archetypal masculine; inducing repression of the chthonic realm of nature into unconsciousness, or *shadow* (both personal and collective).

2. *Son/Mature Ego* Substantiation, or incarnation of the Father in the continuum of history as Logos-made-flesh; transcendent to nature; imparting ego (Logos) power over shadow; bringing ego into full maturation (durability or eternalization) in human consciousness and preparing it for integration in Self; inducing the inevitable formation of, and confrontation with, the Antichrist.

3. *Holy Spirit/Anima* Inner feminine of Father/Son; acts as patriarchal anima in men and, paradoxically, as patriarchal animus in women by imparting mastery of recessive Logos contrasexual in women, or, in other words, continues Logos incarnation in men and women; provides connective link with Self by substantiating Christic ego maturation in the human whole or, in the words of Jung, by continuing the incarnation of Yahweh in the human whole.[3]

---

[2]As Hall (1986) puts it, complexes are the atomistic, cellular components of the personality within the molecular structures of ego-persona-shadow-anima/animus-self.

[3]Jung's interpretation of "continuing incarnation" differs from this view. In Jung's view, the continuing incarnation, which is the work of the Holy Spirit through the eucharist, takes Yahweh into the chthonic. Through the continuing incarnation, or through the eucharistic Christ, the biblical god becomes truly incarnate in the chthonic humanity. Jung recognizes that the incarnation itself is not a true incarnation. The biblical Christ, as Jung points out, is cut off from the shadow (the Antichrist). He incarnates God's "good side" to the exclusion of his

The Satanic Shadow

Conspicuously lacking in the trinitarian formula, as Jung emphasized, is a legitimate place for the shadow, the chthonic syzygy, and thus for the quarternitarian wholeness of the Self. The chthonic syzygy exists on the fringes of trinitarian consciousness, as an unadapted state of consciousness. Both the personal shadow and the cultural shadow derive from the chthonic syzygy. It was repressed at Eden and at the incarnation; it is repressed in the continuing incarnation. Chthonic masculinity came swiftly to the fore in the biblical story, in the figure of the serpent, to oppose the ascendent Logos, to protest its exclusion of other gods, to challenge the false wholeness of its Edenic paradise. It again challenged the Christ in the Jordanian wilderness. It will come (has come?) once more at the eschaton to challenge the durability of egoic humanity.

Another danger to ego is ego inflation, the tendency to usurp, or to claim as its own, the prerogatives and capacities of the Self. This tendency gives psychological credence to the development of trinitarian consciousness and suggests its essential role in the evolutionary scheme.

The danger of ego inflation provides a psychological underpinning to the biblical genesis, wherein is denied the right to know the chthonic world, the serpent wisdom. The Edenic pair are not forbidden to know within their own paradigm (the "good"), only beyond it (the "evil"). The myth would seem to suggest (and depth psychology would seem to bear out) that ego, at the Edenic level of its birth, is too immature to know the chthonic without either collapse into the chthonic (deflation) or without considering itself to be the Self (inflation). The knowing of the archetypal totality, in effect, is a prerogative of the Self. Therefore, expulsion from its paradisiacal state follows ego's epistemological transgression (its wrong choice), and the "tree of eternal life" (or "the tree of the Self") is guarded from ego's premature aggrandizement, its premature tendency "to be like one of us."

Thus, in this light, it is possible to see that the tension between ego and chthonic instinctuality (which so puzzled the patristic theologians) begins in the setting of a second cosmogony pitted against a prior cosmogony, historical time

---

"dark side" (the chthonic aspect of the Self). Jung attempts to compensate this one-sidedness in his treatment of the continuing incarnation and to assign the work of quarternity to the Holy Spirit. It seems to me, however, that it is truer to the biblical myth, and also, to the larger schema of Jung's psychology, to say that the continuing incarnation inculcates the "mind of Christ," or Logos capacity, or mature ego, in the phylogenetic whole. It completes the trinitarian differetiation in the phylogenetic whole of humanity. It does not accomplish quarternitarian wholeness. This is not a function of the biblical god in his trinitarian perfection.

and space pitted against nature. The chthonic was not an aspect of Yahweh's cosmogony. Not created by Yahweh, it predated Eden on the evolutionary time scale. The eucharistic presence, following the Yahwistic incarnation, armors the ego against chthonic (carnal) knowledge (the prerogative of Self) and, at the same time, protects ego against chthonic death. Yahweh's heaven, not the heaven of the Self, is no final heaven. But it functions as ego's holding place in physical death until the Self (the archetypal totality) can be assimilated into human consciousness without ego inflation and/or ego collapse. The "good news" of the New Testament was that Christ descended into the depths of chthonic darkness (into the hell of egoic repression), and the egoic light was not quenched. The Christic Yahweh is able to save his "lost sheep," all egos, those who know and can respond to his voice, whether these be in or out of Judah. He cannot save those not of his fold, however, the pre-egoic, whether these be in or out of Judah. Nor can he effect a rapproachment between the two syzygies, the Logos and the chthonic. The primal split prevails throughout the paradigm of history, for both the quick and the dead of history, awaiting the transcendent function, awaiting a third cosmogony.

The shadow, then, by definition, is unconscious to ego. It contains the repressed (and semirepressed) aspects of the ego personality and finds its chief affinity with the Freudian "id." The shadow is relative to the personal unconscious, although, as we see, there is also the deeper satanic Shadow which permeates the biblical myth and demands theological explication. As Jung saw it, the first task of individuation is to assimilate the contents of the personal shadow into ego consciousness. This calls for mature ego, however, which can master the shadow. Ego must neither collapse into the shadow, nor be inflated by the higher consciousness of the Self, to which it would now have access. In Jung's view, the personal task of integrating the personal shadow connects with the transpersonal and phylogenetic task of integrating the Shadow. The one (assuming the proportions of a critical mass) brings on the other. This deeper integration is a main task of the phylogenetic-macrocosmic process of evolution, and, in Jung's view, it is an undergirding issue of the biblical myth.

Jung recognized this task as the fearsome and uncertain issue of evolution facing us today, involving the extreme agony (or passion) of the ego-centered personal psyche and requiring decisive personal choice. It confronts superegoic choices with a higher consciousness. It confronted Yahweh, himself, with a move into his own higher consciousness. Jung connected this task biblically with the crucifixion/resurrection of Jesus and with the Christic/Antichristic opposition envisioned in the book of Revelation (Jung 1952a). He also associated it with the work of the Holy Spirit, that aspect of trinitarian consciousness which connects with quarternity—that still-latent aspect of evolution held in trinitarian unconsciousness, or in the collective unconscious. The collective unconscious contains the deeper satanic Shadow, the realm of the chthonic syzygy, the forming Antichrist. If, however, one ascribes to it the developmental finality of an ego/Self dialogue (as Jung does), the collective unconscious can also be considered as synonymous with the Self. It contains, in other words, repressed archetypal contents as well as latent contents yet to come.[4]

Along with the shadow, one other constituent of the Jungian psychic anatomy seems to be missing from the trinitarian formula— the Self. The Self, in its ultimate and differentiated form, seems largely to reside still in the collective unconscious. Working from the point of view of his smaller schema, which is that Yahweh accommodates the Self, Jung attempts to remedy the trinitarian deficiency by connecting the Self to the continuing incarnation, or to the work of the Holy Spirit. This contradicts the larger schema of his own psychology; Jung loses the archetypal distinction between trinity and quarternity and does not recognize the distinction between the archetypal feminine and the inner feminine of Yahweh. Jung leaves unexplained how an incarnation so carefully transcendent to nature would bring about a continuing incarnation which was not. In our context, however, it is the Ego, not the Self, that is represented by the trinitarian god, and thus the thrust of the *dramatis personae* of the biblical trinity is toward the maturation of ego.

The Persona of the Father

The persona is the beginning. The persona was active from the first in the primal emergence of the biblical god. It adapts the ego to the exigencies of an outer world, carefully maintaining the rationalistic composure of ego within that world. The outer world is, of course, the patriarchal world that sprang into being at the Word (or the seven Words) of Yahweh. The persona works by introjection of the Yahwistic mores and can be construed as a Jungian parallel to the Freudian "superego." The superego, in Freudian terms, however, was perforce unconscious. This is not necessarily true of the persona, as defined by Jung. On the contrary, serves a useful conscious function. If the persona is conscious (that is, conscious to the ego), it functions smoothly, not only in adapting the personality to society, but in forming a viable society. If it is unconscious to ego, or undifferentiated from ego, the personality is apt to suffer from its rigid, introjected conventionality. The persona, in this case,

---

[4]Transpersonal psychology bears this out. But Wilber, and other transpersonal theorists, are more discriminating in their definitions of the collective unconscious. See Chapter Eight for a further discussion of this aspect of Jungian psychology.

takes on a repressing function attuned to the Freudian superego. The persona/ superego aligns hermeneutically with the law-giving Yahweh. It is reflected in his firm prohibitions, his litany of "thou shalt nots," his wrath against the chosen few, his death threats to the entire human enterprise. The persona/superego also tends to gloss over the deficiencies of the covenant, looks for easy victories, takes naive optimism for genuine faith.

The prophet Jeremiah seemed to sense this socialized dynamic as he complained of a superegoic tendency in Judah to repress the shadow, to cry peace when there was no peace. He seemed to recognize the superegoic penchant of the mental ego as he called for a covenant, not only of the mind, but of the heart—a covenant which could outshine the shadow and bring to consciousness the wisdom (the inner feminine) of Yahweh. Such a covenant, although not immediately forthcoming, possessed a prescient ring. Another champion of this new covenant, the incredible "anti-hero" of the old covenant, the protagonist of the exilic drama of Job, cries out for the wisdom of Yahweh, hoping against hope, beseeching Yahweh against Yahweh. The drama of Job, as Jung makes clear, pits a superegoic Yahweh against an unsuccessfully repressed satanic Shadow. At this point in the biblical myth, it becomes obvious that Yahweh (as persona/superego) is no match for the satanic Shadow, and that he falls into unconscious collusion with the satanic Shadow. It becomes obvious that Yahweh, organically detached from the human milieu, is no match in the human milieu for Satan, who not only has the run of the Yahwistic heaven, but who is alive and well in the chthonic body of humanity as a whole—even of Yahweh's chosen few, the *bene Yisra'el*. It is at this point of recognition in human consciousness (exemplified by Job) that Yahweh brings forth his own feminine and moves into incarnation, into an organic investment of himself, his own unique substance, in the phylogenetic field of human existence. He institutes a covenant of the heart (a eucharistic presence) that aims to move humanity as a whole toward a conscious and radical separation from the satanic, or from the chthonic syzygy, but with a gracious acceptance of his own responsibility for original sin.

This, then, is the mature ego of the Son, the movement from Father to Son as registered in the trinitarian formula. This, as Jung (true to Pauline theology) points out, is the movement from superegoic law-giving to gracious law-giving, from external pronouncement of the Law to internal absorption of the Law, from an emphasis on wrath and exclusion to an emphasis on love and inclusion. This is not, however, a deemphasis of the Law, rather a reemphasis. Jung catches the trinitarian meaning of the Christ when he writes that the Christ was/is the ultimate protection "against the archetypal powers that threaten to possess everyone." And further that the glad tidings of the Christ announce, "It has happened, but it will not happen to you inasmuch as you believe in Jesus Christ, the Son of God" (Jung 1944, par. 41). Jung settles here for mature ego, a mature keeping of the covenant of Yahweh in the power of Christ. He also recognizes here the function of the eucharistic presence, the meaning of the continuing incarnation—to keep the "it" at bay, to prevent the archetypal totality of the Self from inundating the immature ego bred in the pagan world. Jung struggles with the paradoxical good news of the shadowless Son in whom he hoped to find the wholeness of the Self, but does not.

Superego, as an agent of repression, carries an onus from the transpersonal point of view. One would like to be full-born into mature ego. Nevertheless, as noted, Wilber (1981) subscribes to the view that mature ego cannot form in the human psyche without the prohibitive initiation of the superego. Jung, too, would seem to support this as he writes that "the superego is a necessary and unavoidable substitute for the experience of the self" (1954b, par. 394). In this, Wilber and Jung align psychology with the progression of the biblical story, which moves from a superegoic base to a mature, egoic, I/Thou relatedness, defined in both Judaism and Christianity as a person-to-Person, mind-to-Mind, will-to-Will, heart-to-Heart, covenanted (and monotheistic) relatedness.

Holy Spirit as Anima/Animus

To complete our Jungian/trinitarian inventory of the psyche, we need to bring into clearer focus Jung's seminal concept of the anima/animus. As he defined the terms, *anima* (soul) is the inner feminine of the male; *animus* (spirit) is the inner masculine of the female. The two terms, in other words, indicate the contrasexual components of the psyche—femininity (soul) within a dominant masculinity (spirit), and masculinity (spirit) within a dominant femininity (soul). As Jung saw it, the ultimate inner marriage of the two is the *mysterium coniunctionis* of alchemy. It represents an occurrence at the higher levels of the spectrum of consciousness and an experience of the transcendence of historical time/space.

Jung discovered these mysterious entities waiting at the dividing line between the personal and the collective unconscious. He saw them as the elusive psychopomps of the Self, bridging ego and self, reconnecting ego and self across the evolutionary millennia of their differentiation. These components of the personal psyche reflect the contrasexuality of the primal principles themselves—specifically, in a patriarchal world, they reflect, at their most obvious level, the Logos syzygy (Yahweh and the Holy Spirit). The Holy Spirit, as indicated above, correlates with both anima and animus, since "she," as the inner feminine of Yahweh, incarnates the masculine Logos in both male and female. Her femininity, as a matter of fact, is disguised in the biblical myth. As we will discuss in Chapter Eleven, she is largely repressed in the Hebrew canon, and called "he" or "it" in the Christian canon, where, having brought forth the Christ, she cannot be easily ignored. Nevertheless, despite this archetypal slight-of-hand, her "he-ness" and "it-ness" have some validity, since she is the inner feminine of a masculine god, and she does work to incarnate a masculine god in all psyches.

Anima and animus respectively have been largely unconscious to the ego personality, for, as is patently obvious, the patriarchal world in its establishment of Logos masculinity encourages men to be men (and primary in world affairs) and women to be women (the secondary helpmate of the man). Feminism in general, however, and feminist theology in particular, are exploring the outer dimensions of the patriarchal psyche. Logos masculinity is being appropriated for women as well as for men, and, although this is a disputed approach among feminists, it is, in my opinion, a necessary approach. This aspect of feminism, in itself, does not transcend the patriarchy, but it is my contention that it completes it, or translates it, in human affairs. Feminism at this point, it seems to me, is archetypally aligned with the task of the Holy Spirit. In alchemical terms, this in the lesser *coniunctio* that points beyond itself to the higher consciousness of the *mysterium coniunctionis*.

Although, in the patriarchal world, the anima/animus component of personality reflects the stereotypical or fixated sexuality of Logos masculinity, for women as well as for men, ultimately, in a transpersonal world, the anima/animus component reflects the monistic, androgynous wholeness of the Self. Again, attention is drawn to the taichitu (Figure 3.1, p. 29), where we see modeled both the coequal primal syzygy of the transpersonal Self and the contrasexual syzygies of the differentiated primal pair. It is this former wholeness to which we must finally aspire. It designates the transformational dividing line between personal and transpersonal consciousness. It is this dividing line toward which the Holy Spirit moves to effect a conscious link between the primal syzygies. These elements of the psyche are, in fact, basic to Singer's discussion of androgynous being and are ultimately crucial to the development of microcosmic personality and the wholeness of the self.[5]

The Self, then, representing the final totality of the macrocosm, awaits its ultimate fulfillment in the integration of the primal split between the two syzygies. The Holy Spirit, functioning as anima in the patriarchal male, but inculcating Logos animus capacity in the patriarchal female, moves human consciousness toward its ultimate linkage with the Self. The germ of Yin within the masculine Yang moves toward a reconciliation with the total Yin, the archetypal

---

[5]We will discuss this further in connection with Singer's analysis of androgynous being and the development of quarternitarian consciousness. See Chapter Six.

feminine. In other words, the inner feminine of Yahweh (in the third and culminating phase of the biblical trinity) moves toward a reconciliation with the excluded archetypal feminine, thus bringing about the reunion of the primal syzygies and quarternitarian consciousness. This does not invalidate trinitarian consciousness, but emphasizes its essential role in the individuation-evolutionary process. Quarternity is not reached by dispensing with the guardianship of trinity, but by transcending it.

Typology

Thus Jungian psychology presents *ego* and *self*, *persona* and *shadow*, and *anima/animus* as the skeletal structures of the anatomy of the human psyche. These structures both correlate with and go beyond the biblical trinity. Each structure, as we have seen, is composed of the *complexes* of the specific personality, giving each personal psyche its individual psychic "fingerprint" in relation to the transpersonal psyche.

In addition, in connection with the development of ego consciousness, Jung discerned eight basic cognitive modes (or ways of knowing) available to the personal psyche (Jung 1921; Singer and Loomis 1984). The personality, for instance, may focus inward in *introversion*, or it may focus outward in *extraversion*, and these two attitudes (in Jung's opinion, innate in the personality system) are accompanied by four ways of functioning, composing thereby the eight basic cognitive modes. The four basic functions, as discerned by Jung, are *thinking* and *feeling* (which he designated as rational, or judging, functions), and *sensing* and *intuiting* (which he designated as irrational, or perceptual, functions). Each of the cognitive modes, or psychological types, is extensively defined in the Jungian literature, and their finer points need not concern us here. For purposes of a biblical hermeneutic, what is important to grasp is that each personality develops its own specific profile in relation to the cognitive modes. Inevitably some modes are more highly developed than others and seem to govern the ego (the individual personality) as it relates to the inner and outer world. Also inevitably, one cognitive mode (Jung called it the inferior function) is least developed and seems to reside in the shadow and at the anima/animus levels of the personality.

Ironically this *least-developed cognitive mode*, tapping into the unconscious complexes, leads from trinitarian consciousness toward quarternitarian consciousness, or toward the Self. This brings us again to the point that the movement from ego consciousness toward higher, or transpersonal, consciousness is through the lower, repressed aspects of the psyche. It constitutes a reclaiming of chthonic, or prepersonal consciousness. In alchemical parlance, chthonic consciousness is the split-off uroboric "one," which when added to the biblical "three," constitutes quarternity. "Four" connotes a new numerical entity, a new wholeness, a higher, differentiated wholeness, in contrast to the undifferentiated wholeness of the "one."

The individual, then, in the process of individuation is finally (and thus eschatologically) related to the wholeness of the Self, able to operate in four functions and two attitudes (encompassing the eight cognitive modes) and to integrate the archetypal totality. The individuality of the individual is not lost in the whole. The individual is related to the whole each in his or her own unique way, according to the formation of the complexes and according to the cognitive profile. The universal is absorbed in the particular, and the transpersonal is reflected in the personal. Microcosmic personality in its wholeness is not less, but more individual. In ego, paradoxically, individuality tends to be eroded. The trinitarian basis of ego consciousness tends to favor the development of certain cognitive modes (as well as complexes) over others—those modes which reflect and actualize the Logos principle. Thus a certain patriarchal bias affects typology.

PART TWO

Chapter Six

ANDROGYNY

Singer (1976, 1983) has explored this facet of Jungian psychology, tracing the process of evolution in terms of the differentiation and reunion of the archetypal feminine and masculine, and relating the process of individuation-evolution to Jung's concept of inherent contrasexuality of the individual personality system.

Jung's concept of contrasexuality indicates that each individual harbors his or her sexual opposite (the anima or animus respectively) in a recessive, often repressive, way. Singer, following Jung, bases her concept of androgyny on the Taoist monistic polarity of the taichitu, the feminine/masculine principles of Yin and Yang. She aligns the concept of contrasexuality with evolutionary process beyond the personal.

> As we attempt to re-vision sexuality from a transpersonal perspective, it seems vital to emphasize the evolutionary character of human behavior and, most significantly, of sexual behavior. The relations between the two sexes are based upon instincts that are primarily absent from consciousness. *These instincts do not belong exclusively to the realm of the personal unconscious, but to the collective unconscious as well, stemming as they do from residues of archaic and even prehuman social interactions* [italics mine]. (p. 312)

Contrasexuality, in Singer's thought, moves human consciousness into co-equal androgynous consciousness, into the transpersonal *mysterium coniunctionis* of the Jungian tradition, but also into the biblical eschaton of a new heaven/new earth.

Contrasexuality functions on two paradigmatic levels. The anima of the male corresponds to the chthonic Great Mother, but also to the inner feminine (the Holy Spirit) of Yahweh. As Singer puts it:

> [T]he anima appeared in the early matriarchal civilizations between 4000 and 2000 B.C. as Great Mother or fertility goddesses; later under a patriarchy the anima was more likely to appear as frivolous, seductive, trivial ["spiritualized" and secondary to the male]. Today again her appearance has shifted. She becomes stronger. (1984, p. 199)

By the same token, the animus of the female corresponds to the chthonic inner masculine of the Great Mother (the biblical Satan), but also to the Logos masculinity of the Yahweh/Christ.

Thus anima and animus, it would seem, are images of a double syzygy. This notion also connects with Jung's notion of the archetypal "wise old woman" and "wise old man"—those deep archetypal presences who reside beneath the patriarchal world, beneath the patriarchal anima and animus.

The images of a double syzygy, then, encompass the chthonic syzygy (the Great Mother/Satan) and the Logos syzygy (the Yahweh/Holy Spirit). The Logos syzygy (which articulates itself definitively in the biblical myth) relates to ego consciousness; the chthonic syzygy (repressed in the biblical myth) relates to pre-egoic consciousness. Conscious integration of the two, as Singer theorizes, precipitates transegoic, androgynous consciousness, or a newborn, transformed mode of human existence. The *mysterium coniunctionis*, in this sense, can be said to constitute Jung's symbol of archetypal wholeness, the quarternity: the Great Mother/Satan consciously and harmoniously reunited with the Yahweh/Holy Spirit. Quarternity, which symbolizes unity at a higher level than nature's oneness, supersedes the trinitarian primal split.

In contrast to current trends in Jungian thought (notably in Hillman's school of archetypal psychology), Singer makes clear that the archetypal reunion of the feminine and masculine energies (which she sees as the basic propellants of evolution) is not a regression (in the final sense) from biblical monotheism into pre-Yahwistic polytheism. As she puts it, "the guiding metaphor for [this reunion] is still monotheism, but it is not the monotheism of the God of Genesis" (Singer 1976, p. 100). It is rather a trancendence of biblical monotheism into a higher monism, a higher oneness, which she terms *androgynous monotheism* (ibid., p. 88).

Singer encompasses and transcends the biblical myth in an evolutionary framework of matriarchal, patriarchal, and androgynous consciousness. The biblical god, forming patriarchal (ego-centered) monotheism, is reunited in evolutionary transcendence with the matriarchal goddess of the chthonic (polytheistic) realm, and this innovative, transbiblical event (this double-syzygy sacred marriage) forms androgynous monotheism—in biblical terms, a new heaven/new earth, an eschatological Jubilee; in transbiblical terms, a third cosmogony.

Jung correlated phases of evolution with astrological time, with startling implications for our own time. In this correlation, we come face to face with the imminent phenomenon of evolutionary discontinuity, the birth of new form out of chaos, as set forth by Prigogine (1980; and Stengers 1984).[1] This theory recognizes the influx of new energy in an open universe, as opposed to the inevitability of entropy in a closed universe. It makes room for the expectation of transformation.

The concept of androgyny, as defined by Singer, aligns with Prigogine's insights. *"Androgyny,"* she writes, *"is the outcome of a dynamism based on the application of energy in an organic system that is open-ended and that interfaces with an open-ended universe"* (Singer 1976, p. 276). Androgyny, in other words, is emerging from its latency in the collective unconscious into a higher, transpersonal mode of consciousness. Androgynous being, born of the numinosity of the *mysterium coniunctionis,* ushers in a new period of liminality, a new transitional era, a new kind of "infancy" for the human species, a new growing up, a new kind of adulthood, a new cosmogony.

The concept of androgyny (at times discounted as a viable symbol in Jungian literature) is extremely important to maintain. No other concept designates the transformational effect of transpersonal consciousness upon patriarchal human-ity. Note, however, that in Singer's treatment (consistent with both Jung and Wilber) the higher form does not invalidate the lower form. The patriarchal aspect of humanity retains its phase-specific integrity in the open-ended uni-verse. From a clinical point of view, personality may need to develop at each and all of the three levels, or, as Ulanov (1981, p. 31) sees, may need to avoid the concept of androgyny altogether. Nevertheless, clinical readiness cannot dictate psychological theory, as Ulanov, in rejecting the notion of androgyny, would seem to imply.

Samuels (1988) also rejects the notion of androgyny as illusory, preferring to work with the concept of bisexuality, which, as he formulates it, permits "a vision of there being a variety of positions in relation to gender role" (p. 72). Samuel's position is inarguable, as far as it goes. But Samuels does not seem to notice that he has slipped into an "ego" psychology, in contrast to a Jungian "self" psychology, and that his psychology begins to resemble a "pre-Jungian," rather than "post-Jungian," psychology. The "illusion of androgyny," as Samuels puts it, becomes the delusion of Jung in placing his psychology within a microcosmic/macrocosmic context, defining a process of alchemical transfor-mation. In effect, Samuels reduces the archetypal energies to symptoms in an ego world, confusing the primal principles (the archetypal feminine and the archetypal masculine themselves) with their stereotypical fixations in that world. Samuels dismisses them accordingly as needless baggage. Stereotypi-cality, like pseudospeciation, betrays psychic inertia, the blockage of human

---

[1]Prigogine's work in the field of chemistry will be discussed more thoroughly in Chapter Nine as we look at the emergence of new science in the generalized field of transpersonal endeavor.

response to the teleological pull of the Self, or to the archetypal totality. Nevertheless, stereotypicality has an archetypal base: it is caught up in the developmental enterprise gone wrong. Otherwise, we could easily correct the stereotypes and no Jungian analysis would be required.

Jung's psychology suggests that the way beyond stereotypicality is not to dismiss the archetypes, or the archetypal activity which has guided evolution thus far, but rather to listen with deeper comprehension to the archetypes. Jung further suggests that we will hear rumblings of a threatening confrontation between the archetypal energies of the Christ and the Antichrist, expressed in many forms and many ways. We will hear also preparations for a double-syzygy sacred marriage, a reuniting of the differentiated archetypal feminine and masculine. As Singer makes clear, Jung himself does not dismiss the archetypes, but heightens our sense of their activity. Evolution moves at their behest; it depends on our response to them. Dismissal is hardly a Jungian response. Although Samuels moves to the outer limits of the ego paradigm, his tendency to tinker with stereotypical patterns within the limits of the ego paradigm invites entropy, not transformation.

This is not to say that the therapist does not work clinically within the ego paradigm to redeem the stereotypes and to come to terms with the ego world of the client. As Stein (1987) points out (and the biblical myth affirms), the ego world of the individual is, in itself, archetypal. Stein emphasizes that one must be thoroughly grounded in one's own story, one's own ego world (recognizing its stereotypical fixations and complexes), before transformation is a viable possibility. As Stein puts it:

> Jung's . . . account of psychological development includes the personal dynamics of identification, introjection, *participation mystique*, complex formation, *and also the archetypal dynamics of constellation, synchronicity, and spontaneous influences from beyond the horizon of external factors.* (1987, p. 61, italics mine)

Thus, although the ego biography of the individual must not be neglected, the ego paradigm per se must not be considered as the final arbiter of what humanity is all about. The archetypal constellations lie beyond the egoic horizon.

Coward provides pointed rebuttal to Samuels as he writes:

> If we end up with a social situation where women do the odd jobs that men have been doing, exhausting their substance on externality, then— maybe—*we shall at last have a true Patriarchy; and that will be a big change. Then there will be cries for Androgyny after all.* (1988, p. 150, italics mine)

Precisely. The outer limits of ego psychology can only take us to the outer limits of patriarchy and the paradigm of history. This, in itself, as Coward indicates, will be quite an accomplishment. The concept of androgyny, however, defines the theoretical cutting edge of psychological-mythological theory, and, in this theory, evolution accomplishes a quantum leap.

Singer traces the evolution of the androgyne through mythological history, showing that, as a manifestation of the Self, it has been an undergirding, teleological factor in the overall process of evolution. Its ultimate reconstitution of the differentiated primal energies is to be distinguished from a paganistic, semidifferentiated, hermaphroditic state. She rejects Dionysus, for instance, as symbolic of the ultimate Self. He represents an attempt at transformation beyond patriarchy, but an attempt gone wrong. Dionysus collapsed into the chthonic. He was prepatriarchal, not transpatriarchal.

Nor is androgyny to be confused, as it often is, with unisex. Masculinity and femininity are enhanced, not blurred, in androgynous being. Bisexuality, in Singer's definition, is certainly an androgynous option, but androgyny is inclusive of a wider variety of options – heterosexuality, homosexuality, and celibacy among them – depending on the inner androgynous orientation, not the outer expression.

Although she anticipates the development of androgynous society, Singer treats androgyny primarily as an intrapsychic phenomenon. Androgynous society follows from androgynous being, but she declines to speculate in great detail upon such a development. The transformative features of a new heaven/ new earth are not clearly enough in sight for meaningful speculation. But the concept of androgynous being is in sight. It is a concept that clearly reiterates and further explicates Jung's view of microcosmic being.

Singer captures the microcosmic/macrocosmic replication succinctly as she writes:

> The idea of ourselves and the world we live in as microcosmic, reiterating in an imperfect sense the perfection of the all-encompassing macrocosm, may seem like pure philosophical speculation and of little practical use. But if we consider the question from the point of view of the *experience* of the human psyche, as I believe Jung attempted to do, we find a map, a pattern, a model, that helps us understand our place in the entire scheme of things. We begin, as Blake put it:
>
>> To see a World in a Grain of Sand
>> And a heaven in a Wild Flower,
>> Hold Infinity in the palm of your hand
>> And Eternity in an hour.
>
> This means that we exist in both dimensions at the same time. The concept is *non-dual* [italics mine]. It simply points out that we view our existence from more than one perspective. We exist on this earth and we

have to deal practically with the problems of the world in its own temporal terms, cognizant of the linear pattern of the individual life which commences at conception and concludes with organic death. We also live in eternity and are concerned with problems that go beyond the practical and temporal . . . . To the extent that we think in practical everyday terms, we are in touch with the "Edenic Adam" in ourselves, but to the extent that we reflect upon the cosmic scheme, we are in touch with the Archetypal Man, Primal Man, Celestial Man, Zodiacal Man, the Man of many names whose nature is pure existence and who has no manifest form. We are, according to my understanding, both of these. (1976, pp. 109–110)

Singer goes on to identify "Edenic Adam" (biblical humanity), existing in the linear arena of history, with the "ego personality." "Archetypal Man" (transbiblical humanity) is microcosmic. Although microcosmic personality supports the continuity of ego and self, it is nevertheless non-dual. At that level of consciousness, the polarity between microcosm and macrocosm, ego and self, masculinity and femininity is monistic, not dualistic. Thus we see that archetypal differentiation does not lead to polytheistic fragmentation, but to "androgynous monotheism," or to the monistic Self. Ego consciousness, therefore, is not to be *de*centered in polytheism, but instead is to be *re*centered in the monistic polarity of the Self.

Singer, admitting that she carries Jung forward, further clarifies her thought in this regard:

Because the realm of the transpersonal includes an ego that has been fully developed over time [historical time] but goes beyond that ego into a wider consciousness, we can speak of the transpersonal unconscious as the *superconscious*. The vastness of the superconscious is as hard to imagine as that of the Jungian concept of the collective unconscious. The difference lies in the way each relates to the ego. The collective unconscious is the *source of ego development* and the transpersonal unconscious, or superconscious, is the *goal of ego transcendence*. (1983, pp. 240–241)

Thus Singer's work emphasizes the centrality of ego consciousness, its mediating place in the overall spectrum of individuation-evolution. In this statement, Singer indirectly affirms the place of the biblical myth as she affirms the structural necessity of ego. She also invites the feminist movement in a forward direction—to move through and beyond ego and patriarchal consciousness, rather than, as is sometimes the case, to spin its wheels denigrating ego and patriarchal consciousness or bewailing its position therein.

Singer sees the development of ego consciousness as evolving collectively in the direction of meditative, or introverted, intuition, a perceptual function that seems to have been least favored in the development of the patriarchal world. Of the eight possible cognitive modes defined in Jungian psychology as the potential properties of ego consciousness, patriarchy has depended for its development largely on the extraverted/introverted development of thinking, feeling, and sensation. Its development of intuition has been largely extraverted, focused on the outer world. Thus introverted intuition has been the collective inferior function of patriarchy, and, therefore, in Jungian terms, it is the guide to higher consciousness. In Singer's estimation, meditative or introverted intuition now needs to occupy the forefront of evolution, bringing four functions rather than three to fruition, bringing trinitarian consciousness into quarternitarian consciousness. Introverted intuition is the surest guide toward an intrapsychic androgyny, the goal of ego transcendence and superconsciousness.

The sexual act itself, the conjoining of male and female in an act of love, becomes, in Singer's view, a mode of meditative intuition. The archetypal fact of the *mysterium coniunctionis* is thus brought down to earth and actualized in human life in a most basic way. In the language of Eastern tradition, it is a tantric maithuna, but in Eastern life, tantra lacks orientation in ego consciousness and tends to remain pre-egoic. It cannot shape the masses; it can only be reserved for the elite. In the meditative mode of introverted intuition, the sexual act fosters intrapsychic wholeness (the inner marriage), as well as interpersonal wholeness (the outer marriage). This depends, however, on mature ego, two persons who are whole in ego, neither of whom projects unresolved complexes onto the other. In alchemical language, the condition of *unio mentalis* opens to the *mysterium coniunctionis* and a *unus mundus.*

Singer's work makes clear that the transbiblical myth is not new, but ancient and eternal. It is new only in the sense that it now begins to emerge on the edge of historical space/time, to engage the collective consciousness of historical humanity, to dominate the morphogenetic field of human consciousness, and to affect the phylogenetic heritage of the human whole. Singer draws an important distinction between the biblical myth and the esoteric traditions which have, through the years of biblical development, prepared the psyche for transbiblical development. She presents a model, as does Rudolph (1983), in which the process of biblical development must be read in conjunction with a counterprocess, and in which the counterprocess transcends and revisions biblical revelation. This model aligns precisely with Jung's treatment of the biblical myth.

Chapter Seven

WHEN SCIENCE CONFRONTS THE MYTH

*T*he perspectives of both transpersonal psychology and Jung apply to the development of a biblical hermeneutic for a transbiblical age, including the biblical god as a specialized aspect of evolution, but not positing his ultimacy.

Under the umbrella of transpersonal psychology, we will look also at the emerging phenomenon of "new science" in the scientific world of today. This term broadly denotes new and unexpected developments within the scientific world, developments that exhibit a tendency to break through the Newtonian-Cartesian paradigm of science, as Grof terms it (1985, p. 19). This tendency is of interest here since a feature of our hypothesis is that Newtonian-Cartesian science evolves from the archetypal base of the biblical god. In other words, it is my contention that the Newtonian-Cartesian paradigm is archetypally contained within the biblically formed paradigm, and that classical or mainstream science, in effect, is an extension of the biblical paradigm, carrying the work of Yahweh to its logical conclusion.

It seems to be a little known or often overlooked fact that the founding fathers of the paradigm were themselves not unaware of the biblical influence upon their endeavors. Grof, for instance, in defining the Newtonian-Cartesian paradigm, writes as follows:

> For both Newton and Descartes, the concept of God [Yahweh] was an essential element in their philosophies and world views. . . . Newton believed that the universe was material in its nature, but he did not think its origin could be explained from material causes. According to him, it was God [the biblical god] who had initially created the material particles, the forces between them, and the laws that govern their motions. The universe, having once been created, would continue to function as a machine and could be described and understood in those terms. Descartes also believed that the world existed objectively and independently of the human observer. For him, however, its objectivity was based on its constantly

being perceived by God [the biblical god]. . . . . Conceptual thinking in many disciplines represents a direct logical extension of the Newtonian-Cartesian model, *but the image of divine intelligence that was at the core of the speculations of these two great men disappeared from the picture.* The consequential systematic and radical philosophical materialism became the new ideological foundation of the modern scientific world view [italics added]. (1985, pp. 19–20)

Thus, Newtonian-Cartesian science developed originally in response to the biblical god. In the long run, however, as Grof points out, it obeyed that god all too well. Just as Yahweh had displaced "other gods," so the scientific world displaced Yahweh transferring his ego-centered epistemology from "heaven" to the human mind, from suprahistory to history, from Ego to ego. "Philosophical materialism" held that the world was quantifiable, manipulatable, and predictable. Egoic humanity, sprung up from the biblical genesis, lived in a world, which, although harsh and nonparadisiacal, was ultimately comprehensible to the ego-centered mind. This took some time—from the time of "genesis" until Newton—but by then the so-called exact sciences had turned the Cartesian ego inside out, focusing it on the world in which it was set, the phenomenal Yahwistic creation which surrounded it.

This tour de force set the stage for the emergence, in the 1920s, of "behaviorism" or "positivism" as the guiding mythos of the psychological and social sciences, a view that has dominated those sciences until recently. Positivism, following the exact sciences, sought to reduce not merely nature, but the dimensions of humanity itself to the observable, the quantifiable, the predictable, in the form of external stimuli coming in and observable behavior going out. It ruled out of psychological respectability all "mentalisms," all nonobservable process. The inner recesses of the human psyche were left to the debatable purview of a suspect "depth psychology," which, although developing alongside behaviorism, could claim only quasi-scientific status. Depth psychology has become known largely in its Freudian form, for Freud made more of an effort than Jung to remain scientifically respectable, to locate the concepts of his psychology within the Newtonian-Cartesian paradigm. Jung struggled against a too-tight theological and scientific paradigm and found a world less receptive to his conceptual framework. Freud's concept of the "id," although scandalous to Victorian sensibilities, was nevertheless vaguely understandable from the objective standpoint of science. Jung's concept of a still-deeper "collective unconscious," consisting of archetypal contents which could become "objective" to the personal psyche, was scientifically untenable. Any notion of archetypal energies at work in the formation of human consciousness was dismissed out of hand; that is, until recent years, with the advent of transpersonal psychology and "new science," and a rapidly moving paradigm shift.

Positivism, however, is a persistent view. Although discredited and largely dismissed at the leading edge of science, it tends, nevertheless, to creep into the thinking of many who otherwise know better. As previously noted, it is convenient to slip into positivism in order to "deontologize," or rule out of archetypal "reality," certain unpalatable archetypal energies. Biblical theologians, for instance, are selective positivists in regard to the earth mother, the chthonic syzygy. Yahweh can be accepted on faith, but a selective bias deletes the goddesses and gods of nature. Biblical theology takes this stance, however, within the peculiar, exegetical demands of the biblical myth. Selective positivism, in this case, reflects accurately the stance of myth itself. It reflects accurately the actualization of archetypal energy in human consciousness—at least from a developmental point of view and for a specific phase.

Feminist theologians, in seeking to overrule the dominance of the archetypal masculine and to reform the patriarchal culture reflecting that dominance, veer from time to time toward a reverse selective positivism. They tend to deny the reality of the archetypal energy of Logos masculinity and its essentiality in the overall mythic story. In so far as they do this, they are misreading myth and misrepresenting the overall mythic story as it has been actualized during the last four millennia. They are contriving myth rather than exploring myth with the exegetical accuracy it requires. They are revising myth, not revisioning it. They hope to manipulate the future by censoring the mythic heritage of the past, rather than by bringing forth a future that emerges authentically out of an unexpurgated mythic past. Such an approach may succeed in destroying an archetypal image and an unacceptable stereotypical fixation on that image, but, as we know from Jungian and transpersonal psychology, it cannot succeed in destroying the essence of the archetypal energy itself. Ultimately, in failing to deal honestly with archetypal essence, this approach fails to allow the emerging myth to express itself, for new myth emerges through the old, in corrective dialogue with it. The attempt to manipulate biblical myth through selective positivism, rather than by discerning the evolutionary emergence of transbiblical myth, is, in my opinion, an unfortunate detour for the feminist cause, but one which apparently must have its day.

The Newtonian-Cartesian paradigm, including psychological and sociological positivism is a phase of science—"pretransformational science," as Loye (1983) terms it—that obeys the Yahwistic injunction to demythologize and dominate nature. It moves to the tempo of history, not nature, methodically extolling its redundant litanies of cause and effect within the Yahwistic sequence of linear time. Ego epistemology is enshrined in the Newtonian-Cartesian temple of science, and the temple of science is exclusively dedicated to ego's one-sided view of things, its vaunted "objectivity," its absolute quantified accuracy. Ego is featured in the Newtonian-Cartesian paradigm as a transcendent, centralized "subject" analyzing an "objective" material world. Thus a split—a primal split, if you will, a subjective/objective dichotomy—appears in the depths of the psyche, both microcosmically and macrocosmically, both ontogenetically and phylogenetically. It elevates the ego world above the material world, as the ruler and "knower" of the material world. This dichotomy, essential to the pursuit of Newtonian-Cartesian science, correlates precisely with the biblical cleavage between heaven and earth (the Yahwistic heaven and earth), between the human world and the subhuman world, between history and nature, between mind and matter, between the archetypal masculine and the archetypal feminine. It distills the ego god from the pleroma of the archetypal totality. It "monotheizes" the ego god above other gods and then proceeds, as Grof points out, to dismiss him, leaving scarcely a trace, something akin to the smile of the Cheshire cat, a "deus absconditus," a dead god as some see it. These rather convoluted proceedings, however puzzling, nevertheless demonstrate in the infallible logic of science the split between the two primal syzygies—the Logos and the chthonic. The emergence of new science (in Loye's terminology, transformational science), within the arena of an apparently entrenched scientific/biblical paradigm, presents a significant, almost litmus, indication of the emergence of new archetypal activity, of the budding of transpersonal consciousness and of transbiblical myth.

From Jung's point of view, new science connects with an ancient science—alchemical, or Hermetic science—which blossomed esoterically during the Middle Ages, before the Cartesian ego had hardened in the human brain. This little understood and largely forgotten science might be called the original science of hermeneutics, since it stamped all further interpretive endeavor with its name. Jung considered it to herald the approach of Newtonian-Cartesian science. Unlike its modernistic offspring, however, Hermetic science did not function objectively, but in a subjective or projective way. It let in the archetypes. It often functioned in tandem with a biblical outlook, but on the underside of orthodoxy and always on the edge of heresy. Hermetic, or alchemical science, as Jung discovered, was a gnostic science, with a gnostic epistemology, a nonegoic way of knowing. It recognized an archetypal totality larger than Yahweh and a *unus mundus* (a one world) representing a consciousness beyond (or before) the subjective/objective dichotomy (the primal split) of the ego world. New science, in process of emerging on the other side of the subjective/objective split, returns to a gnostic epistemology, a nonegoic way of knowing. It provides formulas for the transformation of consciousness rather than instructions for conditioning. It breathes new life into the ancient science.

New science connects also with Eastern spiritual traditions, which until recently have not been forced to contend at any great depth with the archetypal energy represented by the god called Yahweh. These traditions were freer to develop beyond the biblical god, tuning into levels of consciousness tuned out by Yahweh. Thus, as new science penetrates the Yahwistic barrier, it moves into the hitherto unscientific preserves of Eastern spirituality and Eastern energy.

Nevertheless, new science maintains viable connections to Newtonian-Cartesian science. It moves from a transegoic, not a pre-egoic point of view and, therefore, may find its most congenial base in the theoretical work of Jungian and transpersonal psychology, which makes room for the Yahwistic mental ego while transcending the mental ego. The total spectrum of consciousness is encompassed in these psychologies, but in trans-scientific terms rather than in the arcane, projective views of a prescientific era. In Wilber's format, which owes much to Eastern tradition, the total spectrum of consciousness is resolved in the triphasic spectrum of prepersonal, personal, and transpersonal modes of consciousness. In Singer's more mythological and Jungian format, the spectrum moves from matriarchal to patriarchal to androgynous consciousness. Jung also spoke of a triphasic individuation-evolutionary process that moved from the undifferentiated self, through ego consciousness, to the differentiated self. These three sets of terms are used synonymously here. They describe from different angles the same modes of consciousness and the same triphasic spectrum of consciousness. In our hypothesis, the biblical myth, and the Newtonian-Cartesian paradigm as its derivative, belong to the midphase of the process—the personal, the patriarchal, the egoic.

There is a sense, however, in which the scientific and theological facets of Yahwistic consciousness have not claimed each other. The theological world could not overlook the fact that in appropriating ego epistemology from the archetypal atmosphere of Yahweh, science rejected not only the other gods (as prescribed by Yahweh), but also its own god, Yahweh himself. His archetypal presence was no longer necessary for the pursuit of science. Science could now do on its own what Yahweh had commanded it to do—master nature. Therefore, by implication, Newtonian-Cartesian science could run history. Theology, as the displaced "queen of the sciences," the dethroned dowager of the Middle Ages, bristled at the Logos impudence of an adolescent science. Theological speculation could scarcely draw a distinction between the emerging Newtonian-Cartesian science (the "new science" of its day) and the highly suspect Hermeticism which orthodoxy had thrust aside. It was caught between the Scylla and Charybdis of "no god" and the larger archetypal totality of the Self. I would maintain, however, that the ecclesiastical/scientific imbroglio of today's world occurs within the personal and patriarchal paradigm of consciousness and is an aspect of the outworking, or translation (in Wilber's terms), of this paradigm. From a transpersonal and androgynous perspective, it can be seen as part and parcel of the same mode of consciousness, involving issues confronting that one mode—the issues of ego epistemology and ego ethics, the issues of the primal split between the archetypal masculine and the archetypal feminine. The scientific front of the transpersonal breakthrough is important for biblical hermeneutics precisely because the limitations of Yahwistic consciousness show up in the very exactitude of Newtonian-Cartesian science. By virtue of its overwhelming success, it has painted Yahwistic consciousness into a corner — trapping it in an epistemological/ethical conflict with no solutions. Thus the scientific breakthrough lends an urgency to the formation in human consciousness of transbiblical myth, which the theological world on its own, with its projections on the image of Yahweh/Christ still intact, would be able to resist. New science, in proving to the Newtonian-Cartesian world that ego epistemology is not ultimate, in the final analysis, proves to the biblical world that its god (even in eucharistic presence) is not ultimate. New science is not only new science. It is new theology and new philosophy. It is indeed alchemical hermeticism returned, but at a higher level of consciousness, a transscientific level.

New science has a long way to go, of course, before it proves itself to Newtonian-Cartesian science. News of the paradigm shift has not reached the mainstream. The paradigm being transcended, it would seem, is always the last to know. New science has even further to go before it tackles the Yahwistic mysteries of the "mighty acts" in the Torah experience and in the new Torah experience of incarnation and eucharistic presence. The mighty acts remain beyond the veil of scientific investigation, new or old. They contain the essential, suprahistorical riddle of history and of biblical theology. They are still considered the acts of an ultimate god, or rather *the* ultimate god.

The Newtonian-Cartesian paradigm has posed for biblical criticism the right scientific question, but not answered it. What really did happen in history *qua* history when Abraham left Ur, when a bush burned without being consumed, when the plagues hit Egypt, when the Red Sea parted, when a people were nourished on manna from the skies and water from a desert rock on their long trek through a wilderness, when a god-man called Jesus appeared on the stage of history? And what, if anything, is happening still through his eucharistic presence of Christianity and through the still-living Torah of Judaism, proclaiming the formative experience of Israel with which history began?

The Newtonian-Cartesian question remains unanswered because it cannot be answered. Within the Newtonian-Cartesian framework, it can only be posed. Ego epistemology, versed in positivism, cannot countenance such an archetypal invasion of its native preserve. The left hemisphere of the brain was not born to answer such questions. In order for the answer to be scientific, it would be necessary to trace the causal antecedents of such an invasion, to establish precedent and predictability, to prove beyond reasonable doubt documentary impeccability. But Yahweh's activity is unprecedented, unpredictable, and without traceable antecedents. The mighty acts were not scientifically repeatable, and the recorders of the mighty acts were not trained historians.

They merely witnessed the great Lord of History. No respectable scientist would touch their findings with a ten-foot pole nor, for a time, would any respectable biblical critic simply take their word for it. By a strange archetypal irony, the revelation of "no other gods," which became the revelation of "One God," turned into the revelation of "no god."

Chapter Eight

THE GREAT CHAIN OF BEING

*N*either Wilber nor Jung draws a direct connection between the biblical god and the development of ego or personal mode consciousness. Nevertheless, the overall mythic story or evolutionary framework that each presents begs the insertion of the biblical myth at its midpoint.

This god, who insisted on a personal, covenanted relationship with his personally chosen people, who focused attention on himself, who was jealous of other gods, who prohibited nonpersonal (or noncommitted) relationship (whether friendly or hostile), was, in the biblical accounts, never less or more than personal in his engagement of the human milieu, and, canonically understood, he was never without a reference point in history. Furthermore, never does the biblical god permit "his people" to be less than personal nor more than personal among themselves, nor without historical reference point. The Decalogue (Exodus 20:1–17) locates humanity in interpersonal relationship and in history. Interpersonal ethics (pertaining to friends and enemies alike) permeate and form the chief feature of the biblical story. History is the medium through which we learn to live with each other, or against each other, ego to ego.

From the biblical point of view, escape from the responsibilities of history is mere illusion. Yahweh and his people transcend (or seek to transcend) the natural realm and to march instead to the drumbeat of history – toward the goal of covenant promise, toward the Kingdom of Yahweh, toward the eschaton or fulfillment of history, when Yahweh will reign supreme over the human whole and, indeed (from the perspective of the biblical myth), over the archetypal totality. Biblical ethics, widely recognized as supplying the determining ethic of Western culture, creates a culture which pivots on ego, or personal mode consciousness, a culture invested in history and its fortunes, a culture which seeks to dominate nature. Thus, the connection Wilber and Jung failed to draw explicitly is drawn implicitly: the biblical myth is a myth of history and ego.

East and West

Wilber's work is still in process; nevertheless, among his prolific writings to date, he has achieved a cogent formulation of transpersonal psychology and established its theoretical foundations, primarily in two books: *The Atman Project* (1980) and *Up from Eden* (1981). The first, taking its title from Hindu philosophy, focuses on ontogenesis, the development of the personal "self" in the individual personality system. The atman is not to be confused with the personal ego of Western psychology; it does not designate the ego-centered personality, but rather the microcosmic replication through the personal psyche of the macrocosmic Self, the "brahman" in Hindu terminology. Here, again, we have the distinction between the personal self and the archetypal Self, in contrast to the personal ego and the archetypal Ego. *The Atman Project* takes an Eastern stance, akin to a gnostic stance but with a different tone; the Eastern traditions, unlike the gnostic traditions, have not grappled so intimately with the development of orthodox Yahwism. In today's world, the East/West mythic dialogue gathers global force, intensified for the East by its need of Western technology, but also for the West by its need to find some archetypal reference point outside itself, a reference point beyond ego epistemology and beyond the biblical god.

Both Eastern and gnostic traditions present a distinctly vertical direction of individual development, occurring somewhat in isolation from the flux of history. Ego, or the personal psyche, evolves as the product of a guru/disciple relationship and only through select personalities for whom "self-development" beyond ego becomes a way of life. Ego consciousness per se is not the focus, and these traditions do not develop (in Sheldrake's terms) a "critical mass" for ego consciousness. They do not strike an evolutionary plateau across a linear time span. Ego consciousness does not enter, via the paradigm of historical time/space, into the phylogenetic bloodstream of the general culture, which remains on the whole in a semi-prepersonal state. This remains true in Asian culture even today, although the global East/West dialogue is producing rapid cross-cultural exchange in this regard, and the Asian population seems to be assimilating in a few generations what many generations of biblically-fed Westerners have worked to implant in the phylogenetic field of the human whole.

Nevertheless, the god of the "mighty acts" is not deeply understood in Eastern spiritual tradition, and the tendency in these traditions (until the recent technological explosion) was to escape history, not to translate it. Escape from the turmoil of history can not be construed as a true transcendence of history, but it represents perhaps a prefiguration of that potential, and it serves as a reminder to Western culture that the paradigm of history is not ultimate. The exegesis of the myth which delivered its god to the East most effectively via atomic fission becomes of crucial importance in the global dialogue, for atomic fission can be seen as both the fruit of Newtonian-Cartesian science and also as the incipient, apocalyptic transcendence of that paradigm and its mythic limitations. *The Atman Project* represents Wilber's attempt to set the scene for evolution to work in the depths of the individual personal system, to open a new pathway in the personal psyche through which the strengths and deficiencies of East and West can complement and compensate each other.

The Outward Arc

Up from Eden, as the title suggests, serves admirably in the pursuit of a biblical hermeneutic from transpersonal theory. In this book, Wilber takes into account the sociological and religio-cultural dimensions of consciousness, the effects of which are drawn not only across the paradigm of history *qua* history, but also across the overall triadic process of evolution. *Up from Eden* presents a remarkable compendium of Eastern and Western esoteric and exoteric mythological development, tied into a loose-knit movement known as the "perennial philosophy" which has swept along the intellectual underside of Western culture.[1] Wilber introduces a concept, adopted from the perennial philosophy, wherein life is seen as a "great chain of being." The great chain of being not only describes the archetypal content of being, but delineates a definite order of unfolding. This concept, common to both Jungian and transpersonal psychology, is seen as crucial to psychological well-being. Disorders of the hierarchical process bring about dissociations and complexes in the human psyche. This is reflected in human consciousness both ontogenetically and phylogenetically. In line with Jung, Wilber assumes an ontogenetic/phylogenetic correspondence in human development and recognizes a microcosmic replication of the unfolding macrocosm as the goal of evolutionary process. Wilber is more systematically precise than Jung in this regard, but, in essence, his schema (shown in Fig. 8.1) of the evolution of consciousness, is compatible with the dynamics of Jungian psychology.

---

[1]The perennial philosophy was designated as such some years ago by Leibnitz, but it has been brought to the fore in more recent years by Aldous Huxley (1970).

SUPERCONSCIOUS UNITY

ANDROGYNOUS BEING, SELF, UNUS MUNDUS

8. Ultimate spirit	Spirit and Soul — mysterium coniunctio
7. Causal	
6. Subtle	
5. Psychic	
4. Higher mental EGO	HIGHER SOUL — Mind — unio mentalis
3. Lower mental	
---PRIMAL SPLIT-------- MYTHIC MEMBERSHIP	
2. Body Nature	LOWER SOUL — Body Matter — uroboric oneness
1. Physical nature	

INWARD ARC / OUTWARD ARC

MASCULINE PRINCIPLE / FEMININE PRINCIPLE

EVOLUTION / INVOLUTION

GROUND UNCONSCIOUS

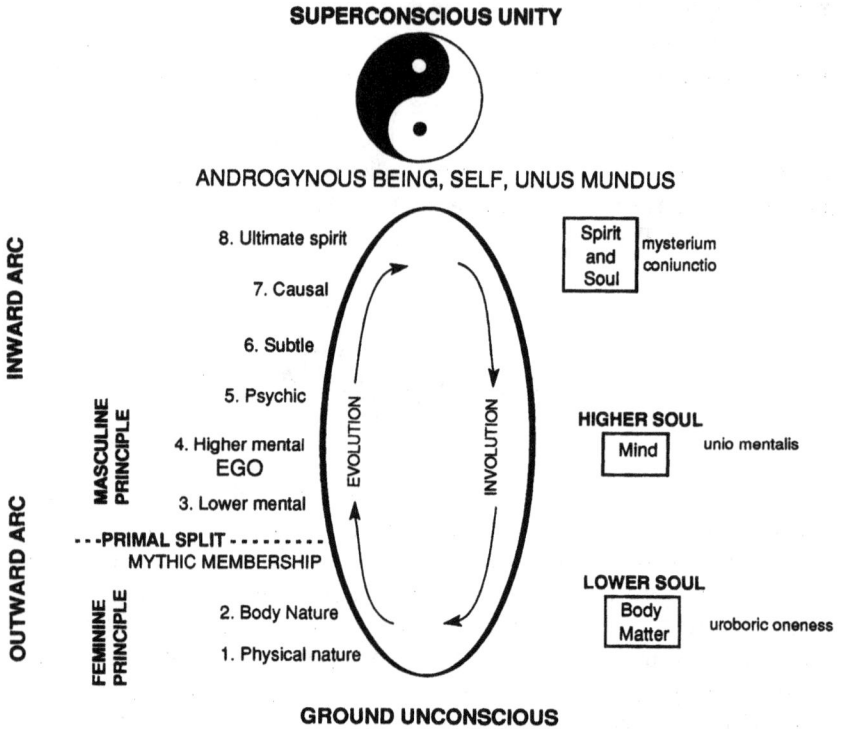

FIGURE 8.1 **The Great Chain of Being**

Ground Unconscious

A dynamic of the process lacking in Jungian thought, which shows up on Wilber's diagram, is the dynamic of involution, drawn largely from the tenets of Tibetan Buddhism. Involution constitutes the infolding of the archetypal principles into a "ground unconscious." The ground unconscious is analogous to Jung's collective unconscious but it is refined by Wilber to the point where the two concepts cannot be considered synonymous. Involution, as presented here, finds its source in the fused monistic Oneness of the taichitu, the feminine and masculine syzygies. Evolution, as Singer postulates, finds its goal in the return of these differentiated principles into the wholeness of the taichitu, the Oneness of "superconscious unity." Thus, the great chain of being connects with the Taoist model emphasized by Jung and the concept of androgyny explicated by Singer (1976, 1983). It also preserves Jung's definition of the overall movement of evolution from undifferentiated to differentiated Self, mediated by ego consciousness.

Wilber recognizes here, with more clarity than Jung, that the movement of evolution per se actually begins from the infolded fullness of a ground unconscious. The ground unconscious holds the full potentiality of both syzygies, bringing these potentialities to life in human existence through the ever-moving resonance of the great chain. The ground unconscious, in other words, is basic to the evolutionary process; each archetypal principle is contained within, infolded in its own aseity. Thus the ground unconscious provides a sort of neutral archetypal territory, hospitable to all principles in potentia, prior to their hierarchical unfolding.

It is this neutral quality that distinguishes Wilber's ground unconscious most significantly from the Jungian collective unconscious. Jung's distinction between the collective unconscious and the personal unconscious was seminal, but it did not go far enough. The collective unconscious, as Jung conceived it, was not neutral. It contained the primal elements, but it was also the place where repressed collective elements were contained, a repression incurred in the process of their evolutionary unfolding. Specifically, the collective unconscious contained the repressed elements of the mother world, the repressed original cosmogony of the Great Mother and her Satanic consort.

Personal Consciousness

Wilber delineates an evolutionary pathway that emerges from the ground unconscious and moves first through physical nature into body nature (both prepersonal modes of consciousness, dominated by the archetypal feminine in the guise of the chthonic earth mother). Wilber distinguishes three subphases within this first phase of prepersonal or matriarchal culture. Following Neumann (1954, 1955), Wilber speaks first of a uroboric stage of fused oneness, when otherness is scarcely recognized as such. The Uroboros symbolized for early humanity the biological great round of birth and decay, circumscribing a cyclical (not linear) sense of time contained in the womblike cosmogony of the Great Mother. A uroboric sense of oneness, basic to the cosmogony of the Great Mother, exerts a regressive pull on the transcendent ego. It exists at the level of physical nature, involved in a largely physical exchange with the environment. Wilber takes the uroboric characteristics of prepersonal consciousness as the sine qua non of the matriarchal phase of evolution.

Second, congruent with a budding sense of bodily being, comes typhonic development. This, it is arguable, is actually chthonic, or phallic, masculinity coming to the fore of human consciousness. It represents the inner masculinity (or animus) of the Great Mother, which later, in the formation of ego consciousness, must be put down by the Logos masculinity of mind. Wilber takes the name "typhonic" from the mythic misshapen Typhon, denigrated as a patriarchal misfit by Zeus. This phase is echoed in the biblical Satan, the chthonic Prince who is denigrated in the continuum of history by Jesus (the incarnate, yet nonchthonic Yahweh).

Third, Wilber distinguishes a mythic membership phase of matriarchal culture. As we discussed in Chapter Three, this phase (a later aspect of bodily being and dominated in large part by chthonic masculinity) represents the apex of matriarchal culture. It is the springboard from prehistory into history, the setting of a discontinuous confrontation struggle with an emerging patriarchal culture. The ghost of mythic membership culture lives on today in the tattered remains of an agonized mother-world torn loose from her roots and a puzzled, somewhat demoralized father-world, unable to read the legendary handwriting on its walls, the archetypal signs of its own times a-changing.

It is at this point that evolution incurs the primal split, a basic and radical division between the archetypal feminine and the archetypal masculine or, in other words, between the chthonic and Logos syzygies. One must make due allowance, as Wilber does, for cultural and developmental lag, for extended transitional periods accompanying paradigmatic change. Nevertheless, the new primal phase—the Logos patriarchal—emerged discernibly at this point from the ground unconscious not only to challenge mythic membership culture, but to alter (as certain research indicates) the very structure of the human brain.[2]

In early patriarchy, a lower mentality is developed which moves developmentally toward a higher mentality. Both are personal modes of consciousness, dominated by the archetypal masculine in the guise of the heavenly father, the great Logos Word-god. Both exercise the hitherto quiescent left hemisphere of the human brain, which is the special domain of the great Logos Word-god.

Wilbur labels the movement of evolution to this midpoint the *outward arc* of evolution. Along the outward arc, evolution moves toward and is guided by the development of ego (or personal mode) consciousness, dominated by the archetypal masculine. The outward arc takes in the first two cosmogonies—the prepersonal cosmogony of the archetypal feminine (the chthonic syzygy) and the personal cosmogony of the archetypal masculine (the Logos syzygy). It thus includes the primal split. Although not brought into focus by either Wilber or Jung, both recognize the archetypal seismic shock, the fury of dissociation and repression heard round the world, as the father god emerges into dominance. They do not incorporate it, however, as a *necessary* developmental aspect of evolutionary process; it has more the tenor of an evolutionary mis-

---

[2]Jung's recognition that archetypal energy is psychoid, affecting matter as well as psyche, makes such research tenable. The human body, including the human brain, is archetypally responsive. In Chapter Nine we will look more closely at the surprising correlations appearing in brain research between consciousness and brain.

take. Nevertheless, neither Jung nor Wilber would dispute the fact that, whether from evolutionary necessity or not, the emergence of Logos masculinity from the ground unconscious does indeed incur a concomitant dissociation from, or repression of, the primal feminine and her chthonic (typhonic/satanic) consort.

The outward arc finds its mythic culmination in the biblical story, a culmination which, according to the internal evidence of the myth itself, could not have occurred without a primal split. Therefore, the biblical genesis of ego is also a genesis of personal and archaic unconscious, which taps down deep into that dark and dubious well of mother-world posterity. When we look at Wilber's schema, or when we follow Jung's excursions into the unconscious, we are left in no doubt as to the origin of the great snake of the biblical genesis.

Exegesis V

He was pre-Edenic. He was also antebellum. He antedated the Holy War, the primal split between the primal syzygies. He remembered more innocent days, when all the fruit in a garden was to be eaten, when there were no forbidden trees, and no good and evil. He remembered when there was no death. Life and death were one in the biological great round of the Great Mother. Not intending to mislead Eve, his advice was a "natural" mistake.

As the Story Goes

As the biblical myth itself makes clear, the first emergence of patriarchal culture was quite primitive in comparison with that rich strata of ancient, but outworn matriarchal culture. Even as mythic membership flourished in the great pockets of agrarian, matriarchal culture, a man named Abram was called out of it by a strange, untested, untried, and unknown god. Abram was called into the wilderness of Canaan, in order to become "Abraham," *father* (in contrast to mother) of the world's great multitude of nations to follow in linear sequence down the corridors of time (Gen. 17:4–8).

A nomadic, nonagrarian existence prepared the Abrahamic people for an allegiance to history, their own personal history with their own personal god, rather than to the nourishment and uroboric containment of the earth mother. They become "Israel," and their story becomes the story of a people whose existence is pitched against the currents of nature. They are those who must suffer and survive the tension of a long and radical struggle between an abstract, transcendent god and a still-chthonic humanity (Gen. 32:27–31). In the tension of that struggle, the rules of the abstract father god were heard and obeyed; other gods, the mother goddess in particular, were repressed.

Still the earth mother at times proved too strong for the *bene Yisrael* and for their desert god (although none among them of Israel would ever think such a thing, much less mention it out loud). In order to escape famine (which their nonagrarian god of the wilderness seemed helpless to prevent), the children of Israel served a long stint as slaves of the "Great Dragon" in a "Great Dragon" of a country, that great matriarchal preserve along the Nile called Egypt. The children of Israel had all but forgotten the god of their fathers when suddenly the call came to remember him and to return to Canaan, the land of their birth. But the wilderness of Canaan, over the intervening centuries of Israelite slavery in Egypt, had itself become a matriarchal stronghold, a land "flowing with milk and honey," a fertile valley, a Baalim delight (Exodus 13:3-5).

The return of the children of Israel, now dubbed *apiru*, or "Hebrews" (meaning slaves, nobodies), was a daring expedition indeed (Mendenhall 1973, p. 90). It would be their first actual confrontation with matriarchal culture in order to defeat it, to displace it and proclaim the archetypal dominance of Yahweh in human consciousness. The nomadic Hebrews, finally straggling in from the desert under the charismatic leadership of the duly appointed Joshua, seemed no match for the rich, well-fed, and well-armed city-states of Canaan. One had to read the signs of the times astutely to be able to recognize the superior evolutionary potential of the Hebrews, bound in some sort of compelling and very personal covenant with their fierce, demanding, appalling, and highly unappealing desert god. His astounding claim of authority over all other dieties preceded him, but no one in Canaan was impressed, until one very strange, rather longish afternoon in Jericho when the sun stood still. This was surely an *opus contra natura*—like that burning bush which did not consume the earth's fuel, like the flowing waters which all of a sudden parted in the middle. What had happened to the goddesses and gods of nature? What on earth had happened to the night? The event fueled the disturbing rumors about the Hebrew god, about the astounding power of his Word, but surely there must be some other explanation. Who could be against nature, outside nature, above nature? How could a god function merely through his Word, apart from the great feminine container of the earth? The children of Israel had an answer—a god who possessed a heaven, a god whose throne room was in heaven, a god for whom the earth of the redoubtable Great Mother was merely a footstool (Isaiah 66:1).

The radical emergence from that throne room, some 2,000 years later, of the Word-made-flesh would seem to represent the supreme actualization in human consciousness of the Word or Logos energy. It took even the *bene Yisra'el* by surprise. Through his incarnation, the Logos cosmogony of the biblical god (as does the cosmogony of no other god) radically transcends and supersedes the chthonic cosmogony of the Great Mother. It supersedes even its own Eden. It is a creation within a creation, an "inner man" within a "natural man," the inner man independent of the *prima materia* of the Great Mother, exorcized at last of the chthonic Prince.

Personal Mode Consciousness

It seems fair to say that the image of the biblical god, as the god of personal relationship and the Lord of History stands out in the archetypal lineup as the purest manifestation of archetypal Ego to emerge from the ground consciousness. Ego begins, as Wilber makes clear, with the emergence of superego, the hallmark of which, in Wilber's view, is its repressing function, its rigidity, its unconsciousness, its blind attempt to assert itself against a threatening archetypal environment. Superego, implanted in the human milieu and representing lower mentality, introjects externally imposed rules and obeys them unconsciously.

The development of higher mentality is reflected biblically in a covenant written on the heart by the Logos-made-flesh, inscribed internally in the personal psyche via eucharistic presence and extended into all the world. This is not, however, to rule out the Talmudic continuation of the Old Testament through Judaism. The superegoic covenant leads toward the development of higher mentality through both Judaism and Christianity. Both covenants (the old and the new) are essential to the evolutionary fulfillment of the human whole, and neither could exist without the other. Their distinction nevertheless cuts into a woundedness still bleeding in the human psyche. It raises above all the specter of anti-Semitism, of modern day Jews being persecuted for the sins of their forebears in the crucifixion of the Christ. It is difficult for the Christian world at large to recognize that the sins of the ancient Jews, as well as their covenant, belong to humanity in toto.

Jung spoke of the outward arc as the ontogenetic/phylogenetic first stage of life, and he emphasized that the final development of ego maturity (Wilber's higher mentality) was of prime importance during this stage. Jung's development of higher mentality correlates with the *unio mentalis* of alchemy, which represents a oneness that splits off from, and opposes, the basic uroboric oneness of the chthonic realm.[3] Higher mentality represents the maturation and centering of ego in human consciousness.

---

[3]*Unio mentalis* is not to be confused with the higher oneness of the alchemical *unio mystica*. It is not a *unus mundus*, a seamless, eschatological heaven and earth. It is not the oneness of quarternitarian consciousness, as defined by Jung, nor is the oneness of transpersonal consciousness, as defined by Wilber.

Recognizing that the outward arc of Wilber's schema culminates in personal mode consciousness and that the development and sustenance of personal mode consciousness correlates with the biblical myth, it may be helpful to explore the biblical myth in the light of personal mode consciousness, to recognize its egoic cast in the spectrum of consciousness.

Personal mode consciousness is most aptly described by Grof. Depicting it as a "hylotropic mode of consciousness," Grof writes as follows:

> It involves the experience of oneself as a solid physical entity with definite boundaries and a limited sensory range, living in three-dimensional space and linear time in the world of material objects. Experiences in this mode systematically support a number of basic assumptions, such as: matter is solid; two objects cannot simultaneously occupy the same space; past events are irretrievably lost; future events are not experientially accessible; one cannot be in more than one place at a time; one can exist only in a single time framework at a time; a whole is larger than a part; and something cannot be true and untrue at the same time. (1985, pp. 345–346)

The struggle with the biblical myth, pronounced in Jung, is muted in Grof. The "basic assumptions" of hylotropic consciousness trace their mythic formation to the god who said, "You shall have no other gods before me" (Exodus 20:3), thereby placing his people in one specific dimension of consciousness — his own. The new covenant consciously extended ego capacity to the human whole, seeking to mature ego from within the personal psyche rather than from without. But it does not transcend ego.

The Inward Arc

The movement from personal mode consciousness to transpersonal consciousness, or ultimate reality, is termed by Wilber as the "inward arc." The inward arc is not to be confused with involution. It correlates rather with what Jung called the second stage of life. It represents the latter stage of evolution and depends, as does the outward arc, on the a priori dynamic of involution, its infolding in the ground unconscious. Along the inward arc, human consciousness is moving beyond ego, retrieving the archetypal totality excluded by ego, including both repressed and latent aspects. Jung speaks of the inward arc primarily as the recentering of the personal ego in the Self. This recentering produces an ego/Self dialogue in the psychic economy. Phylogenetically, it is connected with the emergence of the eschaton. The biblical new heaven/new earth is not established without the apocalyptic overtones of a decisive encounter between the Christ and the Antichrist. This eschatological encounter cannot be resolved by a final defeat of Satan or by exorcism, only by an integration of the Christ and the Antichrist into a higher order of consciousness. In Jung's terminology, it can only be resolved through the emergence of a "transcendent function." Wilber and Jung agree, however, that one cannot transcend what has not been fully developed. Thus mature ego consciousness, Wilber's higher mentality, is an evolutionary necessity for the effectiveness of the transcendent function and the development of transpersonal consciousness. Without it, devolution, or the collapse of ego, occurs, not evolution.

Grof again gives us a succinct description of his "holotropic consciousness." He writes:

> [Holotropic consciousness] involves identification with a field of consciousness with no definite boundaries which has unlimited experiential access to different aspects of reality without the mediation of the senses. Here there are many viable alternatives to three-dimensional space and linear time. Experiences in the holotropic mode systematically support a set of assumptions diametrically different from that characterizing the hylotropic mode: the solidity and discontinuity of matter is an illusion generated by a particular orchestration of events in consciousness; time and space are ultimately arbitrary; the same space can be simultaneously occupied by many objects; the past and future can be brought experientially into the present moment; one can experience oneself in several places at the same time; one can experience several temporal frameworks simultaneously; being a part is not incompatible with being the whole; something can be true and untrue at the same time." (Grof 1985, p. 346)

With this description, Grof makes clear the radical transition from personal (hylotropic) to transpersonal (holotropic) consciousness, the quantum leap between the outward and inward arc. The transpersonal paradigm both accepts and challenges the personal paradigm (and the god of the personal paradigm) at every turn.

Wilber delineates four specific subphases of the transpersonal paradigm. In their hierarchical order, these are the psychic, the subtle, and the causal phases of consciousness/existence, and finally the ultimate phase, characterized by a spiritual mastery of all phases. These phases (although they connect to some degree with biblical mysticism) are, on the whole, exoterically unheard-of in biblical culture. They have developed, however, on the underside of history in both Eastern and Western esoteric traditions and Wilber draws upon these to formulate his depiction of the higher phases. The psychic and subtle phases see the return of the archetypal feminine, although, in Wilber's opinion, she reenters ego consciousness at a higher level than when she left it (via repression). The causal and ultimate phases of evolution return the archetypal masculine to the fore, but, here again, at a higher level. These higher levels—the psychic, subtle, causal and ultimate levels—in Wilber's view (as in Jung's) function largely to reunite the primal principles of being (the feminine and the masculine). They function concurrently as the transcendent function, at a higher androgynous level of consciousness/existence, culminating in the superconscious unity of the Self.

The movement depicted by Wilber parallels the process in Jungian psychology, which moves along a spectrum analogous to the spectrum of light—from matter to body to mind to soul to spirit (or from the carbonic infrared of matter to the transmuted ultraviolet of spirit). Thus mind, or ego, is seen in both psychologies as the point of mediation between prepersonal and transpersonal consciousness. There is a tendency in both Jung and Wilber (perhaps more pronounced in Wilber) to associate soul and spirit with the higher reaches of consciousness (and with the feminine and masculine respectively). Wilber spells this out by assigning the psychic-subtle phases of transpersonal consciousness to the category of soul, and the causal-ultimate phases to the category of spirit. This would appear to eliminate soul and spirit in the prepersonal and personal phases of consciousness, although this does not seem to be the intent. What seems intended is the association of soul with the archetypal feminine, and the association of the psychic and subtle phases with her return to consciousness. The category of spirit designates the higher-than-mind, or ego, capacities of the archetypal masculine. Wilber's soul/spirit gendering here is in line with Jung's anima/animus definitions, and thus Wilber's schema is helpful in orienting us to the evolutionary potentialities of these two contrasexual capacities.[4]

Wilber's psychic-subtle/causal-ultimate gradations of evolution help us to

---

[4]Differentiated qualities of the primal principles permeate the evolutionary process. Hints of this turn up in all of the esoteric systems, but are perhaps most clearly brought out in the kabbalistic system of Jewish gnosticism. In particular, Jung brings the kabbalistic gradations of soul to our attention (1955-1956, par. 592-594). They become an important feature of his later thinking, for gradations of soul (the feminine) seem to mediate the liminal transitions into and out of ego consciousness (the masculine). Gradations of soul supply the continuum for the thresholds of transformation. Utilizing the kabbalistic system, a lower soul or body soul (nefesh) transmits consciousness into the lower mentality of ego consciousness. Ego consciousness (yod) finds its own inner soul (the Shekhinah, the Hokhmah, the Sophia, or—translated into New Testament terminology—the Paraclete, the Holy Spirit) and thus moves into its second phase of higher mentality. In its turn, the inner soul (or inner feminine) of ego transmits consciousness into the higher soul (tifereth). This sphere of the higher soul, tifereth, is Wilber's psychic-subtle sphere which sees the reemergence of the archetypal feminine. In tifereth, however, the archetypal feminine is no longer in the guise of the chthonic Great Mother, but approaches human consciousness in her higher manifestation as the Great Goddess. Likewise, spirit, a higher manifestation of the masculine, emerges through the psychic and subtle spheres, gathering in ego, bringing the causal and ultimate levels of consciousness into play. At the spirit level, the

recognize the nuances of a process that seems to leap off the edge of history into an unknown—a blank eschaton, an alien new heaven/new earth, a weird wedding (who can imagine what the *mysterium coniunctionis* will be like—no doubt it will depart from tradition), a world with no boundaries, no distinguishing marks whatsoever (are we sure we want to live in a *unus mundus*—how will I know what is mine and what is supposed to be yours?). Both Wilber and Jung urge us into the transpersonal, but Jung urges us to look at the journey in terms of the biblical myth and to recognize that our psyches are stamped with Yahweh.

The Growing Tip

An important feature of Wilber's conceptualization with which I will bring the discussion of Wilber to a close, is his notion (garnered from esoteric and Eastern tradition) that evolutionary process incorporates not merely one strand, but two strands of humanity. Wilber recognizes the existence of what he terms a "growing tip" of humanity.

The growing tip represents an advanced ontogenesis, an avant-garde version of humanity, distinct from, in Wilber's terms, the humanity of average mode consciousness. We can recognize in Wilber's definition of average mode consciousness Jung's definition of collective consciousness. This means that

---

archetypal masculine is no longer in the personal, mind-level mode of Ego, or yod, or of Yahwistic monotheism, but at the differentiated level of the monistic Self. Tifereth, it would seem, provides the first transpersonal meeting place (one should say healing place) on the other side of the primal split for the archetypal feminine and the archetypal masculine. Tifereth, in other words, provides the context of the *mysterium coniunctionis* and the birthplace of androgynous being. Thus tifereth represents that point of centering, of ego/Self centering, where ego completes its lonely, monotheistic journey and finds its home in the monistic Self.

It seems clear that the lower mentality of ego connects to a lower soul, and the higher mentality of ego reaches out toward a higher soul. In terms of a biblical hermeneutic, what is essential here is that ego sits in the mediating center between lower mentality and higher mentality, and thus, in the final analysis, between lower and higher soul. Yet the Kabbalah goes on to inform us that "tifereth occupies the middle position." This would seem to contradict ego's position, but it does not. Tifereth occupies the middle position of the unified microcosmic personality. It is known in kabbalistic tradition as Adam Kadmon, in gnostic tradition as the Anthropos (Jung 1955-1956, par. 592), in Buddhist tradition as the *boddhisattva*. To say that tifereth occupies the middle position is but another way of saying that Edenic Adam (Yahwistic humanity), centered in ego, is ultimately to be recentered in the Self. Jung recognizes the egoic paradox when he writes, "[Christ] incarnates God's good will to the exclusion of all else and therefore does not stand exactly in the middle" (1952a, par. 690).

while for both Jung and Wilber the main phases of evolution can be conceptual-
ized in terms of collective, or average mode consciousness, nevertheless, each
phase has within it living representatives of the other phases—some lagging
behind, some representative of the mode itself, some beyond the mode of
average mode consciousness, belonging instead to the growing tip.

Wilber's concept of the growing tip correlates with both the Eastern notion
of the boddhisattva and the gnostic notion of the three strands of humanity—
the hylic, the psychic, the pneumatic—which correlate perfectly with the three
modes of consciousness—the chthonic prepersonal, the logos personal, the
androgynous transpersonal. Gnosticism also makes clear that within average
mode consciousness at any level (whether chthonic, logos, or androgynous)
the three strands of humanity exist. There would seem to be no phase of
evolution that is pure. Average mode consciousness is a matter of dominance.
Gnostic concern, focused on the emergence of Yahweh and his takeover of
average mode consciousness, violently rejected the birth of Yahwistic humanity. In reference to Yahwistic consciousness, those lagging behind it were the
hylics, those within it were the psychics (or in Wilber's terms, the mental
egoics), and those ahead of it were the pneumatics, the growing tip. The
Gnostics, avoiding Yahwistic consciousness, veered toward the two extremes.
They tended either to indulge themselves in the chthonic/hylic depths of consciousness, or to reach toward the androgynous/pneumatic heights of consciousness. It seems likely that their own growing tip was ahead of Yahwism
before Yahwism got started, and a case could probably be made that even their
move into hylic consciousness constituted regression in the service of
transcendence.

Nevertheless, despite gnostic skepticism, the concept of the growing tip
speaks also, it seems to me, to the establishment of Yahwistic consciousness.
We are asked by the biblical myth to subscribe to the theory that Yahwistic
humanity (the mental egoics or psychics) developed in dissociation from a
prevalent (hylic or chthonic) version of humanity. Yahweh's particular strand of
humanity (the Abrahamic strand) was thus, in its time, a growing tip, created
specifically to develop the personal psyche, to center it in ego consciousness
and to insert it into the phylogenetic field of the human whole.

Because a man named Abram responded in faith to a new and untried god,
the personal psyche, centered in ego, exists today in the phylogenetic field of
humanity, invested with the eucharistic presence of its god, still transcendent,
even in incarnation, to the chthonic realm of nature. Thus the personal psyche
is still in conflict with prepersonal instinctuality, the legacy of the prior version
of humanity.

As Wilber and Jung both emphasize, however (in accord with gnostic and
Eastern tradition), beyond the biblical version of humanity a higher version of
humanity can be anticipated—an emerging strand, not as yet obvious, yet

existing esoterically through the ages within the phylogenetic whole. We would seem to be nearing the point where the current growing tip will find its own critical mass and will seek to transcend, to transmute and transform, biblical humanity. In that transcendence, the new growing tip heals the primal conflict (the struggle between a chthonic humanity, subservient still to the claims of the Great Mother, and the egoic humanity of a Logos god).

This conflict, however, as Jung is careful to point out, exists not merely between cultures and nations, but within the personal psyche of each of us, mocking (as Paul lamented) our best intentions, thwarting a shallow righteous-ness and the shallow patina of Christianity. The new growing tip, seeding the phylogenetic field of humanity, has integrated the primal conflict within the personal psyche, has provided the microcosmic container for the archetypal integration of the macrocosm (or the Self), and transforms the whole of human-ity into its own healing image. As we discussed in Chapter Six, Singer (1976) refers to the growing tip of today, those who are forming a critical mass on the eve of Aquarius, as the "New Androgynes." She indicates thereby that the new growing tip is directly concerned with the transformative event which Jung found of ultimate importance – the *mysterium coniunctionis*, the reunion in con-sciousness of the archetypal feminine and the archetypal masculine, the estab-lishment (both ontogenetically and phylogenetically) of quarternitarian consciousness.

The Dynamic of Translation

In order to summarize Wilber's thought, I will utilize another of his dia-grams, again modified to bring forth my own interests. Taken from Wilber's depiction (1981, p. 9), Figure 8.2 orients us in still another way to Wilber's schema. It depicts in generalized, nonmythical terms the archetypal content and principles at work in the overall patterning of evolution. Figure 2 displays the gradual evolution of consciousness along an outward arc and an inward arc, culminating in the final overcoming of unconsciousness in all its forms.

In the background, not depicted in the diagram, is the movement of involu-tion, the infolding of the archetypal principles into the ground unconscious. In evolution, they unfold in hierarchical order, but in reverse. The lowest goes first, and then each in turn from bottom to top, stepwise. The higher move up through the lower, but, in contradistinction to Darwinism, they are not pro-duced by the lower. They unfold along the outward arc from chthonic (preper-sonal) consciousness to ego (personal) consciousness, encountering in the

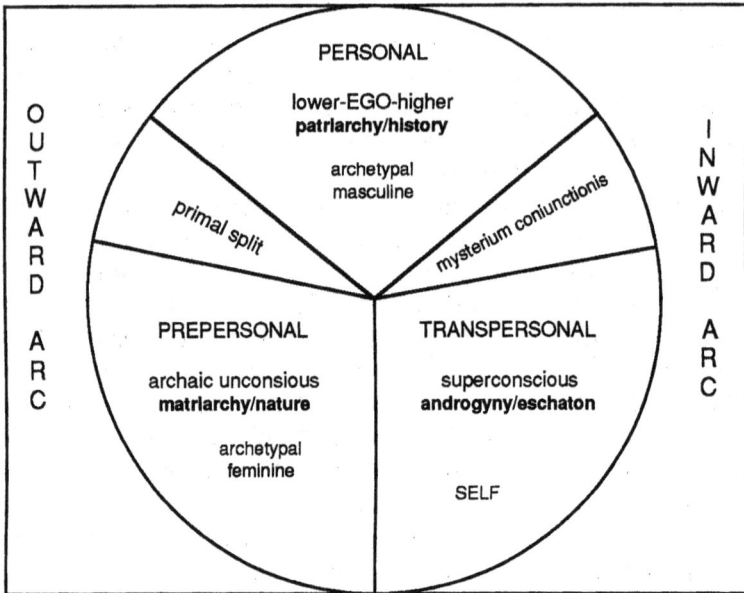

FIGURE 8.2   The Evolution of Consciousness

transition the primal split, or, as Wilber puts it, a primal dissociation rather than a clean differentiation.

Grof's hylotropic mode (and the paradigm of history) is thus orchestrated in human consciousness at the midpoint, or second phase, of the evolutionary process. The third phase of the process (if it is not to be truncated by human fallibility) moves along the inward arc and sees the emergence of the transcendent function in a new order of consciousness. As Jung put it, the transcendent function is the third thing uniting the opposites of prepersonal and personal consciousness. The latter, as we know from the mythic story, is born out of the repression of the former and thus cannot take the former into its oneness.

The new consciousness, the third phase of transpersonal consciousness (as described by Wilber), the holotropic mode of consciousness (as described by Grof), sees the ending of the paradigm of history, the emergence of the eschaton, the establishment of a new wholeness in a new heaven/new earth. Trinitarian consciousness (which is egoic, monotheistic, patriarchal, and hylotropic) becomes quarternitarian, inclusive of the archetypal totality, inclusive of the two differentiated primal syzygies, who, in their differentiated reunion, form the monistic Self.

Thus ontogenetically and phylogenetically, microcosmically and macrocosmically, evolution moves along the outward and inward arcs from the ground unconscious to superconscious unity. *This ultimate state of consciousness, which recenters ego in the Self, exerts a teleological pull on the ground unconscious, actualizing and integrating all aspects of unconsciousness:* (a) the archaic unconscious (which was chthonic consciousness); (b) the repressed personal unconscious (which is the id or the shadow); (c) the repressing personal unconscious (which is the superego or the undifferentiated persona); and (d) the emergent, or latent, aspects of the ground unconscious (which could not function in ego-centered consciousness). Thus, like the sea in the biblical eschaton, the ground unconscious is no more. The Self is totally explicated and known to itself. The overall evolutionary story is complete.

The archetypal content of Wilber's schema seems clear. The phasic dichotomy between consciousness and unconsciousness seems clear. Granted the hypothesis of this study, the fit of the biblical myth in the midpoint of Wilber's schema seems clear. The issues with which we are left to struggle have to do with the dynamics. Wilber's concepts of transformation and translation interface with the biblical concept of the eschaton. The dynamic of transformation in itself presents no problem, but the dynamic of translation, as Wilber defines it, is questionable in terms of the biblical myth and its paradigm—our own.

Translation there must certainly be. No one can argue with the concept that the archetypal energies must be actualized, that the complexes must be resolved, that this is the ultimate demand of the process of individuation-evolution. One wonders, however, if translation can occur at the surface level of a deep structure that is inherently repressive, one deriving from a primal split, one founded on a heavenly wedge thrown across the spectrum of consciousness. Will the translation of such a paradigm not require a transformation, an influx of new archetypal energies? The question is important because the end of the patriarchal era is upon us now. Will its translation be complete? Will it transform quietly, or will we find ourselves in the middle of archetypal combat?

Provisionally, we can say that patriarchy does not end with translation, if translation means that its complexes are resolved, its archetypal frustrations overcome. Patriarchy ends, as it began, on a note of hostility, squared off against its chthonic enemy, a scenario biblically depicted as the Christ against the Antichrist. Translation of the patriarchy occurred, if it occurred at all, in the center of history, as ego maturation reached its highest point. The biblical Christ represents Yahweh's assumption of his own guilt for his own partial creation, for his own sin. In the Christ, Yahweh takes upon himself his wrath against a hapless humanity, which he himself created in chthonic flesh, thus leaving unconscious traces of the chthonic truth and a split in the personal psyche to match the primal split.

Archetypal Ego is now centered in the Christ, and the Christ centers ego within the human whole. Yet ego centering is off-center. As Jung recognizes,

Christ is split off from the shadow. He lacks the chthonic, and therefore is not at the center of the archetypal totality. Tifereth, as the Kabbalah informs us, is in the center, inclusive of the archetypal totality. Thus patriarchy must still face a recentering, beyond surface translation, beyond translation at the level of the Yahwistic heaven. Translation of the paradigm of history does not heal the primal split. And yet the task of translation is no lighter. It is to establish the Kingdom of Yahweh on earth as it is in heaven. This will carry us an evolutionary step in the right direction. It is an essential step, but not a final step. The final translation of both the first and the second cosmogonies, of both matriarchal and patriarchal consciousness can occur only in the subtle-transcendent heavens of tifereth, or in the Self. Translation of the first two phases of evolution can occur only as transformation into the third phase is complete. Judiasm, Christianity, and Islam inherit the biblical myth, in secular as well as sacred form, and each finds it a heavy burden to bear.

Chapter Nine

THE NEW
SCIENCES

*N*ew science has a brief, but intense history. Paralleling Jung's psychology, it reaches back to the early part of the century, when the challenges of quantum physics began to crowd in on classical physics. In particular, the subjective/objective dichotomy of ego epistemology was challenged. Quantum physicists began to perceive that at the nuclear level the material world, which had seemed "objective" on the surface, was not objective at all, but depended upon the framework of observation and measurement, or, in other words, on the subjective position of the scientist. Heisenberg formulated his famous Uncertainty Principle to take this strange nuclear breach of scientific etiquette into account. On this principle, as Jung expressed it, "reality forfeits something of its objective character and a subjective element attaches to the physicist's picture of the world" (1954a, par. 438).

Jung welcomed such advances in the field of physics, at the very core of the so-called exact sciences, for he recognized that such advances undermined the ruling position of positivism, or behaviorism, in the psychological and sociological sciences. Positivism, emulating physics, turned on the objective measurement of observable behavior and ruled out of reality all subjectivity or "mentalisms." Nature, even human nature, had become pure object to the observing Cartesian ego – an ego turned inside out, wandering the academic byways of mechanistic science like a lost soul. The Uncertainty Principle lent support to Jung's own psychology, a psychology also based, as Jung claimed, on objective reality and on empirical methodology. But Jung's objective reality was not merely the reality of the outer world. It was primarily the reality of the inner world, the inner contents of the psyche, the reality of archetypal energies, the very reality that positivists dismissed as mentalisms. These could not now be ruled out of reality by the pure rationalism of the ego-centered psyche, since the ego-centered psyche had now to admit that its rationalism was not pure, that it stumbled over its own subjective feet of clay in its objective world.

The "turning point," as Capra (1982) puts it, has come rapidly, and, the paradigmatic shift from classical science to new science is being detailed by many writers in the field today. The growing realization on the part of the new discoverers that the classical laws of physics had been breached, perhaps fatally, by their own data, was not accepted with pure scientific detachment, but with unscientific dismay. Thus the latter half of the twentieth century has been one of unsettling confusion for the innovators of new science. The breakthrough of classical science is also a breakthrough of classical biblical hermeneutics. If the Newtonian-Cartesian paradigm is not ultimate, then neither is the biblical god, for the Newtonian-Cartesian paradigm comprehends the Yahwistic world, the world of ego epistemology and ego ethics.

The biblical genesis set up the deep structure of a mental heaven ruling over a demythologized earth, opposing history to nature, as the paradigm of the ego world. The Yahwistic heaven, transcending nature, allowed the mental ego to develop and centralize itself in human consciousness, to orient itself in the continuum of history, and to objectify and dominate nature. Newtonian-Cartesian science appropriated the mental ego. There it was, sitting in the middle of an objective world, like a ripe apple waiting to be plucked. Newtonian-Cartesian science had merely to withdraw its projections from the Yahwistic image, from the suprahistorical Lord of History, to harvest it. The Cartesian I AM echoed at last the great Sinai I AM, claiming the archetypal identity as its own. It is as if the fingers of Adam and his god, a millimeter distant on the ceiling of the Cistine Chapel, have met at last. Through the Cartesian I AM, the mind of man learned to hear its own thoughts, to recognize its own authenticity.

It is arguable that the withdrawal of projection could be accomplished during the Christian era, the latter part of it, because the eucharistic presence of Yahweh had done its work, inculcating the mental ego, not only at its highest ethical level, but also at it highest epistemological level, in the phylogenetic field of humanity. Whatever the reason, it is clear that the basic assumptions of Newtonian-Cartesian science were drawn from the archetypal energy represented by Yahweh, and that these basic assumptions work only within the paradigm of the biblical genesis. Where the biblical paradigm is not religiously imposed, it is scientifically imposed on cultures developing under the aegis of Western technology. It is a paradigm that overrides ancient cultural assumptions, ancient rituals, ancient goddesses and gods, reducing them to the status of museum pieces within their own culture. It does scarcely better by its own god. The death of Yahweh within his own paradigm has not been a well-kept secret. We have not learned to withdraw projections gracefully, but then Yahweh was not a very graceful god. Ego had not learned the difference between transcending a god and displacing him.

Thomas Kuhn (1962) introduced the notion of a paradigm to the scientific world, describing its development and the hold it then exercises on the scientific mind. Kuhn's description helped awaken Newtonian-Cartesian science to its possible limitations and shortsightedness. Although Kuhn defined the existence of a paradigm in reference to science, it is not difficult to recognize that paradigms relate to an archetypal background, to the differentiation of archetypal energies as they evolve through human consciousness, to the deep structures of the evolutionary story—thus the direct link of the Newtonian-Cartesian paradigm with the biblical myth. New science, however, would seem to derive from the manifestation of new archetypal energy and from the emergence of new myth—transpersonal energy and transbiblical myth.

Grof affords help in interpreting the work of the new scientists in terms of the new paradigm. Grof's concern is to make it clear that the new paradigm does not invalidate the old paradigm, but rather incorporates it and places it in a larger context (1985, p. 11). The old paradigm, growing out of the famous "cogito," functions still within its own framework, but its framework is no longer to be considered as ultimate.

Wilber has serious reservations concerning the interpretation being put upon the work of the new scientists. Wilber fears what he calls "category error" (1982, pp. 157–185). He means by this that each hierarchical level, or category, delineated on the great chain of being must be scrupulously taken into account and not syncretized or confused with other levels. This provides the basis for our hypothesis—that the biblical myth establishes a paradigm (the egoic) and that it must not be confused or syncretized with other myth. Analogies can be made, but category error must be avoided.

Wilber's warnings are well taken. But he seems to miss the important point that the new scientists, working within the framework of Newtonian-Cartesian science, are breaking through that paradigm from within. In so doing, they show experimentally and empirically, with the hardheaded methods of mechanistic science, the clay feet of that paradigm. In other words, new science offers authentic challenge to the mechanistic paradigm. Granted, it may not grasp, in all of its particulars, the overall dimensions of the great chain of being, nor the theoretical position of transpersonal psychology. This, however, is not its function. Its function is to remain within its own bailiwick—whether physics, or chemistry, or biology, or neurological research—and to show within its own bailiwick, and according to the mechanistic methodology of its bailiwick, that the Newtonian-Cartesian paradigm is not broad enough, that it cannot accommodate a new and totally unexpected influx of data. The new data, in essence, would seem to derive from new archetypal energy, and thus from a higher paradigmatic level than Newtonian-Cartesian science. Using Wilber's own principle, the higher has come through the lower, but it was not produced by the lower. It is discontinuous with the lower and thus calls for a new paradigm, a new myth.

The New Physics

David Bohm burst out of the paradigm of classical physics, in which he had earned a rather comfortable niche for himself, and into the world of new science with a book called *Wholeness and the Implicate Order* (1980). The book, in essence, questioned the wholeness of what Bohm called the explicate order, the order that we see around us, the order of the paradigm in which we live, which sprang into being at the biblical genesis and in which matter is inanimate or passive, molded into shape by a power transcendent to nature. Undergirding, and, in fact, generating explicate order, in Bohm's opinion, is a world we don't see, an implicate order. In this world, as Bohm came to recognize, inanimate matter has a life of its own. This life in matter, not manifested (except negatively) in the explicate order as we know it, is nevertheless implicitly present in matter in the implicate order.

Bohm further recognized that the implicate and the explicate orders relate to each other in a kind of constant and reciprocal dynamic that he called the holomovement. The holomovement represents an energy that cannot be cut off; it is ever-present as an ineluctable and determinative force. As of now, the negative manifestation of the holomovement is the biological great round of decomposition and decay. The explicate is simply pulled back into the implicate, and thus the holomovement describes a closed universe, subject to entropy. As Bohm sees it, however, ultimately the discrepancy between the implicate and explicate orders will be resolved. In the process of the holomovement, matter will be transmuted to a higher energy level, a higher level of consciousness.

Here, Bohm runs into Wilber who rejects this quantum leap out of matter into higher consciousness. In terms of the biblical myth, Bohm's theory suggests that it was transmuted matter which engendered the resurrected body of Jesus. Following Wilber, I would argue that it does not. The body of Jesus was nonchthonic in the first place. It did not come from the lower level of matter. There was no intent, in Bohm's terms, to bring the implicate order of matter to new life. Far from overcoming the discrepancy in the holomovement, Jesus perpetuated it. He proved that the explicate order as we know it need not collapse into the implicate. He gave the explicate a transcendent permanency. Jesus did not reconcile Bohm's two orders. This reconciliation is yet to come.

Bohm's holomovement and its two orders intend to pertain, within the framework of physics, only to matter itself, but in this Bohm is unsuccessful. Since consciousness is implicit in the implicate order, Bohm, to Wilber's dismay, cannot avoid dealing with consciousness, and the ramifications of such an arrangement are all too suggestive in terms of the evolution of consciousness. Bohm's concept of the holomovement would seem, at first glance, to parallel

Wilber's concept of involution/evolution. Bohm's implicate order would seem to suggest Jung's a priori archetypal pleroma or Wilber's infolded ground unconscious. If this were the parallel, Wilber's protests would be on target. However, from the point of view of both Wilber and biblical myth, it is more accurate to say that Bohm's implicate order fits the geological stage, the matter stage of the Great Mother, and thus cannot inform us, via a holomovement, in regard to the higher stages. It becomes clearer perhaps if we say that Bohm's implicate order parallels the chthonic cosmogony and its fall into the archaic unconscious, not the ground unconscious.

If we look at Bohm's work with the biblical myth in mind, it is as though Bohm had peered behind the elaborate production of the mechanistic biblical god (who—like the Wizard of Oz—appeared to be running things), only to find that the atomic building blocks, composing the static forms of this god's cosmogony, were anything but stable. The "nature" created by this god was not natural. The cosmogony created by this god was staged, a kind of pseudo-creation, a facade, for the purpose of glorifying his mind, of promulgating his clockwork way of doing things, not nature's meandering way. The biblical genesis in effect blocked the holomovement, which in Bohm's view (although he cannot say how) would nevertheless have its day, overruling the staged world of inanimate matter and static forms. For a physicist, imbued with the rules of the mechanistic world of the father god (misleadingly billed as "the laws of nature"), it was a dizzying sight, and Bohm's work was perhaps the clearest ringing of an alarm bell in the world of science, signifying that all was not well in the explicate order it called home.

John Bell (1966) had no idea of lending himself to the cause of new science. He still does not claim that distinction, although new science, especially in the form of paranormal science, is apt to claim him. Utilizing a theoretical position of Einstein's, Bell has established an experiment using photons, or particles of light, that shows some physical basis for the proposition that consciousness itself might possibly move faster than the speed of light and—by extrapolation—that consciousness might possibly possess effective intentionality. Bell's experiment was intended to deal with the hidden variables which in classical physics are presumed to exist to explain the as-yet inexplicable. In classical physics, however, the hidden variables are presumed to be mechanistic and locally operative, obeying, as everything must, the infallible "laws of nature." But instead, as Grof (1985, p. 58) puts it, "John Bell presented a proof that in quantum physics such hidden variables . . . would have to be nonlocal connections to the universe operating instantly." Grof goes on to say that "according to Henry Stapp (1971), Bell's theorem proves 'the profound truth that the universe is either fundamentally lawless or fundamentally inseparable'" (1985, p. 60).

Either way, so much for Yahweh's separatist, mechanistic universe, and so much for his "laws of nature." As Einstein recognized in the direction of the new physics – so much for Yahweh himself. Einstein was well aware of, and regretted, the shaking of the paradigmatic foundations and its god. Paranormal psychology, not attached to the Yahwistic laws, does not regret the shaking of the paradigmatic foundations. It finds in Bell's spectacular – but nevertheless repeatable – experiment confirmation of telepathic and other psychic properties of consciousness, properties which defy ego epistemology and its paradigmatic barrier of the speed of light, properties which defy the paranormal proscriptions of the god whose cosmogony began with light, who initiated his transcendent creation with the words, "let there be light."

The New Chemistry

We turn now to the work of Prigogine. As Prigogine saw, the trap of the Newtonian-Cartesian paradigm is the second law of thermodynamics. It is a scientific trap comparable to the mythological trap of a dead god, a god squeezed out of the universe by his own paradigmatic success, a god run down and existing now merely by psychic inertia. The second law of thermodynamics specifies that inevitably, as the universe has run out of god, so it will run out of energy. Energy will give way some day to entropy, and life – the life which the biblical myth had assured us was sustained in heaven and was intended to be on earth as in heaven – would be lost on the earth forever in thermal death. Heaven seems very remote in the face of thermodynamics, not worth the blood, sweat, and tears of history. As Grof (1985) puts it, life to the scientific world had become "an insignificant and accidental anomaly involved in a quixotic struggle against the absolute dictate of the second law of thermodynamics" (p. 61).

Biblical predictions of apocalyptic catastrophe preceding the eschaton found their scientific expression in the second law, but, contrary to biblical hope, science found no room for messianic expectation. Prigogine found it embedded in the chemistry of the "laws of nature" (Yahweh's and Newton's laws of nature). Prigogine studied the so-called "dissipative structures" in the chemical chain of being, structures that are able to dissipate entropy, to let it not accrue and overwhelm energy. Moreover, as Grof points out, Prigogine discovered a new principle underlying these dissipative structures – a principle he christened, "order through fluctuation." As Grof tells it:

Further research revealed that this principle is not limited to chemical processes, but represents a basic mechanism for the unfolding of evolutionary processes in all domains—from atoms to galaxies, from individual cells to human beings, and further to societies and cultures. [How is this for wild extrapolation and category collapse?]

As a result of these observations, it has become possible to formulate a unified view of evolution in which the unifying principle is not a steady state, but the dynamic conditions of the non-equilibrium systems. Open systems on all levels and in all domains are the carriers of an overall evolution which ensures that life will continue moving into ever newer dynamic regimes of complexity. Microcosm and macrocosm are two aspects of the same unified and unifying evolution. Life is no longer seen as a phenomenon unfolding in an inanimate universe [the biblical universe]; the universe itself becomes increasingly alive [the transbiblical universe]. . . .

From this point of view, humans are not higher than other living organisms; they live simultaneously on more levels than do life forms that appeared earlier in evolution. Here science has rediscovered the truth of perennial philosophy, that the evolution of humanity forms an integral and meaningful part of universal evolution. Humans are important agents in this evolution; rather than being helpless subjects of evolution, they *are* evolution [italics his]. (Grof 1985, p. 61)

I have quoted Grof at some length because, in his interpretation of the work of Prigogine, he has captured the very heart of both Jungian and transpersonal psychology. His interpretation makes clear that, in his opinion, new science is "rediscovering" perennial philosophy, not displacing it or revising it, as Wilber fears. Through the advance of new science, a higher cognition is being established in personal mode consciousness, preparing for the development of the transpersonal mode in collective, or average mode consciousness. Through this higher cognition in the personal mode, the wholeness of Bohm's implicate order is finally to be fully explicated in transpersonal consciousness, the mysteries of Bell's minute photons are finally to be penetrated through transpersonal consciousness, the intricacies of dissipative structures will dominate the chemistry of transformation into transpersonal consciousness. This recognizes that humans live simultaneously on all levels, and that as transpersonal consciousness breaks in, and recenters ego consciousness, it revises the Newtonian-Cartesian paradigm, aligning it with the perennial philosophy. And furthermore, it aligns the god of the Newtonian-Cartesian paradigm with the overall story of evolution.

In his interpretation of Prigogine's work, Grof has also captured, unwittingly, the heart of a biblical hermeneutic and its connection with transbiblical myth. The apocalyptic message of the biblical myth is that the domain of the biblical god is eternal. It cannot be destroyed. It will transmute into a new structure, a structure of higher complexity, an eschaton (a new heaven/new earth) which sustains it. Thus the biblical myth in itself is a dissipative structure. The mistake of the biblical myth, however, is two-fold: it does not recognize that the chthonic realm also cannot be destroyed, and it does not recognize that the biblical myth represents an essential phase, but not the ultimate phase of evolution.

It is intriguing to speculate, in the light of Prigogine's work, that chemistry may indeed play a part in the transition from biblical to transbiblical, or from personal to transpersonal existence. The resurrection of all flesh, the creation of a new heaven/new earth are images of chemical transformation. The incarnation of Yahweh in itself gives some hint of a chemically unique composition of human flesh, the effects of which may be organically registered in the human brain.

We simply do not know what role dissipative structures in the chemical chain will play in paradigmatic transformation. We do know, as we have noted, that in Prigogine's theory the transformation, or transmutation, from domain to domain, from level to level, from old myth to new myth, has always an element of discontinuity about it. The principle of fluctuation is just that. The new order derives from a newly emerged element from the ground unconscious, an element which was not conscious, and not operative, in the old order. Thus, although it connects with the old order and incorporates it, the new order, in Prigogine's view (as in Wilber's), is not produced by the old. It is at the point of transition that a kind of reflex in the process of evolution occurs. The entropy of the old order is dissipated. A new thing is born. Jung's transcendent function is brought into play. Wilber's categorical differentiation from one level into the next is set in motion. The Great Chain fluctuates in tempo with the process of evolution.

The New Biology

Sheldrake (1987) is the very latest of the new scientists to move out of the laboratory and into the public eye. His work at this point commands interest because he offers experimental confirmation to transpersonal theory of one of its most cherished assumptions: that evolutionary process is not dependent on genetic inheritance and environmental influence alone, transcending the cause-and-effect syndrome of linear time. It is transcendent to the paradigm of history. Jung's discovery of the archetypal energies of the collective unconscious,

Wilber's concept of the ground unconscious, Bohm's recognition of an implicate order, all bespeak an energy field of consciousness beyond the energy field of history. We can recognize especially in Jung's concept of synchronicity the delineation of a dynamic playing across the paradigmatic dimensions and energy fields of consciousness. In Sheldrake's terms, this is the dynamic of "formative causation." It is not merely genetic (or biological) nor merely environmental (or historical). It incorporates causation, but it transmits these influences into "morphogenetic fields" which effect phylogenetic change in whatever species is being addressed. Sheldrake's theory is reminiscent of a discredited Lamarckism, which theorized the inheritance of acquired characteristics. Sheldrake differs, however, in that he posits morphogenetic fields, not linear genetics, as the transmitting agent.

Genetic and environmental influences are transmitted into the morphogenetic field of a species via the formation of a "critical mass" within the species. In the words of Grof (1985), "if a critical number of members of a species develop certain organismic properties or learn a specific form of behavior, these are automatically acquired by other members of the species, even if there are no conventional forms of contact between them [including genetics]" (p. 63). A cumulative effect on the species – "morphic resonance" – seems to attach to the formative causation of a critical mass. Morphic resonance seems to tilt phylogenesis irreversibly. Sheldrake has been able to demonstrate his theory by experimental work with animals, especially rats and monkeys. He is well aware, however, of the far-reaching implications of his work for the individuation-evolutionary process as delineated by Jung and the transpersonalists. Sheldrake's theory of formative causation echoes Jung's theory of the archetypes and their synchronistic causation:

> [The term *archetype*] is not meant to denote an inherited idea, but rather an inherited mode of functioning, corresponding to the inborn way in which the chick emerges from the egg, the bird builds its nest, a certain kind of wasp stings the motor ganglion of the caterpillar, and eels find their way to the Bermudas. In other words, it is a "pattern of behaviour." This aspect of the archetype, the purely biological one, is the proper concern of scientific psychology. (Jung 1948a, par. 1228)

But, as Jung well knew, psychology (unless behavioristic) cannot be confined to biology and ethology. Biology provides the base or the grounding of the psyche, and, in this sense, it is of primary importance, but it cannot contain the entire spectrum of the psyche.

Sheldrake's concepts afford an invaluable grasp of archetypal activity and the dynamics of evolution. In the light of his theory of formative causation, the biblical myth can be construed as the archetypal formation of a people who seed the phylogenetic field of humanity, or form critical mass within it. They are those who are to grow from the tiny proportions of the mustard seed into the vast proportions of a mustard tree sheltering all of humanity (Mark 4:31). The history of Israel in ccvenant with Yahweh is the story of the formation of critical mass, dependent for a time on genetic and environmental influence, but then moving beyond genetic and environmental influence into a "morphic resonance" affecting the phylogenesis of the human whole. The basis of formative causation was Abraham and Torah, but, as we learn, Yahweh could raise up children of Abraham from the stones (Luke 3:8) and go out on the highways and byways to find guests for his eschatological banquet, his finishing touch on the human psyche (Luke 14:23).

The Christic influence, or the new covenant in the Christ, bases itself on the formative influence of Israel in the phylogenetic field of humanity, but the new covenant requires its own institutionalized container – the church. The separateness of Israel had protected Israel from collapse into the still-seething chthonic mass of humanity, but at the same time had curtailed its effectiveness in formative causation. The church sought to close the gap, to move into the four corners of the earth, to establish critical mass, to set in motion the morphic resonance of the god called Yahweh. If our hypothesis has merit, the biblical mission was/is to instill within the phylogenetic field of humanity the properties of ego, so that every human infant born anywhere, on any part of the globe, has within him or her the capacity of ego consciousness. Biblical ethics revolve around the development of, and the honoring of, this capacity in everyone, even in "the least of these my brethren" (Matthew 25:40).

A biblical hermeneutic which sees the function of biblical myth as phylogenetic ego-building puts Judaism and Christianity (and Islam) in a very different position vis-a-vis humanity as a whole than has been traditionally the case. It prevents the condition which Moore has referred to as pseudospeciation (1987, p. 159), for it recognizes that ego is not the final destiny of humanity. In the terminology of Wilber and Moore, it enables the Judeo-Christian tradition to reclaim its unfinished ritual task of inculcating mature ego, rather than performing the shallow persona-restoring ceremonial to which it has become accustomed. The emergence of the eschaton and Islamic fundamentalism on the horizon of Pisces requires nothing less. The plight of third-world countries, lacking ego refinement and human necessities, let alone human rights, requires nothing less.

Moore and others in the Jungian field still hope to assign this new task of formative causation to the church, but, since the church is without myth in this regard, this seems to me archetypally untenable. The most we can hope from the church (as from the Judeo-Christian tradition in general) is to allow it its ritual task of the translation of strong and durable ego capacity in the morphogenetic field of humanity. I would hope, however, that the church would do so with a greater degree of consciousness concerning its myth than it now possesses. However, the new setting of transformation beyond ego (and beyond the aegis of the biblical myth) is, in my opinion, to be looked for in the psychological world, not the theological. Jungian psychology supplies the cognition necessary to grasp and interpret it. It also supplies the sacred space/time continuum for the conjunction of opposites within the personal psyche. The biblical process ends with the splitting off of the shadow; the Jungian process of individuation begins with its integration.

According to Sheldrake, we cannot change the biblical myth; its morphic resonance is set in motion. It is valid so far as it goes and must stand as it is. But we can accept new myth that compensates the biblical myth. We can become a part of a new seeding of human consciousness, members of a new critical mass, working from a base within the Judeo-Christian tradition, if that is a part of our calling, but yet beyond the Judeo-Christian tradition and its god.

The New Neurology

We come now to the work of MacLean on the evolution of the human brain. The nebulous relationship between mind and brain is important in the formulation of a transbiblical hermeneutic of the biblical story. The brain is the seat of the actualization and translation of the archetypes in human affairs, reflecting the psychoid nature of the archetypes, their physical as well as their psychical imprint. Consciousness, in this view, is not an epiphenomenon of the brain; rather the reverse, consciousness is a priori, and the brain is its instrument. As such, it seems probable that the development of the human brain reflects the evolution of human consciousness, developing correlatively with the overall mythic story of evolution and fits hand-in-glove with the overall spectrum of consciousness.

As Jungian and transpersonal psychology depict a triadic process of evolution, a process composed of three fundamental phases, so MacLean pictures three brains in one, a kind of organic homoousia encoding at its current apex the mythic trinity. Both aspects—the three and the one—are important. MacLean himself emphasizes the threeness, the triadic process, while Pribram emphasizes the oneness, the incredible holographic properties of the brain.

A depiction of MacLean's "three brains in one" is given below in Figure 9.1. Immediately apparent is that the "three brains" are developmental and that each reflects an evolutionary phase in the development of human consciousness. Taken together they are roughly correlative with the three aspects of Wilber's prepersonal, matriarchal phase of consciousness. Beyond MacLean's

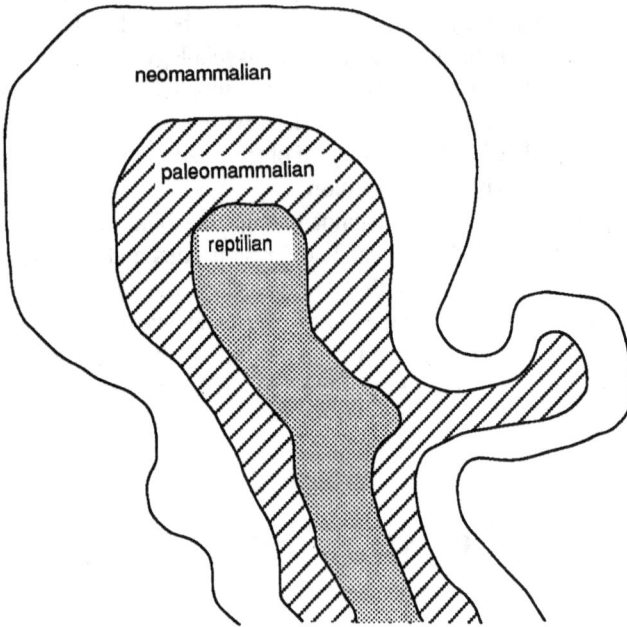

FIGURE 9.1   MacLean's Brain

depiction, we recognize a continuing evolution of the brain; most important development, for instance—hemispherical lateralization—is not depicted. This further development carries us into the personal, patriarchal phase of consciousness and suggests that further evolution of the brain will comprehend the overall format of Jungian and transpersonal psychology, its entire prepersonal-personal-transpersonal triadic spectrum. Studies have been made that are suggestive along this line.

The earliest brain is the reptilian brain, the dark inner core of the brain stem. For many millennia that's all there was. Humanity slept in reptilian slumber, embedded in a fused oneness, a consciousness mythologically depicted by the huge uroborus. As Stevens (1982) puts it, "emotions had not yet emerged, nor had cognitive appreciation of future or past events. Behavioral responses at this level are largely governed by instinct and appear to be automatic" (p. 264). The human potential is there, waiting for its full complement of consciousness to emerge, teleologically prepared to be receptive to higher modes of consciousness. The higher modes, which will come through, but are not produced by, the lower modes. In this sense, human consciousness is already distinct from animal consciousness, but at the uroboric stage of development it is scarcely noticeable.

The next stage of brain development – the paleomammalian, or paleocortex, stage – can be identified with Wilber's typhonic level of consciousness. Although still in the prepersonal, matriarchal mode of consciousness, the brain is more aware of the body *qua* body. It is most likely that at this stage the mind could look back in rudimentary self-reflection, in dim recognition of where it had been. The midbrain, as the paleocortex is sometimes called, is composed of the limbic system, which includes the hypothalmus and pituitary glands, the homeostatic mechanisms of the body. The major emotions of fear and anger develop, imparting a fight-or-flight stance to the body. The chthonic, "idian" sexuality discovered by Freud would have emerged into consciousness here, in thrall to the Great Mother and exhibiting a tendency toward incest and thus arousing the castrating tendencies of the Great Father. Behavior at this time is still largely determined by instinct, although less automatically so. The "rules" of the superegoic father have not yet been inculcated, but, nevertheless, they are being dimly anticipated. A kind of judgmental capacity, an affective capacity, is in evidence, but it is based more on feeling than on thinking. It is not based on abstract regulations, an abstract covenant, an ego-to-Ego relationship, a Word.

The next stage of brain development, the neomammalian (or neocortex), represents the apex of brain development to date, at least in so far as average mode consciousness is concerned (we cannot be sure, unfortunately, of the brain development of the growing tip). So far as we know, the neocortex, in its totality, represents the apex of matriarchal consciousness, and also, ironically, the apex of patriarchal consciousness. However, in the transition between the prepersonal and personal modes of consciousness, lateralization of the neocortex occurred. The "new human brain" – the neomammalian – was divided into two hemispheres, known simply in the literature today as the right and left hemispheres of the brain,.

The right hemisphere, as we know, controls the left side (the passive Yin side) of the body. The right hemisphere and the left side of the body are associated, and for good developmental reasons, with the archetypal feminine, the Great Mother, the chthonic syzygy, the archaic unconscious. The right brain "is more holistic, working to provide us with perceptions, intuitions, nonverbal processes, 'illogic,' and nonsequential activities" (Litvak and Senzee 1986, p. 76). The right brain correlates with the mythic membership phase of consciousness: persons are not yet persons, they belong to a group, existing en masse. They are beholden to a king or a tribal leader who simply tells them what to do, who directs them. They are embedded in the forces of nature, placating and cajoling the goddesses and gods thereof. There is no personal relationship, except through the king, for there is no person otherwise. Sexuality is still chthonic or phallic, intended to fertilize and make productive the Great Mother, who nourishes the body. The king is her spouse, king as long as he is sexually potent, deposed as his potency fails. Old kings must die, but death is not viewed with great horror. It is a part of life, a part of a natural process. This is not, as it might seem superficially, a transcendence of ego, or faith in the power of the ego god to defeat death. It is simply the pre-egoic acceptance of the fact that one comes from dust and one returns to dust. In any case, one who is not fully one is not lost from the Great Mother. Her geological/biological great round recycles everything. Everything the Great Mother creates is biodegradable. The fertile valleys of the world are her sacred space, and also the high places, where among the druidical trees the moon is visible. Her timing is lunar, based on the waxing and waning of the moon and the feminine menses. It follows the seasons, stretching from planting time to harvest time (summer to autumn) or from dormant time to flowering time (winter to spring). Her calculations of time are cyclical, contained in a small circumference, comprehended completely in the biological great round.

By contrast, as Litvak and Senzee go on to say, the left brain "specializes in logical, verbal, sequential, symbolic, and analytical functions" (1986, p. 76). As we gather from this pithy description, the left brain, controlling the right side (the active Yang side) of the body, resembles in every respect the mental ego. Wilber quotes Gebser in this regard:

> We have two reasons for choosing the designation "mental" [or mental-egoic] to characterize the structure of consciousness still prevailing. . . . First, the word harbors an extraordinary abundance of relations in its original root, which in Sanskrit is *ma*, . . . all the words formed from this root [expressing] definite characteristics of the mental structure. Secondly, the word is one which stands at the beginning of our Western culture . . . . This word "mental" is contained in . . . *Menis*, [the word] with which the *Iliad* begins . . . a statement which for the first time within our Western world . . . describes a ceremonial act directed by man (not exclusively by the gods), in an *ordered or causal course of events* [italics mine].

> Thus, we are dealing with directional thinking, which comes tentatively out in the open. If mythical thinking [or paleologic] . . . was an imaginative, symbolic projection, which took place within the confines of the [uroboric] circle . . . directional thinking is radically different. It is no longer polarized, that is, enshrined in and mirroring [cyclical] polarity; it is *object-oriented and hence turned toward the objective world* [italics mine]. (1981, pp. 182–183)

It is not difficult to recognize the paradigm of history in directional thinking which is aligned with the causal course of ordered events. Nor is it difficult to recognize the Newtonian-Cartesian paradigm in the description of an object-oriented world. Gebser appropriately associates the development of the mental ego with the *Iliad*. The Greek gods, swooping down upon the matriarchal goddesses of the Greek world, certainly took over the goddess world. The Great Mother is separated from her daughter, her Kore, her own self-contained inner source of renewal. The Kore, too, is appropriated by the gods and placed in the underworld of ego consciousness. A new daughter, a new kind of feminine, replaces the Kore in consciousness, springing directly from the head of Zeus. Gradually a new kind of polis begins to emerge, developing slowly over the long haul of kingship. Human consciousness begins to embrace the ideal of a political democracy, which favors the development of the personal psyche, of individual rights and responsibility. In the new myths emerging, the patriarchal myths (or the left brain myths), "the individual triumphs over the Great Mother—breaks free from her, transforms her, defeats her, or transcends her" (Wilber 1981, p. 183). Greek myth tells the archetypal story well, and Greek culture moves consciousness into patriarchy where the heroic ego (the budding mental ego) prevails.

Nevertheless, there is another myth that tells the ego part of the evolutionary story even more radically, and in the long run more accurately. Wilber, somewhat unwittingly, pinpoints this myth when he writes:

> In ways never really seen before, the ego did not just transform up and out of the typhonic and membership stages, it violently *repressed* them. The ego rose up arrogant and aggressive, and . . . began to sever its roots in a fantasy attempt to prove its absolute independence [italics his]. (1981, pp. 181–182)

The archetypal energy thus described belongs, of course, to Yahweh, not to Zeus.

The point for now, however, is to recognize that something momentous occurred in the lateralization of the "new human brain," its neomammalian cortex—a radical leap from the first major phase of consciousness (the matriarchal) to the second major phase of consciousness (the patriarchal), or, in effect, from a first to a second cosmogony. When did this momentous event occur? Can a date be established for the breakthrough of the mental ego out of the maternal darkness into a paternal light, and its consequent effect on the brain? Wilber quotes Campbell in this regard:

> Toward the close of the Age of Bronze (c. 2500 B.C.) and, more strongly, with the dawn of the Age of Iron (c. 1250 B.C. in the Levant), the old cosmologies and mythologies of the goddess mother were radically transformed and set aside in favor of those male-oriented, patriarchal mythologies . . . that by the time a thousand years had passed, c. 1500 B.C., had become the dominant divinities of the Near East. (1981, pp. 184–184)

It is interesting to note that Campbell, although he scarcely seems to notice it himself, slips patriarchal mythology into the Levant, into Canaan, into Judea and Samaria. He thus, somewhat off-handedly, associates it with the biblical myth and the god of the Hebrews. He merely fails to recognize that the patriarchal divinities of the Levant are not plural, but singular. A monotheistic Ego is at work in the mythology of the Levant, as in no other mythology.

Approximately around the beginning of the time frame set by Campbell, 2500 B.C., we hear the voice of the strange father god whispering to Abram: come out of Ur of the Chaldees into a land that I will show you; enter into covenant with me and I will make you Abraham, the father of a multitude of nations. And, again in Campbell's time frame, around 1250 B.C., a young Hebrew (nobody or slave) named Moses, descendent of Abraham (but yet, under strange circumstances, reared in the palace of Egypt) hears the voice of Abraham's god addressing him: go and tell Pharoah, who holds my people enslaved, to let them go; tell Pharoah, if he should ask, that the great god, I AM, is sending you. This is the myth, I would submit, that is the true myth of lateralization, the true myth of the left hemisphere of the human brain. Conversely, the lateralization and the development of the left hemisphere of the brain offers a salient hermeneutical principle for the biblical myth—the correlation of the biblical god with ego.

As the left brain gained cultural dominance, the right brain sank into a kind of slumbering unconsciousness, the hidden property of artists and lunatics, only to be discovered and pulled into prominence at the turn of the twentieth century by depth psychology. The development of left brain dominance has been, roughly speaking, a four-millennia process, with considerable developmental and cultural lag and pronounced individual differences. Nevertheless, it dominated average mode consciousness and was discernible to brain researchers. The right brain became the source, not of conscious everyday activity, but of dreams. The right brain tapped down into the ancient brains—the paleomammalian and reptilian brains, into the still-living mythic energies of the mother world, into the phallic realm of chthonic instinctuality. It found, in the pre-ego world, personalities, or subpersonalities, which were conscious, but not conscious to ego. These subpersonalities, or archetypal images as Jung called them, found their centers deep down in the mythic realities of evolution, and they reflected these mythic realities.

The pre-ego goddesses and gods of the chthonic realm still lived in these subpersonalities, and also the pagan deities, the patriarchal gods and goddesses of the Greco-Roman world, and other such cultures. These too had been displaced by Yahweh and thus thrust out of the left hemisphere of the neocortex (which they had helped establish) and into the right hemisphere. There, in the ancient brain system, the ancient archetypes still lived, speaking through dreams or fantasy, their voices heard in the world only when the left brain was unguarded. Jung can perhaps be credited as the first to trace these strange voices to their source, to take seriously their archetypal validity, their challenge to ego and the monotheistic god of ego. He made room in the compendium of his psychology for a further development of consciousness, a consciousness that would envelop the archetypal totality.

What happens to the brain beyond the development of its left hemisphere? Where in the development of the brain is a setting for the eschatological event? Research at this point can be only suggestive and based largely on speculative intuition. But speculative intuition and educated guesses have been the mainstay of scientific discovery more often than positivistic research cares to admit. Speculation at this point focuses on the dividing line between the two hemispheres of the neocortex, the corpus callosum. Its dormancy has been more or less taken for granted through the years of concentration on right-left specialization. The corpus callosum seems to act primarily as a line of demarcation, functioning mainly to differentiate (and to dissociate) the two hemispheres, as evidence of the primal split, to protect the budding left brain from its once dominant, unmarked off other side (its dark side). But, given the psychoid nature of archetypal energies, Jungian and transpersonally oriented psychologists have begun to suspect is that the corpus callosum may not play merely a blocking role, one to be breached only at night. In response to the demands of evolution and to new archetypal activity, its role may be subtly changing.

Singer's definition of androgyny gives psychological substance to the growing speculation concerning the function of the corpus callosum. "Androgynous love is essentially transpersonal in nature," she emphasizes (1976, p. 330). This distinguishes androgynous relationship from purely interpersonal relationship, although it does not exclude erotic love (as Christian agape tends to do), but carries it into a higher dimension, a truer maithuna. Androgynous love, as a new quality of love, is thus tied in with Jung's transcendent function and, therefore, in Stevens's view, with the function of the corpus callosum. "All the while, however slowly, evolutionary consciousness is increasing in the world," Singer concludes (1976, p. 335). In terms of brain development, this would mean that the corpus callosum, and perhaps other parts of the brain as well, are beginning to function differently. It would mean that new archetypal capacities (specifically the androgynous) are being brought into play, and that, concomitantly, the brain is responding.

The work of David Loye (1983) contributes a different point of view to the general speculation concerning brain development and the evolution of consciousness. He focuses on the future development of precognitive capacity in the brain. Loye recognizes that pretransformational science, as he terms it, could not come to grips with this capacity, except superficially. Precognition can only be studied by new science as it breaks through the Newtonian-Cartesian paradigm. Loye suggests that this latent capacity, as it develops under the dictates of evolution, will locate itself in, and affect the further development of, the frontal lobes of the brain. He points out that the frontal lobes are embedded in both hemispheres of the brain, thus drawing from both. Also, they are situated on either side of the *ajna chakra*, the third eye, the transcendent function of the Kundalini system of higher consciousness. Furthermore, the corpus callosum itself, besides bridging the left and right hemispheres, also connects *ajna* with the typhonic and uroboric brain structures (the paleomammalian and the reptilian brains). Thus the frontal lobes, functioning in conjunction with *ajna*, receive tremendous stimulus from the total brain.

Loye also points out that there is another form of lateralization of the brain, of lesser renown than the corpus callosum, but perhaps as important. This is the central sulcus, or fissure of Rolando. This "wrinkle" in the brain divides the front and posterior parts of the brain, the frontal lobes from the brain stem. Concomitantly the central sulcus provides potential connection between right and left brains. Thus two connective avenues, the corpus callosum and the central sulcus, function first to differentiate consciousness, but are available also to reunite consciousness (and the archetypal totality) as the transpersonal paradigm emerges. These two avenues meet at the top center of the brain, and it is tempting to wonder about the meeting point. Could this location in the brain be analogous to the *sahasrara chakra* of the Kundalini system, or perhaps the *kether* of the Kabbalah, each representing the epitome of consciousness? We cannot be sure what kind of development will follow in brain structure, or for that matter in the organic constitution of the human body, but we do have a sense of the archetypal direction. The pattern to be actualized is holistic, involving a mysterious conjunction between the feminine and masculine principles, leading toward the formation of a new world unity, what Jung called *unus mundus.*

With uncanny accuracy, MacLean's charting of the "three brains in one" has led us to see an evolutionary correlation between mind and brain. His work suggests that the actualization of an archetype in human consciousness is not without specific encoding, and thus not without structural alteration, in the brain. MacLean's work affirms Jung's notion of the psychoid nature of the archetype and also makes clear that consciousness is not, as positivism had led us to believe, an epiphenomenon of the brain. Rather the structural capacity of the brain correlates with and is determined by the evolution of consciousness. The encoded archetypes may be transcended, but they cannot be ignored, as even today a selective positivism would have us believe. Singer, in her conceptualization of androgynous being—utilizing the full complement of archetypal energies that have thus far developmentally confronted us—leads us toward that transcendence.

To move from MacLean to Pribram seems on the face of it to involve us in an abrupt switch, a change of direction, a contradiction. MacLean's work emphasizes the compartmentalization and specialization of the brain. Pribram's work emphasizes holographic properties of the brain, which seem to deny specialization. And yet, as we have seen, when we consider the brain's specialization, we arrive at a vision of the brain's development in the direction of wholeness, the developmental contradiction resolved. Differentiation and specialization make wholeness possible. Transpersonal consciousness cannot form where consciousness has remained undifferentiated. We see by MacLean's work that the process of archetypal differentiation and dissociation is reflected in the brain's specialization. Pribram's work gives room for speculation that the recentering of the archetypal totality in the differentiated consciousness of the Self is to be reflected ultimately in the brain's holography, but a holography which includes specialization.

Pribram, looking for the distribution of memory traces in the brain—a distribution that did not seem to be as localized as specialization of the brain would suggest—came finally to base his research on the model of holographic photography, or on the hologram. The hologram, a lensless form of photography employing lazer beams, was the brainchild of physicist David Gabor. The hologram is a three-dimensional image, but, more surprisingly, the fragmented pieces of the hologram retain the whole image. This model of reality corroborated Pribram's rapidly accumulating data that memory is nonlocalized and seems to be held, in the manner of a fragmented hologram, in the very cellular structure of the brain, its tiniest and well-distributed entities. After much finely tuned research, Pribram's conclusion is that the brain itself is holographic, reflecting a holographic universe, and that each cell of the brain is a faithful replication of the whole brain (the microcosm replicating the macrocosm). No matter its location in the brain, no matter its specialization, each cell of the brain contains, encoded within itself, the whole of the brain (and thus, in principle, the whole of the macrocosm). In principle, each and every cell of the brain can function in each and every specialized way. In principle, each and every cell of the brain can function as the whole brain. In principle, each and every brain (microcosm) can function as the macrocosm. Odd to think that each microcosmic personality might reside in toto in any one of its brain cells.

The New Psychology

Sperry (1988) chronicles the paradigm shift in the field of science from behavioral research to consciousness research. Sperry is best known for his work in mind-brain research. He is no stranger to the issues discussed above.

He was among the first to perform experiments with the corpus callosum, leading thereby to the much heralded discoveries of the properties of the right and left brains. His early work with the corpus callosum was governed by a positivistic conception of human behavior, a positivistic view of science, a tendency to dismiss archetypal realities as a mentalisms. His views, therefore, on the paradigm shift in the field of science are of interest today.

Sperry traces the shift from positivistic thinking to the scientific acceptance of "mentalisms." For Sperry, the shift is a foregone conclusion, not merely a shift still in process. It has happened, although, of course, it is happening still. As we have seen, positivism is with us still as a sort of semi-conscious selectivism, but not in principle. Sperry attributes the shift in the final analysis to mind-brain research. Positivism was toppled, in Sperry's opinion, not by the new physics, or systems theory, or any number of other presumed causes, but by researchers in the field of positivism itself, as their data became less and less explicable within the constraints of the old paradigm. Sperry's contention is that the paradigm shift is a consequence of the resulting "changed concepts of brain and consciousness" (1988, p. 54). From the cumulative data of mind-brain research a new principle took shape. It is referred to by Sperry as "the principle of emergent or molar determinism." He defines it as follows:

> According to this view . . . things are controlled not only from below upward by atomic and molecular action but also from above downward by mental, social, political, and other macro properties. Primacy is given to the highest level of controls rather than to the lowest. The higher, emergent, molar or macro phenomena and their properties throughout nature supersede the less evolved controls of the components. (1988, p. 44)

Or further, "The mentalist position is emergent, holistic and antireductionist" (1988, p. 53).

Thus the new principle of brain and consciousness, as stated by Sperry, controverts the mechanistic approach which sought to reduce everything to its least common denominator and to analyze the whole from its parts. It controverts behaviorism which reduced human psychology to its least common denominator of measurable behavior and analyzed the whole from its parts. It also controverts the Darwinian cast of positivism, which saw evolution as moving from the most elementary forms of life into an inexplicable higher complexity, or which saw the higher as produced by the lower — whether materially, organically, or in terms of behavior. In the Darwinian view, there was no ground unconscious, there was no teleological principle, there was no emergent determinism. Human consciousness was produced by the ape. The human psyche was defined by its observable behavior. One can see that these reductions were absurd and severe. Little wonder that the old physics responded to this worldview with the second law of thermodynamics. Where the whole was a product of its parts, where the universe was closed to higher energy, the energy supply of the universe would be finally depleted.

Jung, in his clinical work with the psyche, had long ago recognized and pinpointed some fallacies of behaviorism. In the face of reductionism, Jung held firm to the teleological properties of the Self. Wilber, in his insistence that the lower does not produce the higher, has championed Jung's stance and counterposed transpersonal psychology to positivistic science. In Sperry's new principle, however, the behavioral point of view and the transpersonal point of view would seem to meet. In the half century since Jung first challenged it, positivism has come full circle, recognizing that it can no longer be so positive, and that, as Wilber puts it, science must admit spirit. The principle of emergent determinism echoes Jung and Wilber, and it echoes Sheldrake's principle of formative causation. It aligns with the principle of the emergence from the ground unconscious of the determinative, organizing principles of an a priori, infolded archetypal totality.

The important point to be made, however, and the note on which to end our discussion of new science, is that in Sperry's estimation the paradigm shift has occurred. The world of science now exists in it. We have spoken as if new science were a thing of the future. We hear from Sperry that new science has transcended, but also incorporated, the Newtonian-Cartesian paradigm. Furthermore, in Sperry's view, the shift registers not only in science and psychology. It "represents a fundamental correction applying not only to all the sciences but also to the humanities and to contemporary thought in general" (Sperry 1988, p. 53). As applied to biblical hermeneutics, it would suggest that the world created by Yahweh is no longer supreme. Its categories have been transcended in human consciousness. The potential exists today for humanity to look down on, and back on, the Yahwistic creation, to recognize the principles that define it as phasic aspects of consciousness, to penetrate the paradigmatic barriers that have divided it off from a higher consciousness, to utilize the hitherto undeveloped capacities of the corpus callosum, the central sulcus, the frontal lobes of the human brain, to approach *ajna*. Evolution seems to be moving on, beyond the heaven of Yahweh, into an open universe.

Here, on the eve of the Newtonian-Cartesian paradigm, Boorstin (1985) takes us on an exploration of the amazing clockwork world of the old order. His hero, he writes, is "Man the Discoverer" (p. xv). His hero, in other words, is the heroic ego, moving out of the biblical pages into the world of nature to subdue it. We conclude our breathless exploration of the new sciences with the following remarks from Boorstin:

The mysteries of the atom multiplied with every new discovery. The limits of mathematics were increasingly disclosed. In the mind of Einstein the unity of phenomena . . . brought "scientific" problems and paradoxes beyond the ken of any but Hermetic philosophers. Time and space came together in a single tantalizing riddle, which led Einstein to conclude that "the eternal mystery of the world is its comprehensibility." (1985, p. 684)

Perhaps. But one senses a willingness on Boorstin's part to travel beyond the universe in which God doesn't play dice. He writes, "The most promising words ever written on the maps of human knowledge are *terra incognito* — unknown territory" (1985, p. xvi).

PART THREE

Chapter 10

THE RELIGIOUS WRITINGS OF C. G. JUNG

*T*wo approaches to the biblical myth that become apparent throughout Jung's work are illustrated in his autobiography, *Memories, Dreams, Reflections* (1965). I call these two approaches "the smaller schema" and "the larger schema." The smaller schema is based on an Ego god, while the larger schema associates God with the Self. In his youth, Jung rejected an Ego god and was looking in vain to the biblical tradition for help with his developing concept of the Self. It never became quite clear to Jung that he could find help with his concept of ego in the biblical myth's traditions or that ego could not have developed in the human milieu without help from an archetypal source, an Ego god.

Jung recounts a significant dream of those early years, one which became highly pertinent to the later development of his psychology, and one which he might have connected with the archetypal necessity of an Ego god. In the dream Jung had to make headway against a mighty wind. His hands cupped a tiny light which threatened to be extinguished by the mighty wind. Yet "everything depended," as Jung writes, "on my keeping this tiny light alive." Jung found himself being followed in the dream by a gigantic black figure—his own shadow cast against the swirling mists behind him by the tiny light. Jung recognized this tiny light as his own ego which had to be kept alive within the vastness of the Self, against the winds of transpersonal transformation, and against the shadow of prepersonal regression. The dream provided a tenet that became a mainstay of Jungian psychology—the essentiality of ego in the human constitution.

Jung might have amplified this dream by the biblical myth—particularly by one of his favorite texts in *The Gospel of John*—where the Logos light shines triumphantly in the darkness of the undifferentiated Self. The biblical myth, Jung might have recognized by his dream, recounts the psychological work of

Yahweh (the mythic I AM) as he sought to keep alive the tiny light of ego within the prepersonal and transpersonal vastness of the archetypal totality of the Self (1965, pp. 87–88).

Again in *Memories, Dreams, Reflections*, Jung almost suggests a correlation between Yahweh and ego, as he writes:

> By virtue of his reflective faculties, man is raised out of the animal world, and by his mind he demonstrates that nature [I would say evolution] has put a high premium precisely upon the development of consciousness. *Through consciousness he takes possession of nature* by recognizing the existence of the world and thus, as it were, confirming the Creator. The world becomes the phenomenal world, for without conscious reflection it would not be. If the Creator were conscious of himself, He would not need conscious creatures; nor is it probable that the extremely indirect methods of creation, which squander millions of years upon the development of countless species and creatures, are the outcome of purposeful intention. Natural history tells us of a haphazard and casual transformation of species over hundreds of millions of years of devouring and being devoured. . . . *But the history of the mind offers a different picture. Here the miracle of reflecting consciousness intervenes—the second cosmogony.* (1965, pp. 338–339)

One easily recognizes here the process of ego formation at work. Jung does not distinguish the work of the two syzygies (the chthonic and the Logos), but he speaks of a second cosmogony, which is associated with the development of the mind, and which takes possession of nature. (One is tempted to substitute the name of Yahweh when Jung speaks of the Creator.) Furthermore, Jung goes on to connect this passage with the Piscean era—the Christian era formed by and responsive to the biblical myth. In effect, Jung has given us here the larger schema of his psychology.

There are several main aspects of Jung's treatment of the biblical myth and the myth's traditions, drawn mainly from *A Psychological Approach to the Dogma of the Trinity, Transformation Symbolism in the Mass*, and *Answer to Job*. These works seem to inhibit to some degree Jung's view of the larger panorama of the archetypal totality. They seek, as the youthful Jung sought, to find this totality within the biblical god, rather than beyond the biblical god. They seek to claim the biblical god for the Self by expanding him. The opposite effect results, however; the archetypal totality tends to shrink. Jung sees the danger and he moves with bewildering inconsistency between his view of a larger schema and his hope to encompass that schema in the figure of Yahweh, which I have termed a smaller schema hidden within.[1]

These two schemata offer a rough guide for the intertwining complexities of Jung's thought. They are mythic variations on a theme—Jung's constant theme of transformation, of the evolution of human consciousness. Jung (as one soon discovers in the voluminous collection of his work) was a heuristic, not a systematic, thinker, and Jungian psychology offers both orthodox and gnostic versions of Yahwistic consciousness. The two schemata reflect strategic approaches in this regard: the smaller, moving out of a narrow, theological context, was directed to a theological audience; the larger, encompassing a broader mythological context was directed to the world at large.

To the theological audience, Jung says, "If Christianity claims to be a monotheism, it becomes unavoidable to assume the opposites as being contained in God" (1954b, par. 358). This provides the framework of his smaller schema. He sets himself to prove, if he can, that the opposites are contained in Yahweh; but the results are less than satisfactory.

To the broader, more amorphous audience, Jung seems to be saying that the biblical myth is neither broad enough nor elastic enough to contain the opposites. One needs to read carefully the mythological literature of the world. One needs to take seriously the esoteric as well as the exoteric literature in regard to the god called Yahweh, and the development of the alchemical as well as the orthodox point of view.

The Larger Schema

Although the overall mythic story, in which the biblical myth is but the midpoint, permeates the body of Jung's work, *Aion* (1951), *Psychology and Alchemy* (1944), and *Mysterium Coniunctionis* (1955-1956) seem most representative of this point of view. Alchemy, in Jung's opinion, encompassed the overall mythic story of the evolution of consciousness in its strange processes. It encompassed, as Eastern traditions did not, the Yahwistic story, and therefore, provides the most trenchant basis for the larger schema of Jungian psychology.

---

[1] In *Aion: Researches into the Phenomenology of the Self*, Jung develops a view of the ongoing validity of the orthodox view of Christ in the human psyche, the symbolic place of this Christ in the ongoing evolutionary story. Thus *Aion* seeks to provide a transition from the smaller to the larger schema, but the paradigmatic distinction between biblical and transbiblical myth cannot be clearly recognized in this writing.

Alchemical materials, proceeding from a different orientation, do not seek to reduce the larger schema to the proportions of the biblical god, nor to identify the biblical god with the Self. Rather they place the biblical god (though somewhat surreptitiously) within the context of the larger totality. Throughout the Middle Ages alchemy had conveyed an esoteric, gnostic counterpart to the exoteric, canonical (or standardized) tradition of orthodoxy. The orthodox tradition which succeeded in rendering gnosticism heretical, also gradually ushered in the world view of modern science, which internalized ego capacity in the personal psyche and detached it from the mythic dimension altogether (including its own myth). The overwhelming success of the scientific world view relegated the mythically alive discipline of alchemy to prescientific obscurity. Jung's struggle to return alchemy to consciousness, and through it to bring ego to a higher level of consciousness, is a measure of the importance he attached to psychological wholeness.

The alchemists, in Jung's opinion, were engaged in the evolution of human consciousness, seeking practical as well as theoretical ways in which to accomplish this. The dynamic of psychic projection enabled them to discern in matter the comprehensive spiritual propensities of human consciousness, while the biblical myth elevated ego into evolutionary dominance over matter. Moreover, the biblical myth accomplished an epistemological centrality which denied the archetypal totality, including, in the extremities of science, its own god. The alchemists, in contrast, were concerned with the archetypal totality and could be content with nothing less. Thus they looked for a formula which connected this unearthly, heavenly god with the dregs of matter – which, in the words of Blake, married heaven and earth – and, in this conjunction of the opposites, birthed a new heaven and earth.

As he was struggling with his revolutionary thoughts on alchemy, the essential truth of this esoteric science was affirmed for Jung in a dramatic vision, which he recounts in *Memories, Dreams, Reflections* (1965, pp. 210–211). The vision was of an unusual crucifix, a green-gold Christ on the Cross. This vision convinced Jung of the ultimate truth of the "undisguised alchemical conception of Christ as a union of spiritually alive and physically dead matter" (ibid.). It represented a Christic experience, evolved beyond the orthodox version of Christ, that connected the biblical Christ (of physically dead matter) with an alchemical Christ (of spiritually alive matter). In the assurance of this vision, Jung went on to complete *Psychology and Alchemy* (1944), his first in-depth presentation of alchemy. In this work, he positions the evolutionary procedure at the beginning of the first, not the second, cosmogony. He explores the definitive distinction between a mother-world and a father-world (a mythic distinction basic to Jung's psychology) and ponders the evolutionary relationship between the two.

In *Psychology and Alchemy*, Jung recognizes the primal split and suggests (though he sometimes takes the obverse point of view) that the enmity (the impulse of the primal split) is largely on the side of the father-world (the biblical tradition). He veers between a positive evaluation of the primal split and a reluctance to accept the implications of primal enmity. He takes the biblical god and the biblical traditions to task for the negative aspects of such a dissociation and for the continuance of this condition in the human milieu. The mother-world, he points out, shows signs (through the medium of alchemy) of adapting to the father-world, the Great Mother producing her own "son" in response to the sonship of the father-world. This represents, in Jung's view, a chthonic willingness to transcend the essential mother-daughter relationship that had characterized the Great Mother realm, the willingness of the archetypal feminine to find a means of rapprochement with the evolutionary ascendency of Yahweh.

This alchemical son of the mother-world, the *filius macrocosmi*, presents a fabulous chthonic counterpart to the *filius microcosmi*, who is the son of Logos masculinity, the very incarnation of Yahweh himself, the supreme manifestation of archetypal Ego. Of the *filius macrocosmi*, Jung writes, *"We know that the mask of the unconscious is not rigid — it reflects the face we turn towards it. Hostility lends it a threatening aspect, friendliness softens its features"* (1944, par. 29). Alchemy, in other words, having turned a friendly face toward the chthonic world, had discovered the friendly *filius macrocosmi*. This is in direct contrast to the orthodox Judeo-Christian tradition, which has perpetuated the primal split and which, therefore, has produced that great satanic shadow of the ego world, the Antichrist. We catch a glimpse of the grim visage of the Antichrist, staring down the ages of the Christian era and stalking its accomplishments, in *Revelation,* the concluding book of the biblical myth. It is an enmity which is experientially and dangerously alive in many areas today, an enmity that can no longer be averted, but which must be met for the ongoing task of evolution.

Jung recognizes and seeks to make clear that the mother-world, despite repression, despite the hostile disenfranchisement of the father-world, will not disappear from the ontological parameters of the psychic economy. The mother-world (the chthonic syzygy) constitutes a permanent aspect of the Self. Yahwistic (egoic) repression thus offers no final resolution to the problem of the opposites that emerge in the linear arena of history. The macrocosmic problem of the opposites will need to be dealt with beyond the biblical solution, as set forth in the book of *Revelation*. The apocalyptic defeat of the chthonic world, or of Satan as its most militant representative, is not a macrocosmic possibility. From the Jungian perspective, only the integration of Satan and the chthonic realm will do. The teleological imperative of the Self insists upon it.

"The self is a union of opposites par excellence " Jung tells us, *"and this is*

where it differs essentialy from the Christ-symbol" (1944, par. 22).[2] This dynamic
of the Self as a union of opposites is, in Jung's thought, operative ontogenetically as well as phylogenetically, and it is his opinion that the final outcome of
the phylogenetic establishment of the Self in human consciousness depends
upon the willingness of each individual to claim and integrate the personal
shadow. Ontogeny must lead phylogeny to the Self, seeking a critical mass
which will permeate the whole.

Jung goes on to speak of the "androgyny of Christ." He recognizes that
despite an undeniable androgynous consciousness in the trinitarian incarnation
of Yahweh, *"the Trinity is a decidedly masculine deity, of which the androgyny of
Christ and the special position and veneration accorded to the Mother of God are
not the real equivalent"* (1944, par. 25). I believe Jung means by this that neither
the androgyny of Christ as the incarnate Yahweh, nor the androgyny of the
preincarnational Yahweh, connects with the chthonic world. The Mother of
God (the Holy Spirit in conjunction with Mary of Nazareth) is not the equivalent
of the Great Mother, the archetypal feminine herself. Mary of Nazareth represents the Holy Spirit, the inner feminine of Yahweh in a kind of semi-incarnation
(via immaculate conception). The chthonic realm is not venerated in the Christian veneration of the Virgin Mary. Thus Jung implicitly distinguishes the inner
feminine of the Logos syzygy from the primal archetypal feminine. The androgyny of Christ is placed on a mental level of consciousness (characterized in
alchemy as a *unio mentalis*), and it is recognized that the Christic level of
consciousness (the incarnation of Yahweh) does not include, but rather
represses, the chthonic syzygy. In other words, the Christic incarnation of
Yahweh does not signal a rapproachment on the part of Yahweh with the
chthonic, but rather a more radical departure from the chthonic, a unique
archetypal victory over the Great Mother.

This insight draws Jung's seminal distinction between the archetypal properties of trinitarian and quarternitarian consciousness. Although this basic distinction permeates the greater body of his work, the difference between the
chthonic syzygy and the Logos syzygy is not one that Jung consistently maintains. Especially in the smaller schema, in which he seeks the Self in Yahweh or
attempts to treat Yahweh (and the biblical myth) as ultimate, Jung tends to
collapse the inner syzygistic distinctions, treating the feminine and masculine
principles unilaterally, as nonsyzygistic. Thus femininity often refers unilaterally to the archetypal feminine, and masculinity often refers unilaterally to the
archetypal masculine. Jung tends, for instance, to speak of the inner feminine of
Yahweh and the union, or sacred marriage (*hieros gamos*), between Yahweh

---

[2]By Christ-symbol Jung refers, in this instance, to the orthodox Christ, or to the
Christ of the biblical myth as interpreted by orthodoxy. In Jung's thought, there
are other possible Christ-symbols such as his green-gold Christ.

and the inner feminine, as if the archetypal feminine has been included in the biblical trinity. This is particularly obvious when he associates the recent dogma of the "Assumption of Mary" with the inclusion of the archetypal feminine in the heavenly councils of Yahweh (1952a, par. 743). It is as if his hope for the final conjunction overleaps his insight into the lesser *coniunctio* or the essentiality of the self-contained drama of the trinitarian god.

Jung is truer both to the larger schema of his own psychology and to the meaning of the biblical myth when he says:

> But the marriage [between Yahweh and the Holy Spirit] takes place in heaven, where "nothing unclean" enters, high above the devastated world. Light consorts with light. That is the program for the Christian aeon which must be fulfilled before God can become incarnate in the creaturely man. (1952a, par. 743)

In *Answer to Job*, one sees interwoven the threads of his larger and smaller schemata. The two strands of thought are not really resolved in this book; they simply flow through each other without too much recognition of inconsistency. Nevertheless, this exercise in biblical hermeneutics seems to prepare the way for a fuller resolution. In the statement quoted above, Jung recognizes the inner *coniunctio* and its connection with the incarnation, and that only this *coniunctio* (the trinitarian) is operative for the Christian era. In line with this, Jung also sees clearly that "Christ, owing to his virgin birth [from an immaculately conceived mother] and his sinlessness, was not an empirical human being at all. . . . He remained outside and above mankind" (1952a, par. 657). Such statements, it seems to me, negate Jung's own tendency to see in the work of the Holy Spirit a "continuing incarnation" that collapses the distinction between Christ and "creaturely man" (ibid., par. 744).

From the point of view of Jung's larger schema and the biblical myth itself, it makes more sense to interpret the work of the Holy Spirit as continuing the incarnation of God's "good side," so to speak, in order "to create the most durable basis for a later assimilation of the other side" (1952a, par. 741). The continuing incarnation, it seems to me, must be consistent with the incarnation itself, a continuing creation of the durable basis. The work of the Holy Spirit is the work of implanting the transcendent-to-nature Christ, of bringing the whole of humanity into the paradigm of history (or into Yahweh's story), of armoring the ego-centered personality against the chthonic instinctuality of creaturely being.

An alchemical treatise quoted by Jung speaks to this point. It places the biblical myth within the context of the overall story of evolution encompassed in the alchemical formulae of transformation, promising new understanding of the biblical myth of creation and resurrection. The resurrected body, it proclaims, is not "this body that we have received from Adam, but . . . that which we attain through the Holy Ghost, namely . . . such a body as our Saviour brought from heaven" (1944, par. 347). The eucharistic presence, the "kinship by blood," as Jung speaks of it, does indeed work "profound changes in man's status" (1952a, par. 658), but, I would submit, that these profound changes lead to a deepening of the primal split and an extending of the primal split to the human whole. The separation between the Christ and the Antichrist is maintained in the depths of the human psyche until the end of history, until the end of "the program for the Christian aeon." Reconciliation between the Logos and the chthonic, the archetypal masculine and the archetypal feminine, is transbiblical. The larger scheme of Jung's psychology prepares us for transbiblical myth and overcomes the inconsistencies of his smaller schema. The monotheistic god of the biblical myth can remain both monotheistic and pure if he is seen as archetypal Ego (temporarily and developmentally a one and only god) rather than as the monistic Self (the ultimate conjunction of all opposites, an archetypal totality, a pleroma).

In *Aion* (1951), Jung explicates most clearly, but without systematically conjoining, the orthodox and gnostic symbols of the Self. *Aion* puzzles, as does *Answer to Job* (1952a), at the Christic separation from the satanic shadow. Both of these works decisively reject the ultimacy of such a separation, but in neither work does Jung quite come to grips with the distinction between Yahweh's unconscious (regressive) collusion with Satan (an Old Testament phenomenon) and the biblical thrust toward ego formation which necessitates the total repression of the shadow, and the completion of the evolutionary primal split (a New Testament phenomenon). Jung sees, and yet does not see, the evolutionary necessity of the primal split. In *Aion* he recognizes that the final solution is implicit in the double *quaternio* of gnosticism (akin to the kabbalistic ladder of life) which does conjoin the developmental worlds of the personal and the transpersonal. The paradigm of history that guides the biblical story is not brought clearly to the forefront in *Aion*, however, nor is it associated with the development of ego consciousness per se. The particularities of history tend to be lost in the entangled forest of symbology.

Nevertheless, *Aion* clearly recognizes the transitional nature of the biblical Christ. As Singer (1976) has reminded us, Jung places the canonical Christ in a zodiacal context, a perspective admittedly outrageous for traditional exegesis. Jung calls our attention to the fact that the canonical Christ is Piscean. Christ makes his entry upon the center stage of history precisely as the astrological age of Pisces emerges in the circling aeons of the heavens. The era of Pisces, with its affinities to the archetypal masculine, moving from the age of Aries in effect, pronounces the eternal characteristics of the Christian era and the potentialities of the postbiblical world which it initiates.

The Piscean era is symbolized astrologically by two fish moving in opposite directions. Jung took this antithetical duality of the Christian era to represent the Christ and the Antichrist. Humanity, he warns us, may integrate this duality and move forward from the Christian era into the further reaches of the Self, or humanity may be demolished by the emergence of the Antichrist. Nevertheless, despite its dangers, the fierce pull of consciousness out of the chthonic realm necessitated the temporal repression of the chthonic syzygy, the temporal repression of the numinosity of the Great Mother. The primal split was necessary for the Arien/Piscean paradigm of history but, if perpetuated, it will prove devastating. The new age of Aquarius, demanding the return of the chthonic energies, will not accommodate the primal split. The Yahwistic ego, entering a new phase of consciousness, must learn to integrate, rather than to repress, the archetypal totality.

In this, one is able to recognize a mythic outline of the larger schema in which the biblical Christ fits comfortably if Yahweh is the historical point of the transcendence of nature rather than the eschatological point of reconciliation between the Logos and the chthonic. One is able to see that what was accomplished by Yahweh in the Christic incarnation was his own total separation from the Great Mother. Both Johannine and Pauline theology supports this line of thought. "This is the bread [the body of Jesus] which came down from heaven," writes the Johannine author (John 6:58). Paul writes, "The first man [Adam] was from the earth, a man of dust; the second man is from heaven" (I Cor. 15:47). The second Adam was not constructed of the *prima materia*, the maternal clay (and, therefore, could not be snuffed out by the maternal clay). The second Adam was begotten of the inner *coniunctio* of Yahweh, the self-contained trinitarian unfolding. The second Adam was transcendent to nature (and thus free of original sin), but fully present in the milieu of history. The second Adam was Yahweh, himself, incarnate in his own unique substance in his own unique creation and inimical still to the maternal realm. The biblical myth unfolds the Self into mature ego consciousness, but—as if awaiting its own maturation in human consciousness—it prohibits the further unfolding of the Self. The biblical myth ends with two fish still pointing in opposite directions. Like Moses, its great protagonist, the biblical myth merely peeks into the next dimension. It sees the realm of the differentiated Self. It does not enter.

The alchemical formula of the larger schema of Jungian psychology is worked out conclusively in Jung's last major work, *Mysterium Coniunctionis* (1955-1956). Jung saw his way past the primal split in this work. Here, Jung utilizes alchemical insight in order to articulate in greater depth the archetypal event of the eschaton, which has the potential of carrying humanity past the dangerous shoals of the primal split and its threat of final destruction.

Jung emphasizes that the evolutionary enterprise carries no guarantee of success. It calls upon human response and human cooperation. Jungian and transpersonal psychology both inform us that humanity holds within its own power the outcome of its own planetary evolution. This emphasis is completely compatible with biblical ethics, although the ethics of ego consciousnesss (biblically evolved) fail to provide the final key to ego's ethical dilemmas. The biblical myth would seem to assure us of the survival of ego in the Self, but one is less sure of the survival of the Self in ego. The disconcerting biblical position is that ego crucifixion would seem to be an unavoidable event on the path to transcendence. Paradoxically, the crucifixion of ego seems to be essential for its survival and durability. *The crucifixion of ego is not the dissolution of ego, but a new centeredness of ego in the larger totality. The question of human survival hinges on the question of whether ego will forego its small centrality of consciousness for the larger centrality of the Self.*

Briefly formulated along alchemical guidelines, the larger schema developed in this last major work would seem to read as follows:

1. The formation by the Great Mother of matter (or of the *prima materia* of evolution) and the establishment of a cyclic state of biological oneness. Biological oneness indicates a biological great round, known mythically as *uroboric oneness* symbolized by a great serpent — the Uroborus — devouring its own tail. It revealed the lack of a sense of otherness in the chthonic realm. Real differentiation had not yet begun.

2. The rendition of a primal split in the psychic economy as the nonbiodegradable ego is formed by the Great Father and transcends the uroboric great round of the composition and decomposition of matter. The biblical myth begins here with the emergence of the trinitarian god as the superegoic Yahweh, or the Father.

3. A deeper rendition of the primal split as the Son, or the Christic Logos, establishes the alchemical *unio mentalis* of the maturation of ego, accomplishing a trinitarian oneness that sustains a radical transcendence over the chthonic realm of biological decay. This is made palpable in the continuum of history by the resurrection of Jesus. Since biological decay happens in history, it required a remedy which happened in history. The Christic incarnation and resurrection was not "natural," but neither was it "docetic," a mere apparition. Its reality was in the continuum of history.

4. The Holy Spirit (the inner feminine of the trinitarian god) picks up the task of the continuing incarnation of the trinitarian god through the eucharist.[3]

5. Proceeding from this primal, now antithetical, duality between trinity and quaternity (or between ego and self, or between the archetypal feminine and masculine) a rapprochment between the chthonic and the mental realms is necessary if evolution is to acheive its ultimate wholeness. This calls for the *mysterium coniunctionis*, a double syzygy sacred marriage between the Logos and chthonic syzygies into a differentiated wholeness.

This wholeness contains the biological realm. It brings about a mysterious transmutation of the material realm into a spiritual realm (known biblically as a new heaven/new earth), comprehending the quick and the dead (a general resurrection which loses no jot or iota of the egoic realm). The *mysterium coniunctionis* heals the primal split in the human psyche, and thus the split world is now experienced as one world, the *unus mundus*, representing quarternitarian unity. Quarternitarian unity is a higher unity than uroboric-biological oneness, or than the trinitarian oneness of the *unio mentalis*. The *unus mundus* is a world of androgynous being. The individual personality system in that world is microcosmic, reflecting the macrocosm.

Of the mysterious alchemical move from *unio mentalis* into the *unus mundus* Jung writes:

> Despite all assurances to the contrary Christ is not a unifying factor but a dividing "sword" which sunders the spiritual man from the physical. The alchemists, who unlike certain moderns, were clever enough to see the necessity and fitness of a further development of consciousness, held fast to their Christian convictions and did not slip back to a more unconscious level. They could not and would not deny the truth of Christianity [the truth of ego consciousness], and for this reason it would be wrong to accuse them of heresy. On the contrary, they wanted to "realize" the unity foreshadowed in the idea of God [the higher unity of quaternity] by struggling to unite the unio mentalis with the body. (1955–1956, par. 773)

---

[3]Jung's smaller schema tends at this point to merge the archetypal feminine and the inner feminine of the biblical trinity, and to blend trinity into quaternity. His larger schema, as we have discussed, supports the view that the Holy Spirit is distinct from the archetypal feminine, that she belongs to trinity and not quaternity, that the eucharistic presence of the Christ is consistent with his incarnation.

Jung establishes three things here that are important for the formulation of a Jungian hermeneutic of the biblical myth. The first is that Christic consciousness (the *unio mentalis*) must be maintained and at the same time transcended. The second is that, through the *mysterium coniunctionis*, the chthonic realm of matter and the world of ego become one, although the way for that event to happen and the form it will take are still mysterious. The third is that the *mysterium coniunctionis* is possible because an essential and encompassing unity underlies the primal split between the realm of nature and the realm of history. This is the unity of the *unus mundus* waiting to unfold. This is the potential world to which we belong in a *unio mystica*. The *unio mystica*, in other words, parallels the recentering of the ego in the self.

The Smaller Schema

Somewhat earlier in his career, Jung had made his first major approach to the biblical myth itself in his seminal essay on the biblical trinity, "A Psychological Approach to the Dogma of the Trinity" (1948). Jung's smaller schema of evolution emerges here, although the larger schema provides a counterpoint. It is as if Jung resists being pulled into the smaller schema, but cannot ignore the importance of the biblical god; he finds that to begin from the point of Yahweh, as if Yahweh were the Self, leads into hermeneutical contortions. Jung's willingness to explore strange avenues, however, and to follow difficult paths of thought, has cut a clearer path for us all.

He based his approach to the biblical myth on the concept of trinitarian homoousia—the biblical trinity as one-in-itself. Homoousia indicated for the early church (struggling with the unprecedented implications of an incarnation of the Hebrew Word god) that the three "persons" of the trinity were not separate gods, but one god. Homoousia, in effect, preserved for orthodox Christianity both the notion of Yahwistic transcendence and of Yahwistic monotheism. Incarnation did not dispute Yahwistic transcendence of the chthonic; "Father, Son, and Holy Spirit" did not dispute monotheism.

Jung maintains this definition of the biblical god, and yet, he sometimes treats the homoousia (the radical transcendence of Yahweh over the chthonic forces of nature) as an evolutionary mistake, rather than a differentiation and an essential aspect of evolution. The thrust of the smaller schema is to seek the properties of the Self (including the chthonic) in the biblical god. This quest, which he ultimately rejected, nevertheless at times throws Jung's work awry of his own larger schema and distorts to some degree his reading of the biblical myth.

Jung was reluctant to let Yahweh part with the Shadow, and he was perhaps overly eager to reintegrate the Shadow of Yahweh. He resisted the biblical repression of the chthonic realm, the emergence of archetypal Ego and its disruption of the monistic Self. He sought to convince the theological world of the importance of the monistic Self, but, as that world well knew, his arguments carried him against the grain of the biblical myth. The biblical myth had its hands cupped around a tiny light, and it could not let go.

Alongside his struggle with the trinitarian limitations of the biblical god, however, Jung also recognized the implications of Platonic and Pythagorean philosophy for the biblical myth. In these two philosophical traditions, which influenced the later hermetic tradition of alchemical science, the archetype of trinity indicated process. Threeness in itself indicated incompletion and moved toward the higher unity of quarternity. Although Jung is off target in looking for biblical myth, rather than transbiblical myth, to move into quarternity, he is on target, and within his larger schema, in defining the biblical trinity as representative of the masculine perfectionism of ego consciousness. Jung comes to recognize that the biblical trinity, although inclusive of the Holy Spirit as the inner feminine of Yahweh, rejects the archetypal feminine. Jung recognizes that the potential evolution of the Self is inherent in Yahweh, even as, from the psychological point of view, it is inherent in ego. The Self in its undifferentiated state undergirds Ego, and, conversely, the centrality of Ego undergirds the higher centrality of the Self. Yahweh disrupts the Self. Yet with his tiny light (the Logos light that shines in the chthonic darkness), he also perpetuates the Self.

We might conclude that Jung had a double intent within the smaller schema: first, in a world that could not see beyond Yahweh (an orthodox world), to somehow connect the monotheistic god with the archetypal totality of the monistic Self; second, however, in a world that tended to reject Yahweh (a gnostic world), to uphold the necessity of ego and the maturation of ego. Jung warned of the danger of gnostic inflation in this regard and endorsed the long trek through the paradigm of history to which orthodoxy has subjected us (1954b, par. 438).

Jung's basic recognition of the biblical trinity as a homoousia is of foremost importance in the development of a Jungian hermeneutic. His gradual recognition that the trinity contained an inner feminine was an archetypal pattern leading toward quarternity, would have been meaningless without his acceptance of the homoousia. Jung, somewhat precognitively, stressed the importance of not considering the biblical god as triadic in his "psychological approach to the dogma of the trinity." He makes a careful distinction between the biblical trinity and the "father-mother-son" triads (composed of three deities), which were concurrently developing in other patriarchal systems (the Greek, for instance). The homoousia of the biblical trinity meant, in effect, that the biblical god was exclusive of the chthonic syzygy. He was/is thoroughly transcendent to nature, to the mother-world, to the nature gods, as the triadic schemes are not.

This consideration seemed so important to Jung at the time that it caused him to deny the gnostic contention of the femininity of the Holy Spirit, since a concession to femininity ran the risk of regressing the biblical trinity to the father-mother-son triads. Furthermore, the Holy Spirit, in this regard, is not the second (or mother) person of the biblical trinity, but the third person. Jung rescinded this judgment later and most emphatically in *Answer to Job*, where he recognized the femininity of the Holy Spirit. Her thirdness in the trinitarian scheme need not indicate her place in the intrapsychic aseity of Yahweh. The Holy Spirit was co-creator at the beginning, thus certainly a secondary help-mate of Yahweh.

Her thirdness, I would suggest, serves to emphasize the temporal, historical point at which "she" becomes dominant in the further evolution of the biblical god. The age of the Spirit is of signal importance in both biblical theology and Jungian psychology. For both disciplines, it conveys a new injunction, effective both historically and eschatologically. The age of the Spirit must be identified, however, with the postbiblical world of the Christian era and with the paradigm of history. It belongs to the development of trinitarian consciousness. It is an aspect of the Piscean era and should not be confused with the new age (the Aquarian Age) to come.

In Jung's view, the postbiblical work of the Spirit was to effect the continuing incarnation of Yahweh in the phylogenetic field of humanity, to instill the eucharistic presence (forming a critical mass), to permeate the globe with Christic consciousness, to inculcate mature ego in the human psyche, all in preparation for the eschatological integration of the chthonic syzygy. Jung tends to collapse the distinction between trinitarian and quarternitarian consciousness at this point and to make the work of the Holy Spirit quarternitarian, but this tendency is counterbalanced by his recognition of the homoousia, the trinitarian roots of the Holy Spirit, and the Logos purity of the Christ. The success of the evolutionary enterprise, as Jung emphasizes, depends upon the work of the Holy Spirit, the human absorption of Christic consciousness. Otherwise, collapse into pre-ego consciousness occurs, a sort of devolution rather than evolution, with the loss of the tiny light.

In his essay on the trinity, Jung traces the unfolding of the trinity through the biblical story. He speaks of this unfolding as a self-contained divine drama. The trinitarian unfolding is, in other words, a *hieros gamos* (an inner, or lesser *coniunctio*) resulting in an incarnation which owes nothing to any other deity. If this is to be accepted (and the concept is inherent in orthodox Christianity), it is difficult indeed to avoid positing an inner feminine of Yahweh. Nevertheless, it has been avoided. Yahweh's "germ of Yin," his inner feminine, suffers from a canonical tendency toward disguise, derived in large part from an orthodox paranoia concerning the numinosity of the Great Mother. The New Testament authors, aware of the tremendous implications of the incarnational scandal, approached the trinitarian unfolding with great caution. They were eager to avoid a gnostic interpretation of Yahweh, which in effect devalued the Ego god, but they were forced, nevertheless, to recognize that the traditional Hebraic conception of a celibate Yahweh (married to Israel, but that by the Word alone) had been shattered.

In the opinion of orthodox Christianity, however, it had not been shattered in the gnostic direction of an acceptance of the archetypal feminine and her chthonic consort, nor of the acceptance of a higher unknown god beyond Yahweh. The New Testament dilemma was how to portray the startling, unprecedented trinitarian activity, intimately involving the inner feminine of Yahweh, without arousing the specter of the Great Mother and her fertility gods and without conceding an archetypal totality beyond Yahweh. These intricacies of biblical hermeneutics are still germane today. For now it is important simply to recognize that the Holy Spirit, as the inner feminine of the Yahweh/Christ, is essential to trinitarian oneness, and, as the third "person" of the trinity, she reaches beyond patriarchal psychic inertia to connect with the archetypal feminine, to prepare for the quantum leap from trinity to quarternity.

This function of the Holy Spirit is reminiscent of the whimsical warning of Jesus that the Holy Spirit blows where it will, and also of his more ominous warning that sin against the Holy Spirit is unforgiveable (Luke 3:28–29). Pitted against the overall evolutionary story, one recognizes the precognition of Jesus concerning an egoic resistance to evolution, the probability of patriarchal, ecclesiastical resistance to the third movement of its trinitarian god. Sin against the Holy Spirit, however, as Jesus saw, is sin against the thrust of evolution, which ineluctably incurs the destruction of the human species. The "forgiveness of sin" against the first and second persons of the trinity cannot extend to the third person. Resurrection, the end result of Yahwistic grace, presumes her evolutionary activity.

In *Answer to Job*, Jung opens the scandal of incarnation (the scandal which patristic Christianity sought to avoid) for all to see. He speaks evocatively of the trinitarian unfolding as a *hieros gamos* (a sacred marriage) between Yahweh and Sophia, and he associates the goddesslike heroine of Proverbs with the Holy Spirit. She is thus deprived of her own aseity, but she is granted a place in the aseity of Yahweh himself. We see here that the Son, begotten by the biblical *coniunctio*, is clothed by the Holy Spirit in flesh and blood, but not clothed in chthonic flesh and blood. The *coniunctio* between Yahweh and the

Holy Spirit was a lesser *coniunctio*, not the *mysterium coniunctio* which is to come between Yahweh and the Great Mother. The trinitarian *coniunctio* did not utilize the *prima materia* of the Great Mother. It begot rather, in the person of Jesus, a "second Adam," and the "second Adam" was of the unique substance of Yahweh. In the trinitarian *hieros gamos*, the Logos which had been previously disincarnate in the chthonic world, previously related to the mind of man abstractly, was made flesh, but a flesh transcendent to nature, a flesh that had come down from heaven like manna, a bodily being that expressed itself concretely in the Yahwistic milieu of history, not in the chthonic milieu of nature.

Thus, in the trinitarian unfolding, we come to the conjunction of Jungian psychology with the eucharistic presence of the orthodox Christ in the human milieu. Jung struggles with the problem of a nonchthonic incarnation, which, as he recognizes, did not really reach the chthonic. The trinitarian *hieros gamos* did not really incarnate the heavenly god, nor thus could it heal the primal split. In his smaller schema, he seeks to reach the chthonic through the work of the Holy Spirit, and yet ultimately here, too, he sees that although the Holy Spirit moves toward quarternity, she cannot effect quarternity. As the orthodox Christ remains transcendent to nature, so the eucharistic presence of this Christ remains transcendent to nature.

In his essay, "Transformation Symbolism in the Mass" (1954b), Jung initiates discussion of this important issue. He parallels the Mass with the gnostic "visions of Zosimos" (and other primal god-human communions, including the Dionysian) in order to establish the fact that the Mass, "although a unique phenomenon . . . would be profoundly alien to man were it not rooted in the human psyche" (1954b, par. 339). Jung's main intent in this, as it seems to me, is to show that the Mass, even though on a spiritually higher plane than the primitive "god-eating" of the polytheistic children of nature, is, nevertheless, of the whole cloth of evolution (1954b, par. 340). The orthodox Christ entered the Yahwistic milieu of history, not nature, in preparation for the fulfillment of the overall story of evolution, in which history would commune with nature. The incarnation of Yahweh, and the eucharistic presence deriving from it, exhibit a radical discontinuity and yet are held in continuity, within the individuation-evolutionary process.

My argument that the orthodox separation of the eucharistic presence from the chthonic element of the human psyche ("the natural man") is substantiated (although sometimes lost sight of) by Jung. Jung makes clear that the eucharistic Christ, as conveyed through the medium of orthodoxy, is not ultimate, but phase-specific. Humanity, receiving the eucharistic presence, is not whole, not yet complete, not yet microcosmic, and—as Pagels (1988) takes issue—still dependent on the patristic heritage (largely Augustinian) of ecclesiastical authority.

Included in this phase-specific stage, however, is the trinitarian work of the

Holy Spirit which continues the incarnation (the inculcation of eucharistic presence) in the human milieu. For the duration of the Christian era, Yahweh, under the aegis of the Holy Spirit, is organically investing himself in the individual personality system. This sets up a "kinship by blood" that makes of humanity "sons of god" (1952a, par. 744), and, if we can grant credence to Sheldrake's work (1987), this sets up in turn a potential for a morphic resonance able to accomplish what indoctrination cannot accomplish—a covenant of the heart, a covenant of mature ego capacity, a covenant phylogenetically present to the whole of the human species. The Holy Spirit maintains, and gradually conveys, a certain independence of ecclesiastical authority, and, concomitantly, a higher capacity in the individual personality system for the exercise of free will.

In order to discuss this higher dimension of consciousness, Jung again resorts to alchemical formula. He speaks of Hermes Trismegistus (the thrice-greatest) as an expression of the archetype of trinity higher than the biblical manifestation. This mercurial spirit (prominent in alchemy) is defined by Jung as "the soul of the bodies," the "anima vitalis," the "spirit which has become earth" (1954b, par. 356). Hermes, Jung tells us, wields the "alchemical sword [which] brings about the *solutio* [the dissolving]. . . of the elements [of the biblical world], thereby restoring the original condition of chaos, *so that a new and more perfect body can be produced by a new* impressio formae, *or by a new imagination* [italics mine]" (ibid., par. 357). The alchemical Hermes bears a remarkable resemblance to the biblical Satan, who is also Lucifer, the bringer of the larger-than-ego light. The new and more perfect body (the body of wholeness in contrast to the Christic body, which is not whole) is the body of the androgyne, the gnostic Anthropos, the kabbalistic Adam Kadmon. The new impressio formae is, of course, the anticipated new heaven/new earth, the new form out of chaos affirmed by Prigogine's work.

Answer to Job

Jung pursued his comprehensive synthesis of human consciousness in *Mysterium Coniunctionis*, concluding there the larger schema of his work. Just prior to this, however, as if leading up to this task, he bursts forth with his personal reaction to the biblical Yahweh, his controversial and seminal *Answer to Job*. This book (Jung's most extensive treatment of the biblical myth per se) expresses his emotional reaction to the god who was not, and yet who claimed to be, ultimate. It is as if the synthesis of a new unity of consciousness through the biblical myth cannot be accomplished intellectually. It must include the emotional complexities involved in the process.

In *Answer to Job*, Jung takes the god to task. Still, the book reflects Jung's final acceptance of the evolutionary necessity of this god. Despite his admittedly emotional indignation, Jung comes to terms with the god who both colluded with and repressed Satan, who both demanded and violated justice and mercy. He comes to terms with the god who finally remembered his own feminine, who activated her wisdom rather than his wrath, and who through her wisdom entered into his own creation. He explores the evolutionary requirement of a radical primal split between the Christic Yahweh (latent in the Old Testament Yahweh) and Satan (in collusion with the Old Testament Yahweh). He explores, as always, the necessity of an eschatological healing of the primal split in the Self. He tends to bemoan the Christic separation from the satanic Shadow. In this, he falls into his smaller schema which seeks the wholeness of the Self in the biblical god. It pushes Jung to elevate the pre-Christic Yahweh over the Christic Yahweh, for the pre-Christic Yahweh contained the satanic Shadow. Nevertheless, this does not prevent Jung from berating the pre-Christic Yahweh for his unconscious collusion with the nether world. The distortion of the smaller schema is obvious here. The larger schema allows us to see that the pre-Christic Yahweh was not fully differentiated from the chthonic; in the Christ, a full differentiation is accomplished, but not wholeness. Wholeness lies beyond the Christ, in transbiblical myth.

Despite this defect, which deflects the developmental direction of the biblical myth and does less than justice to Jung's own psychology, Jung achieves in *Answer to Job* a rare combination of gnostic and orthodox theology, which perhaps sets in motion a pattern for the synthesis of today. In true gnostic fashion, Jung lays the onus of "original sin" at the feet of the creator of the ego world, rather than the created, and suggests that Yahweh must consult his "omniscience" (implying the higher god of the gnostics), in order to connect his floundering creation (via his own incarnation) with the on-going thrust of evolution. Furthermore, Jung takes up the gnostic belief that human consciousness has the potential of moving beyond Yahweh and contends that, in the drama of Job, human consciousness did move beyond Yahweh. Job sees through Yahweh, recognizing the relativity of the absolute god.

The first answer to Job is the Piscean Christ, because only through incarnation, only through entering his own creation in his own unique substance, could Yahweh truly experience himself and elevate his consciousness above Jobian consciousness. In incarnation, Yahweh takes up the burden of his own covenant, the covenant of the mind. He suffers his own moral demands, his historical "mission impossible." He invests himself organically, through his eucharistic presence, in the human milieu. Never thereafter will Yahwistic insufficiency be charged from on high against a hapless humanity, cowering below. Yahweh has charged his own insufficiency against himself. He has contracted in a covenant of the heart to pay up the deficits of his own creation. The final, yet-to-be-given answer to Job will occur when Yahwistic, or Christic, conciousness is able to incarnate Satan, when ego is able to come to terms with the "natural man," to withstand the higher centrality of the Self.

For this resolution of the Piscean conflict, we await the Aquarian Christ. The Piscean incarnation demonstrates, however, the great truth of Yahweh, that Yahweh is proof against the Great Mother. He can and does avoid the biological great round. He establishes the durability of ego, the durability of the tiny light, against the darkness of biological death. The sting of death, the great enemy of ego, is dead. It becomes clear that ego – mature ego – can surrender to the Self, without dissolution, through the Christic medium of Yahweh, and that transformation beyond Yahweh is effective for the phylogenetic whole of humanity, inclusive of the quick and the dead. Thus it becomes clear that evolution can proceed beyond Yahweh.

As Jung took up his position in *Answer to Job*, he claimed not to be a biblical scholar. He disqualified himself as a bona fide exegete. And yet he pinpointed the archetypal issues at stake in the drama of Job as no other exegete has. Jung came to it because he already knew the overall story of evolution. His exegetical endeavors had extended far beyond the biblical myth. He had looked into the gnostic Pleroma and knew many of its archetypal secrets. He was not put off by the majesty of the god. Despite the prohibitions of the biblical god, Jung had encountered many goddesses and gods, and he knew that one engages them where they are and in the fullness of one's own being. Jung employs his own two methods of mythic exegesis, active imagination and amplification, and in so doing he brings to life the drama of Job, but more than this. He brings to life the drama of the god of Job, the extraordinary career of an extraordinary god, and yet a god in whom we can find no ultimate home. In *Answer to Job*, Jung stamps his own exegetical methodology upon biblical exegesis. As previously noted, it would be impossible to consider a Jungian hermeneutic of the biblical myth apart from Jung's methodology.

Jung sums up the gist of his position in *Aion*, as he writes:

> The irreconcilable nature of the opposites in Christian psychology is due to their *moral accentuation* [a differentiation between "good" and "evil"]. This accentuation seems natural to us, although, looked at historically, it is a legacy from the Old Testament, with its emphasis on righteousness in the eyes of the law. *Such an influence is notably lacking in the East, in the philosophical religions of India and China. Without stopping to discuss the question of whether this exacerbation of the opposites, much as it increases suffering, may not after all correspond to a higher degree of truth.* I should like merely to express the hope that the present world situation may be looked upon in the light of the psychological rule alluded to above. Today

humanity, as never before, is split into two apparently irreconcilable halves. The psychological rule says that when an inner situation is not made conscious, it happens outside, as fate. That is to say, when the individual remains undivided [caught in ego] and does not become conscious of his inner opposite [the shadow], the world must perforce act out the conflict and be torn into opposing halves. (1951, par. 126, italics mine)

If the biblical myth in its moral accentuation (its chthonic transcendence) does correspond to some higher degree of truth, or if it leads developmentally to a higher degree of truth (as Jung hints), then the basis for the myth (and a global dialogue between the biblical myth and the esoteric and Eastern traditions) can be established. This is to say that Yahweh is not a god to reject, but to go beyond—to make conscious his inner opposite. This, in Jung's thought, is the true answer to Job.

Chapter 11

YAHWEH AND THE MIND OF MAN

*T*he field of biblical criticism has developed adjunctively – somewhat in the nature of an addendum – to the process of biblical development. The struggle to explicate and codify the biblical Word, which began, experientially, some three to four thousand years ago, is carried on apace in the field of biblical criticism. From a Jungian point of view, however, biblical hermeneutics must include material which, although dealing with biblical experience, moves against the grain of biblical development. A Jungian hermeneutic asks why, and thus roots itself in an explication of both the process and the counterprocess of biblical development. During its tenure in human consciousness, the biblical myth has confined us within the closed universe of ego, or personal mode consciousness. Transbiblical myth opens the closed universe of ego and brings personal mode consciousness into transpersonal fulfillment. It is important to note, however, that the canon itself is not opened. The canon remains intact. The canonical experience of Yahwistic consciousness is transcended in transbiblical myth, but not rendered obsolete.

From a Jungian point of view, the counterprocess of biblical development is as important as the process. The hermeneutical questions become: What archetypal purpose was being accomplished through this interplay? How does the polarized process relate to the overall process of evolution? What was the essential aim of the canon (the orthodox rule or standard which guided the process of biblical development), and why did evolution require a counterprocess, an extracanon? Such questions bring us to the point of division between two bodies of literature pertaining to the biblical god – the canonical and the extracanonical.

I use the phrase "mind of man" advisedly. I am aware of, and not unsympathetic to, feminist protest of the association of the biblical god with masculinity and of the association of masculinity with ego. Such protest reflects the mythic vacuum, the lack of mythic leverage, sustained by women of the patriarchy under the dominance of the mind of man. My point is, however, that we must confront the archetypal picture as it is. No amount of positivistic denial will

contravene the mythic energies. We need to recognize that Yahweh differentiates and develops the archetypal energy of Logos masculinity in human consciousness. In the paradigmatic parlance of a patriarchal age, he shapes "the
mind of man." He shapes the mental ego, a patriarchal capacity which
empowers men and disempowers women, a capacity radically conveyed into
human consciousness by Yahweh, above all other gods.

As we have seen, however, Jung's concept of contrasexuality, based on the
syzygistic nature of the primal principles of being (the archetypal feminine and
the archetypal masculine) permits us to recognize that Logos masculinity, the
mental ego, is intended ultimately for men and women alike. In other words,
women can claim, indeed must claim, this quality, without denying the archetypal essentiality of Logos masculinity. This is not to deny the need for patriarchal men to claim the Logos feminine. Only thus can patriarchal men and
women reflect the syzygistic nature of the Logos god. The canon of patriarchy,
the biblical myth itself, indicates contrasexuality, but it indicates also the difficulty of contrasexual endeavor. The primary concern of patriarchy is to invest
power, the power of Logos masculinity, in men. The Logos feminine, the inner
feminine of the biblical god, is deeply hidden in the myth and repressed in the
myth's traditions. This is an ironic deception from the Christian point of view,
since the Christian era is the age of the Spirit, and the third person of the
biblical trinity, the Holy Spirit, is increasingly recognized as the inner feminine
of Yahweh. A Jungian hermeneutic challenges the canonical deception, and,
simultaneously, it challenges the ultimacy of trinitarian consciousness, making
room for the inner feminine of Yahweh.

The recent reappearance of a banished "her-ness" in the mythic lexicon still
shakes the theological and cultural rafters of a patriarchal world. The patriarchal world does not yet grasp the psychological recognition that patriarchal
development is not complete until the Logos syzygy is differentiated and
reflected in patriarchal men and women alike. Nor does it grasp an even deeper
recognition—set forth, as we have seen, in Jungian and transpersonal
psychology—of the need to retrieve the archetypal feminine, the need for
patriarchal men and women alike to claim the chthonic syzygy and to heal the
primal split. The inner feminine of Yahweh, even granted her proper place in
human affairs, is no substitute for the archetypal feminine. The Logos syzygy,
even fully developed in consciousness, is no substitute for the chthonic syzygy.
Humanity did not begin in ego and is not fully developed in the full development
of ego.

The Canon and the Extracanon

Rudolph (1983) speaks of two texts, or two accounts, that deal with humanity's experience of the biblical god. He speaks of an "external text" and a text which runs "counter to the external text" (p. 54). Process and counterprocess respectively are the producers of these two texts of the human soul, which history has sought, out of its inner ambivalence, both to destroy and to preserve. The external text can be characterized as exoteric and canonical. The text which runs counter to it is esoteric and extracanonical. These two bodies of literature have been traditionally considered as mutually exclusive, with the canonical text representing "truth," and the extracanonical text representing "error." If we apply the Jungian categories of ego and self, however, we can recognize an intrinsic and complementary relationship between them, a point/counterpoint in the process of evolution, with the larger and more encompassing movement of the self belonging to the counterprocess, and with the canonical process relating specifically to the formation of the mental ego (the mind of man) in human consciousness. *From this perspective, each text can be recognized as true, but only as each is relative to the other.*

The Canonical Process

The *canonical process* produced the Bible. To speak of the canon is to speak of the Bible itself. "Canon," as Terrien (1978) informs us, "was originally not a dogmatic structure imposed from without by institutionalized collectivities but an unspoken force which grew from within the nature of Hebrew-Christian religion" (p. 32). Thus he affirms, as does Jung, the archetypal integrity of the biblical myth and validates its claim to tell the authentic story of a god from within the authentic tradition of that god. The Bible, then, is the "external text," and in the Judeo-Christian tradition, this text has assumed the elevated status of ultimate revelation. The Bible is considered as the authoritative Word of Yahweh, possessing the stamp of approval of the god himself. Since, in this tradition, Yahweh is considered to be ultimate god, the canon is a major source, and for some the sole source, of archetypal truth. A problem arises, however, within the canonical tradition, in that not one, but two Bibles exist in this category (leaving aside minor variations within each): the Hebrew Bible and the Christian Bible. These two canons exist alongside each other in the postbiblical world, each claiming the high authority of Yahweh and generating separate fields of scholarship, unfortunately with little interaction between the two.

Thus not merely the canon but the split canon must be considered as a part of the authentic tradition of the biblical god.

The Hebrew Bible lays the basic canonical foundation. It includes the Torah (the basic "Law," or covenant) by which Israel (the chosen people of Yahweh) was brought into existence in the world's arena. The Torah sets biblical revelation within the medium of history. It carefully distinguishes the god of the Bible from the deities of nature. The Torah distinguishes the god of the Bible as masculine. He directs the affairs of history, enters into history, while remaining transcendent to it. The heavenly god utilizes nature. He creates with it. He is a god at war with the archetypal feminine, the high point (and archetypally definitive point) of which is the eighth-century (B.C.) struggle between Elijah and Jezebel, or between Yahweh and Baal (I Kings 18:20–40).

The Christian Bible includes the whole of the Hebrew canon (christening it the Old Testament) and adds the New Testament. The New Testament focuses on the story of the incarnation—the birth, the ministry, the death, the resurrection and ascension of Yahweh (in the Christ), and of the formation of a "new Israel" (the church). The new Israel is the agent through which the biblical god now reaches into the phylogenetic field of human consciousness. The New Testament proclamation of incarnation seems to contradict the Torah. It was a long leap in consciousness from the two stone tablets of the Decalogue and the proscription of graven images, to the flesh and blood incarnation of Yahweh in a man called Jesus. No matter which way you look at it—as a homoousia (Christianity's final definition), or as a Zeus-like merger with chthonic flesh—scandal stares back.

Jewish and Christian scholarship, meeting at the canonical divide, might help prepare a bridge, but interrelated exegetical endeavor is complicated. Christian interpretation of the Hebrew canon, for instance, is freer, oriented more toward narrative (the "Haggadah") and toward a theological exposition of the themes of the biblical story, than is Judaic scholarship. Judaic scholarship is focused on the cumulative layers of commentary which have augmented the canonical material since the formation of the canon (nearly two millennia ago). Thus Judaism, focusing on Law, has developed an orthopraxy (correct practice) in contrast to Christian orthodoxy (correct doctrine). It is beyond the scope of the study to do more than acknowledge this difference, but I would like to suggest that both orthopraxy and orthodoxy function as important components of ego formation, modeling ego in the image of the biblical god. (The positivistic tendency to reverse this, to see the biblical god as projected in the image of the human ego, is a misunderstanding of the dynamic of projection. The source of a projection is archetypal energy, no less real for being recognized through projection.)

It is important to acknowledge the ramifications of the canonical split. They have dominated the development of Western culture and cannot be glossed over. The hiatus, the sudden turn-about-face of Yahweh in his lordship of history, has resulted in two millennia of discrimination and pogroms, a holocaust, and now the crisis of militant Zionism in an Islamic world—a world which in itself is split off from the Judaic world. The resolution of these difficulties is crucial to the resolution (or translation) of the paradigm of history, the setting of the biblical cosmogony. The biblical cosmogony revolves around one god, but that god has established three people, with three different avenues of worship and three different types of national identity, and, somehow in the course of four millennia, he has given all three a stake in the same numinous piece of real estate.

The canonical world, on the wane of history, seems to veer into the specter of pseudospeciation, as defined by Moore (1987). Its internecine conflicts appear unresolvable. Agape, the Christic prescription for the resolution of conflict, is not a reassuring strategy, except to one's enemies. And somehow, after two millennia of militant Christianity, agape still does not seem to fit the god of the Holy War.

As Rudolph reminds us, however, this is not the larger problem. Beyond the intracanonical problem looms the extracanonical problem. We must deal with the fact that the canonical text (whether Hebrew, Christian, or Islamic) is confronted by a counter-text. It deals with the archetypal totality of the Self and challenges the canon in its dedication to Ego monotheism, transporting us into a far different theological and psychological landscape. From the vantage point of this new mythic landscape, the three canons seem quite consistent.

The Extracanonical Process

The extracanonical process has produced a body of literature which consists of a volatile mixture of mythic themes and motifs, oriented around notions of divinity, directly or indirectly concerned with Yahweh and often concerned specifically with the Christ. These themes and motifs seem to have run rampant, out of control, as if no divinity were guiding them, as if some unhinged mythic imagination was running amok. From a canonical point of view, this is precisely the situation. The god of the canon was not in charge of the extracanonical accounts. They respond to a different teleological impulse and a different paradigm. New discoveries of extracanonical collections indicate that the extracanonical accounts of Yahweh fail to satisfy canonical standards, not by accident, but by deliberate, archetypal design. In other words, human consciousness is divinely, or archetypally, guided in these accounts, but not by Yahweh.

Extracanonical accounts divide themselves into two major sections, not clearly drawn in the literature. One section is supportive of the ultimacy of the biblical god. The other section repudiates that ultimacy. This latter category, which can be designated as gnostic, is the material which holds forth the possibility of mythic transformation beyond Yahweh. The former, although it emphasizes the reality of the chthonic realm (the "sons of darkness"), does not essentially challenge the biblical paradigm. Its emphasis is on the defeat of the powers of darkness and the ultimate victory of Yahweh.

Biblical hermeneutics, for the most part, has taken for granted the ultimacy of canonical criteria and over the years has regarded all other religious literature as inauthentic. Extracanonical literature, although acknowledged in recent years as a rich source of background information, has not been and is not currently granted divine (or archetypal) legitimacy. Its theological content is largely discounted by biblicists, and its allegedly erroneous excesses are considered to be decisively corrected in the canon. In the light of Jungian and transpersonal psychology, however, it seems possible to consider that there might be a dimensional, or paradigmatic, difference between the two bodies of literature, particularly in regard to the gnostic material. It would account for the hermeneutical puzzle of how the same archetypal phenomena could draw such different perception, and of how one body of literature could seem to be entirely "right" and the other, entirely "wrong." In this, we would be driven to conclude that different "sets" of people, functioning within separate paradigmatic parameters, exist in the ongoing evolutionary venture.

This seems farfetched on the face of it, but, as a matter of fact, this is fundamental to the biblical myth itself. Implicit in the biblical myth are the paradigmatic features of nature, history, and an eschaton—three paradigms. And there is the clear assumption that the people of Yahweh compose a special breed of humanity peculiar to Yahweh and inconsistent with the prior, then dominant, breed. The people of Yahweh had to be kept separate from, and uncontaminated by, the other peoples of the earth. It seems possible to surmise that they represented a phylogenetic mutation in consciousness, which was not yet secure and thus had to be guarded in the evolutionary scheme of things. The canon comes from the people of Yahweh, the phylogenetic strain of humanity which has developed Western culture and with which we are, therefore, most familiar.

The appearance of Islam on the stage of history is a special case, to be included in the general development of a biblical humanity even though it writes its own canon. The Koran, or canon, of Islam moves, although somewhat obliquely, out of the biblical myth, and, like the biblical myth, it has its gnostic interpreters. Islam gained its covenant moorings slowly, a half century after Christianity and, emerging from a pre-Yahwistic culture, recognized the paradigmatic difference. The "people of the book," as Islam saw it, were qualitatively different from pre-Yahwistic people, people who had not yet fully emerged into the egoic paradigm. Islam exalts Islam, of course, but it attempts to pay some homage to its Yahwistic predecessors. This ethical position is strained to the utmost these days, as whose is not.

The distinction between pre-Yahwistic and Yahwistic humanity is not difficult to grasp as we read the evolutionary story. What presents a problem is the parallel existence of what we must call trans-Yahwistic people. These are the mysterious people of the extracanon, surviving the onslaught of biblical/koranic humanity, not as a well-defined group, not in an identifiable institutionalized form, but esoterically. Their ancient literature, premature in its day and even today, now seems to illustrate Wilber's "growing tip," Singer's "New Androgynes." They are the progenitors of the perennial philosophy, which gives philosophical antecedent to transpersonal psychology. In Jung's opinion, they are also the philosophical forebears of depth psychology. The genus of the growing tip – the New Androgynes – seems now to be emerging into the light of day. How they will express themselves in the world we do not know. We only know that they represent a "hyperedification and hyperformation of being," a mutation unprecedented in human phylogeny (Vysheslawzeff 1968, p. 14). Although their transformed and transformative capacities are far from fully visible, we can assume that androgynous cultural forms will displace the patriarchy. This potential of radical transformation is basic to the formation of a Jungian hermeneutic of the biblical myth. It puts a different stamp, a different valuation, on the body of literature we categorize as extracanonical.

The Canon and History

The canon emphasizes the prophetic and priestly core of Israel's theology. The prophets and priests were those who interpreted Israel to Israel and conveyed the Word of Yahweh, both ethically and liturgically, to his chosen people. The Word was not always a pleasant Word (the canon does not whitewash Israel), but it was always a definite Word, based on Torah. The Word of Yahweh that speaks through the canon is dynamic and dialogic, personal and interpersonal. It specified the personal will of the personal god in specific, historical situations: the time and space of history was yoked to heaven. "In the thirtieth year, in the fourth month, on the fifth day of the month, as I was among the exiles by the river Chebar, the heavens were opened," a biblical prophet began, thus nailing the visionary concerns of heaven into history, and vice-versa (Ezekiel 1:1).

In the early days, the canonical deity was known as "El Shaddai" (Gen.17:1), the high mountain god, who, like a high mountain goat (the zodiacal Aries), was transcendent to the valleys and the agrarian ways of the earth. El Shaddai was the instigator of history through Abraham, and he would one day in history bring all nations into covenant relationship with himself. Only later was he known as "Yahweh," the great I AM (Ex. 3:14), the transcendent ruler over all, who had intervened in history to lead Israel out of slavery in Egypt and who, by a sort of mind-to-mind combat unparalleled in human experience, had lifted Israel out of its embeddedness in nature.

In still later times (ca. 300 B.C.), it was considered sacrilege to refer to the god by name. The mind-to-mind god must be heard and related to personally, by choice and by covenant. Thus, since around 300 B.C., the sacred name has been cloaked in silence in Judaic precincts. The famous tetragrammaton, YHWH, is converted to "Adonai Elohim," the great Lord of all, when the Scriptures are read in public. There was little in the canonical tradition to indicate the mysterious fact that the name Elohim, by a linguistic sleight of hand, concealed a feminine cognate, or that the tetragrammaton itself contained a linguistic connection to an ancient dove goddess (Singer 1976, p. 81). The canonical text focuses on the god's masculinity, and on his conduct of history, turning consciousness away from the ways of nature. With perfect canonical attunement, Jesus will ask, "Who is my mother and who are my brothers?" "Whoever does the will of my Father in heaven," he will answer (Matthew 12:48–50).

From the canonical point of view, Adonai Elohim of the old covenant and the heavenly Father of the new covenant, without human manipulation, could be depended upon to keep covenant promises, to provide for his people what is needed, and to lead history, all history, to a successful conclusion. Through the biblical story, we enter a world of straight time. Time has a definite beginning (a genesis) and a definite end (an eternal Sabbath, or an eschaton). Between the beginning and the end of history, time takes a linear route, a pathway which marks itself off into past, present, and future. The categories of historical time/ space seem absolute, but, in fact, as we now know—not only from mysticism and psychology, but from physics itself—they are relative to other dimensions of consciousness.

The new New Testament situation reflected a new relationship with Yahweh. The remote "Adonai Elohim" became "Abba"—the familiar, intimate, childhood term for "father." Its unprecedented use in relation to Yahweh indicated new terms of intimacy between Yahweh and humanity. Newly invested with the incarnate god, the human person—whatever his biological and ethnic origin—now belonged to Yahweh. All persons (potentially the human whole) were eligible for adoption into the unique "sonship" of the Christ, to become carriers of the living Christ, and thus, in their own unique being, to become personalities who would not dissolve in nature. Christian insistence on the incarnation of Yahweh in history, in this man known to the Judaic world as Jesus of Nazareth (an itinerant, blasphemous, ne're-do-well rabble-rouser), and on a new covenant open to all who believed in this Jesus, was a stumbling block for the Jews, producing the historical impasse that split (and still splits) the canon.

Exegesis VI

It would have been better if they could have squelched those rumors of resurrection and ascension, but it was simply amazing what some people would believe (or so their post-crucifixion thoughts might have gone). Still one would never have expected Paul to succumb to such nonsense. Light from heaven indeed. Light from a light head was more like it. It was one thing, as the Pharisees made clear to Paul, to believe in a general resurrection at the end of history, marking the Jubilee year of the Lord, the establishment of his Kingdom, his power over all nations, his power over death. Quite another to believe that this obviously misbegotten son of Nazereth could be the Messiah, the eschatological son of man — the son of god himself. If it were so, if resurrection had really occurred, then where were the trumpets? Why were the bones of Israel so still? Why were the tombs so quiet? Why was Zion silent? Why were the dispersed not gathering in? Why were all the nations of the world not there to bow down to Judah and her God?

Split Canon and Split History

In the postbiblical world of the Christian era, history and canon go together. The center of the paradigm of history is the Christ. The historical basis of the Christ is the Torah, the covenant between Israel and Yahweh, the struggle of Jacob at the ford into a new kind of consciousness, a Logos consciousness, unembedded in nature. The historical future of the Christ is that moment when the covenant work will be complete, when every person everywhere is a son of Abraham, not through circumcision, but through the receiving of Yahweh's own flesh and blood, through the organic investment of Yahweh in the chthonic flesh, through an inner Christ. Then of course the trumpets will blow, Israel will be made whole again, the dispersed will come forth to join Judah, the dead will come forth to join the living, every knee will bow in Zion, the great Jubilee will occur, for every person will belong to Yahweh. Every person will be a person and safe from collapse into the chthonic. The will of Yahweh will be done on earth as it is in heaven.

The eschaton (the eternal Sabbath of Yahweh), which is yet to come, will be marked by the return (Parousia) of Jesus to a humanity fully invested with his presence and, as Tillich puts it, by a resolution of the ambiguities of history. In this, the great theologian, witness to the twentieth-century holocaust, gives a mild description indeed of the biblical Parousia, involving an apocalyptic confrontation between the Christ and the Antichrist. Jung has a more biblical sense of the transition of history into the eschaton. But Jung would argue that the evolutionary requirements of the eschaton are not fully understood in the biblical myth. Jung looked for a final integration, not a final defeat of the chthonic forces. Enmity between the two great archetypal sons—the *filius microcosmi* of the Logos syzygy, the *filius macrocosmi* of the chthonic syzygy— must be turned to compatibility. Jung's psychology gropes for the incipient beginning of transbiblical myth.

To gain our canonical moorings, we must return from the precipice of history to its center. There at the volatile center, which seemed like an eschaton to some, we find the event of events, the mighty act of all mighty acts, the incarnate Yahweh, the Logos-made-flesh, the Christ. Time occurring before the event of Christ (B.C.) is counted backward from the event of Christ. The Hebraic era, the era which preceded the Christian era, dates back to ca. 3700 B.C. In biblical terms, this was the beginning, the "bereshith" of existence, the genesis of the world. In the biblical view, prior to the Hebraic era, there was nothing—only chaos and an insidious serpent who popped up mysteriously out of nowhere. Prior to the beginning of Israel, the biblical story merely looks for its own mythic foundation, and finds it in a strange, ambivalent "paradise," called Eden. Time after Christ (A.D.) moves forward into the Christian era.

The Christian era (the postbiblical era) continues the incarnational process which begins in Christ. It is continued on two levels—the sacred level, caught up in the numinosity of the biblical myth, and the secular level, which attempts to appropriate the Christic ego for its own use, detached from its myth. The Christian era, by astrological calculations, is afforded two millennia, which makes good biblical sense because it balances the Christic center of history with two millennia of history on both sides. The first millennium is dedicated to capturing the world for Christ, to exorcising the chthonic, to developing a Christic purity of personality with no shadow. The venture is not totally successful. It is circumvented by the problem of "original sin" and requires the constant supervision of the church. (Jesus, of course, as the begotten son of god, had no original sin, so his problem was not the same as that of his followers.) Ethical adjustments had to be made by the church, the guardians of Christian orthodoxy and righteousness.

The second millennium of the Christian era (now drawing to a close) has been dedicated to discovering the secrets of the chthonic realm through the formation of Newtonian-Cartesian science. Now, at the end of the second millennium, we can see where it has led. It has led to a powerful and unexpected unleashing of the chthonic forces, which a church, schooled in repression, can scarcely be expected to accommodate. Jungian and transpersonal psychology seek to prepare human consciousness for the new archetypal demands upon it, for a confrontation between the Christ and the Antichrist, and a transcendence of the time and space of history. The point for now is that history, in the biblical sense, is more than a recording of the events of time. History assumes a theological position and proceeds from within its own myth.

In the early days of the Christian era, the standard measurement of histori- cal time was converted by the Roman Empire from the ancient, agrarian-based, lunar calendar (by which time revolved around the earth) to the solar calendar (which measured the march of the days of history into a purposeful future). Solar timing reflected the dynamic of the masculine principle. It recorded the advent of the gods. It celebrated their triumphant entry into human conscious- ness, their displacement of the goddesses and gods of nature, the abject defeat of the lunar world. Solar timing reflected the biblical sense of history more accurately than the ancient lunar calendar, by which Israel had functioned to distinguish herself in a lunar world. Thus, as Christianity came into prominence—becoming at last the official religion of the Roman Empire—it adopted the new Roman calendar, adapting it to the specifications of its own myth, looping the Hebraic era into solar history—although counting it back- wards, as we have noted, from the christic event.

The new religion, carefully aligning itself with the Hebrew canon, thereby distinguished its god (its solar god, its god of new light) from the pagan gods, who, although they managed to usurp the powers of the goddess world, were, nevertheless, still embedded in nature. Christianity gradually assimilated the solar analogues of Yahweh (Zeus, Apollo, Mithras, to name the most promi- nent) to its own singular, transcendent myth. The god whose first words in human consciousness were "let there be light" was not the sun god. This god was totally transcendent to the sun. He was the solar creator, creating the sun as a measure of his ongoing creative activity. The first day of the biblical week was the first day of "light," the new light of Yahweh (later to be invested in his created sun). Thus the first day of the solar week became the sun's day, or Sunday. On Sunday, the "old history" had begun, the story of human conscious- ness lifted out of the lunar light of nature. Therefore, it was probably no accident that the "new history" began on Sunday with a resurrection. This, the central moment of history, is the moment of Yahweh's supreme triumph over the dark, chthonic realm of nature. It commemorates that moment when the light of ego shone unquenchably, even in the darkness of physical death, even in the realm of decomposition and decay.

New Testament theology had at last to recognize that the eternal Sabbath was not yet, but the new history of Yahweh moved toward it, and toward the general resurrection of the egoic dead. Paul, the great theologian of the day, strikes the salient note:

> For as in Adam all die, so also in Christ shall all be made alive. But each in
> his own order: Christ the first fruits, *then at his coming those who belong to
> Christ* [italics added]. (I Cor. 15:22–23)

I underscore Paul's wording here because it blends the Judaic and Christian
concepts of the resurrection of the dead. Paul has merely converted Jewish
eschatology to Christianity and transposed the eschaton from a first coming to
a second coming of the Christ. Those who belong to Christ, in essence, are
those who belong to Yahweh.

There was a catch, however. Judgment was an important feature of Hebraic
theology. Those who did not justly belong to Yahweh would be rejected by
Yahweh—Israel, if it did not keep its covenant; the individual, if he or she failed
the covenant. There could be mercy, but not at the expense of justice. Justice
could not be compromised. Emphasis on judgment of the individual became
more pronounced, not less so, in Christian eschatology. Christ offered grace, a
grace that brought the ego god into his own process, a grace that abrogated the
wrath of the ego god, and made his Law accessible to the human whole. But
grace did not abrogate the Law, the demand that the person be on one side of
the primal split or the other. Nor, therefore, did it abrogate judgment. The "last
judgment" was depicted in highly personal terms in the New Testament (Matt.
25:31–46). It was the curse (the other side of the blessing) of ego formation,
this demand of personal choice and responsibility, this inability of egoic humanity ever again simply to sink into pre-egoic oblivion, the inevitability of judgment until the task was done.

Christianity establishes more than the ego, however. It establishes what
Jung has called the shadow of ego. It represses "the elemental spirits of the
universe" (Col. 2:20) and puts to death what is "earthly" in the human constitution (Col. 3:5). It discounts, in other words, the ancient lunar-based values. It
sends the chthonic deities to the dark side of the moon. It forms the archaic
unconscious.

Biblical myth indicates, it seems to me, that the mythic and scientific merger, which centers our solar system in the sun, is psychologically analogous to
the centering of ego in human consciousness—not the Self, as is usually supposed. Copernicus merely discovered scientifically what had already been discovered at the mythic level. He brought science up to date, not the soul. The
centering of the Self, in the terms of Jungian psychology, cannot be attributed
to the biblical myth. The biblical myth is the Western solar myth par excellence. It might well be that a scientific discovery of the future will have some
cosmic correspondence to the centering of Self. New science probes in that
direction.

We need to take note of a recent movement in connection with the split
timing of history that attempts to deemphasize the canonical split by renaming

the two eras of history. The Christian era becomes the "common era" (C.E.), and the Hebraic era becomes "before the common era" (B.C.E.). This is a mild concession, certainly not a major overhaul of time, but it seems to have come about out of a desire to minimize the residual tension between Judaism and Christianity, and to release the non-Christian world from calendrical bias. It is indicative perhaps of a new spiritual climate in the Western world, a new Christian humility, a growing awareness that other meaningful faiths (essential in the process of evolution) exist alongside the Christian. Such awareness at a scholarly level gradually raises the general level of collective consciousness, and, as the canonical split loses its divisive charge, the psyche is better prepared to face the other side of history, to meet the extracanonical.

The Forming of Ego

At its inauguration nearly 2,000 years ago, the Christian era considered itself to represent a new era of Yahwistic development, one radically superseding its basic, or "fathering," era, the Hebraic. The Christian era claimed to represent not a transformation of, but the valid continuation of the Hebraic era into the postbiblical world. The New Testament claimed to continue the Old Testament to its orthodox conclusion. This claim, taken on the face of it (as it is usually taken), would seem to render Judaism obsolete. Judaism in its own right was something of an anomaly, and the continued existence of the Jews as a religious entity was therefore problematic. As "killers of the Christ," Jews held a precarious existence in the Christian era. Christianity conveniently forgot the christic words of forgiveness from the cross and seldom recognized that its own actions "killed the Christ," that its recurrent atrocities splashed across the pages of the Christian era violated the Christ within.

Needless to say, Judaism did not accept the Christian verdict of obsolescence. It continues, with obvious justification, to claim its own heritage. In itself, Judaism represents an only slightly less radical accommodation and continuation of the Hebraic era into history. As mentioned previously, in contrast to Christian orthodoxy (correct doctrine), Judaism developed an orthopraxy (correct practice). At the inauguration of the Christian era, at the time when Judah itself was being ground into the dust, Judaism uplifted the Torah. In the constant remembrance of its primal experience, in its constant renewal of its inner being, Judaism continued to find its way in the world's wilderness. I am suggesting that this Torah of the Jews is not merely the primal experience of the Jews, but the core experience of ego formation for the human whole. In line with the psychological view of myth, Judaism enshrines a particular and highly exacting moment in human evolution which belongs to us all, and which has entered the phylogenetic bloodstream of humanity through the Jews.

Christian exegesis must concede that the roots of its faith are as essential to the truth of its faith as the fruit. It is one thing to recognize a developmental process, quite another to discount the earlier features of that process. The New Testament cannot be used without the Old, nor can it be used, as is sometimes the case, in contrast to the Old. The Old Testament can stand on its own; the New Testament cannot. To its credit, biblical theology, based on the theology of Barth, honors the developmental process wholistically and exegetes accordingly. A Jungian hermeneutic, based on Jung's assessment of the trinitarian homoousia, also takes the biblical myth wholistically and gives the framework of ego/self for orienting the monotheistic work of Yahweh within the archetypal totality.

Judaism, for its part, preserves, as Christianity cannot, the historical roots of the biblical myth. The Jewish presence offers history irrefutable proof that Yahweh has acted in history, is acting in history, and it strongly suggests that Yahweh will act again in history in the old way, through the Jews. No other energy could have kept Judaism alive, and it is hermeneutically inconceivable to think that it would be for no purpose. One suspects that the ultimate role of Judaism in the Kingdom of Yahweh will be commensurate with the difficult role of Judaism in the history of Yahweh, that Yahweh will act to justify his firstborn. Translation of the paradigm of history must fulfill Yahweh's unfulfilled promises to the Jews. The struggle of Jacob at the ford between nature and history, between the chthonic world and the Logos world, has yet to receive its eschatological blessing.

What we know now from the Judaic struggle is that history—in itself the paradigm of struggle—is not to be avoided, but encountered. The psychological message is that to move human consciousness prematurely beyond the struggle of history is to prevent an essential actualization, the actualization of ego (the mental ego). This does not mean that we never transcend the paradigm of history; it means that we cannot escape it. In the overall panoply of the world's myths, the biblical myth is the only myth that seriously attaches itself to history. Yahweh, if not the Lord of History, is no Lord at all. And yet, minus the Jews, there is a strong possibility that the biblical myth, particularly the Christian myth, would have gone the way of all myth, detaching itself from history, taking on the qualities of mystery religion, or allegory. Despite the Jews, there is a tendency in this direction.

It becomes hermeneutically crucial to comprehend the difference between an authentic transcendence of the biblical myth into transbiblical myth and an inauthentic detaching of the biblical myth from history. A Jungian hermeneutic is able to take seriously the canonical attachment to history as the medium of ego; but, through the medium of self, a Jungian hermeneutic leads past the dead end of biblical fundamentalism into transbiblical myth. Through the medium of self, a Jungian hermeneutic avoids an absolute concretization of the paradigm of history, and thus Moore's pseudospeciation and fixation.

Judaism (cultivated in the modern world by the biological sons of Abraham) awaits the outcome of the Christian era and looks toward a messianic era, still to come. What for Christianity will be a second coming, for Judaism will be a first coming, and in that event, history, which began with the creation of the Jews, will find its culmination through the messianic restoration of the Jews. Impressed into the soul of Judah is the eschatological expectation of the "great return," the regathering of the diaspora into Jerusalem. Furthermore, in the early, pre-Christian days of Judaism, the diaspora was ontologically expanded to include the resurrection of the living dead of Israel. The Greek vision of an impersonal, ineluctable, unembodied immortality of the soul, which did not connect with history or with personal decision for the god of history, was not for Judah. In the Judaic vision, the end of history affirms the meaning inherent in the beginning of history, and the eschaton is as concretely and personally realized as the genesis of history. Eschatological emphasis is on wholeness and restoration. It completes and makes permanent the work of Yahweh in an eternal arena. In Wilber's terms, it translates the work of Yahweh. Judaic eschatology sees the cessation of the paradigm of history, but it "eternalizes" that paradigm. However, this does not "ultimatize" the Yahwistic paradigm.

Deep in the Christian soul is the same notion, the Judaic notion of the great return. In the deeper struggle of New Testament theology with the canonical split, the culmination of history begins with a restoration of the Jews and a firm rerooting of Christianity in its Hebraic ground. New Testament theology canonized a position best worked out by Paul, who saw and felt keenly the effects of the canonical split. I will summarize Paul's thinking briefly, for it speaks to the mythic destiny of ego and history.

As Paul saw it, in the Christ, the incarnate god of the Jews had opened his presence and his covenant to the human whole. The intention of incarnation was to eliminate the ancient distinction between Jew and gentile, and to bring the whole of humanity into the oneness of Yahweh (Eph. 2:14-16). To Paul's way of thinking, the New Testament way of thinking, this reaching out to the human whole was a move in history by the god of history, a concrete manifestation of the Hebrew god in Jesus of Nazareth. The divisive effects of the incarnation were thus of real theological concern to Paul, and he dealt at some length with the problem (Romans 9-11).

Paul echoes Job in his struggle with the evidence of blatant injustice on the part of Yahweh—his favoritism, his choosing of some but not all, his choosing of one over another, first the Jews, now the gentiles. These strange inconsistencies are not to be equated with the impersonal, whimsical fluctuations of nature. Yahweh does not function by whimsy, but by deliberate and personal choice—"Jacob I loved, but Esau I hated" (9:13). Thus Christianity, although faced in the incarnation with a new situation vis-á-vis god, is not faced with a different god. The god who approaches humanity through a new covenant in the Christ is the same god who approached humanity through the old covenant with Israel.

In the Pauline description of Yahweh, we can recognize the Jungian description of ego. Paul grapples with the troublesome characteristics of an ego god and sets forth the ethical problems of an ego world. Lacking the category of Self, Paul remained embedded in the god. It was his understanding that he dealt with the ultimate god, whose purposes for the continuum of history were ultimate. In Paul's day, the archetypal energy of Yahweh was consistent with the cutting edge of the Self. From a Jungian perspective, it is possible to construe the work of Yahweh as the formation of ego in the phylogenetic field of human consciousness and as the cutting edge of the Self. Paul was keenly aware of the evolutionary importance of the work of Yahweh, and he dedicated himself to its effectiveness, its intended inclusiveness of the human whole. Thus he knew that the wounds inflicted in history (inherent in the very process of the god) would require the healing of history.

It is important to point out, however, that Pauline theology does not lead to the healing of the primal split. Archetypally, the primal split has to do with separation between the archetypal feminine and masculine. Phylogenetically, it is between nature and history. Ontogenetically, it is between body and mind. There is in Paul no sense of an ultimate reconciliation between the old nature (still chthonic and infested with the elemental spirits) and the new nature (initiated in Christ, who had conquered the elemental spirits) (Col. 2). Paul works toward the formation of the christic ego (the mature ego which could master the elemental spirits), but not toward a transcendence of the christic ego. New Testament eschatology stops at this point, with the christic ego as the crown of evolution.

Jungian and transpersonal psychology throw light on the Pauline dilemma. Both of these psychologies suggest that evolution proceeds, both ontogenetically and phylogenetically, by a process of differentiation and transcendence. Splits (or dissociations) in the psyche are produced inevitably as ego (the mental, or logos, ego) is differentiated in human consciousness. Thus evolution also encompasses a kind of inner movement, a reversal of energy, a movement backward or downward to heal the splits and dissociations. Paul seems to have sensed this dynamic. His own mission was at the cutting edge of evolution, the opening of the Jewish covenant to all peoples. Yet he came reluctantly to the conclusion that the intended integration was not an immediate possibility. Its *kairos* (or fullness of time) was not yet. Further differentiation was required— an elevation of the gentiles and a concomitant depression (but not a rejection) of the Jews. In Paul's view, the work of the integrative Christ was proleptic, a seeding of the present for the future; but that future, for which Jews and the early Christians both yearned, was still to come.

Paul writes of the situation of a budding Christianity branching apart from the Jews: "If their rejection means the reconciliation of the world, what will their acceptance mean but life from the dead" (Rom. 11:15). Thus we see that to Paul's way of thinking the healing of the canonical split will precipitate the eschaton, and this in turn will precipitate the resurrection of the dead. Resurrection establishes the completion and the durability of the kingdom of the god of history. Those of this eternal kingdom, whose names are written in the book of heaven, will be clothed with Christic bodies not susceptible to decay nor in any way in thrall to nature. In Paul's words, "the creation itself will be set free from its bondage to decay and obtain the glorious liberty of the children of God" (Romans 8:21). The chthonic world will pass away, but the ego world and all (Jew and gentile) who are debtors not to the flesh, but to the Holy Spirit, who belong essentially to the ego world, will not die. Pauline eschatology does not extend beyond this point in evolution. Biblical eschatology does not embrace what Jung calls the incarnation of Satan, the assimilation of "the dark God who also wants to become man" (1952a, par. 742).

Chapter Twelve

THE ROLE OF ISLAM

The Judeo-Christian myth finds a challenging and disturbing confederate in the Muslim myth. The Koran is, of course, outside the scope of this book. Nevertheless, from a Jungian point of view, biblical hermeneutics cannot ignore the Koran. The science of biblical interpretation must become sensitized not only to the two canons of ego monotheism, but to the existence of that other sacred book of "one god." The postbiblical world is heir, through Abraham, not to two monotheistic faiths, but three. Alongside Judaism and Christianity, Islam represents a third strand of history continuing the Hebraic myth into the postbiblical world. If we subscribe to the thesis that myth holds essential truth, it becomes obvious with each day's news that the exegesis of the Islamic myth, no less than the Judeo-Christian myth, is of crucial importance to the outcome of history.

Islam is a postbiblical development. It was born in the Christian era, but it rejected the underlying assumptions of the Christian era (the begotten Son, the Trinity). It rejected the mighty act of Yahweh in incarnation, thereby reducing the paradigm of history to a pre-Christian level. Islam accepted Jesus, but only as a prophet in a line of prophets beginning with Abraham and culminating with Muhammad. It refocuses covenant history to point beyond the Christ (and Christianity) to Muhammad and Islam. Nevertheless, Koran and Bible, though different in format and tone, stem from the same god, the same general orientation toward history, the same general theological point of view. Although the trinitarian cast of Christianity is suspect to Judaism and Islam, all three canonical strands can be accredited with an uncompromising monotheisim. The chants of the three "people of the book" (as Islam expresses it) essentially mingle: Hear, O Israel: The Lord our God is one Lord—I believe in God, the Father almighty—There is no God, but God. In those chants, we hear the centralizing effects of ego consciousness and its concomitant divisiveness. We hear the beginning of the phylogenetic spread of a universal consciousness.

According to Islam, Muhammad was the last of the prophets of Allah (the one god, the god of Abraham, the ultimate god), and his work set the final seal upon prophecy. The messages of Allah through Muhammad brought to completion all of the messages of Allah to humanity. In a somewhat bizarre twist of mythic irony, the angel Gabriel, who had announced to Mary of Nazareth that she was to bear the begotten son of Yahweh, appears to Muhammad to announce that he, Muhammad, is to become the supreme Messenger of Allah. The angel Gabriel, who seems to have forgotten the "annunciation," makes clear to Muhammad that Allah is not a begetting or a begotten god. Thus, by implication, Christianity is built on a false foundation and cannot be considered as a final faith. Gabriel then proceeded, over an intense period of time, to transmit the Koran (recitation of the divine words of Allah) word by word to the illiterate, but receptive prophet, for the founding of Islam (submission to the will of Allah). Islamic submission to the god of history is through covenant, but a covenant that rejects the biblical covenants, both old and new. Muslims (those who submit to the will of Allah) submit to a covenant viewed as prior to either of the biblical covenants, and yet basic to both.

Islam exists to restore the primordial covenant of Abraham, which was given to Abraham when the paradigm of history was whole, before the splits of history began. Islam, in Muslim eyes, is the original and true covenant of the great god of the covenant with humankind.

The Koran, sent down from heaven, is actually a book of oracles, not a book of history. It is based on history gone astray, a history in which Islam must find its own unique place. It lacks the sharp exchange between humanity and Yahweh, characteristic of the Hebrew/Christian experience. It does not hone the mind in the daily grind of history, thus it retains a rigid superegoic cast, a reliance on external authority, which (despite their quarrel) both Pharisaic casuistry and the Christian emphasis on grace have moved beyond. Muhammad is commanded to say, and he says. Islam is commanded to do, and it does. Nevertheless, these oracles which Muhammad is commanded to say and Muslims to do, are the oracles of the god of history, who, in Muslim eyes, now takes his history out of the hands of Jews and Christians, gives it into the keeping of Islam. Islam thus considers itself to be the religion of the eschaton, and Muhammad is its prophet. On the last day of history, in a familiar eschatological scenario, the dead will be raised from their graves, either to the rewards of heaven or to the fires of hell, according to one's submission to Islam.

Thus the most recent of the monotheistic faiths sees itself as the original. Islam establishes its historical roots not in the Christian era, but in the early beginnings of the Hebraic era, in the pre-Isaac covenant with Abraham. The first traces of Islam are to be found in the Hebrew canon. It roots itself back before Abraham through Shem (the son of Noah who fathered the Semitic peoples). The sons and daughters of Ketura (Abraham's Arabic wife after the death of Sarah) are also the ancestors of Islam. Most notably, however, Islam picked up the ancient tale of Abrahamic Yahwism which pitted Ishmael (Islam) against Isaac (Judaism). The Koran seeks to reverse the effects of this strange domestic intrigue, which was not merely a domestic intrigue, but an episode in the epic struggle of an age—the struggle between matriarchy and patriarchy.

In the biblical tale, Isaac was Abraham's second son, not his first son, and so, by rights of primogeniture, Isaac should have sunk into oblivion, not risen in the egoic ranks of patriarchy. Isaac's own second son, Jacob, would one day follow in his father's footsteps, so a precedent was set which made primogeniture (as everything) subject to the will of Yahweh.

Isaac was born of Sarah, who, despite a certain marital flexibility of the cultural norms, was recognized as Abraham's true wife. Sarah was the wife who was recognized by Yahweh, and this was important. No longer was every woman to be considered sacred because she represented the goddess. Only women in proper relationship to Yahweh were sacred. Not just any woman would do, and the men of the covenant could not be trusted to choose. The patriarchal couple in particular had to be personally chosen by Yahweh. Thus, as Abraham was chosen to "father" the covenant people, so Sarah was chosen to "mother" them. Isaac himself, his birth in Sarah's old age, was of Yahweh's choosing. Isaac was a child of the covenant, the special promise between Yahweh and Abraham. Isaac's belated conception obviously owed nothing to nature and nature's fertility. It obviously owed everything to Yahweh and Yahweh's fertility. So it seems that Isaac was quite a feather in Yahweh's cap. He was Yahweh's answer to the fertile prowess of the earth mother. Isaac's conception, long after the possibility of natural conception, was an early demonstration on the part of Yahweh that he could raise up sons of Abraham on his own. Such a conception and such a birth would go a long way to impress upon a skeptical humanity that anything "She" could do, "He" could do better.

We might say that the birth of Isaac (god laughs) was Yahweh's abiding joke on the earth mother. It was a joke which somewhat later he extended into a macabre charade of human sacrifice, a strange, seemingly uncalled for maneuver that put Abraham's faith and loyalty on the line in a questionable manner. Nevertheless, in the throes of a traumatic interplay between masculine and feminine power, Yahweh succeeded in eliciting a quality of faith from Abraham that no one could ever forget, least of all Yahweh. Abraham's loyalty, in the face of extreme provocation, bound Yahweh to his covenant with Israel for all time. Such faith in the promises of a god was unprecedented in the world before Abraham. It represented a mutation in consciousness that became the basis of the continuing covenant with Yahweh and the Pauline watchword for the opening of that covenant to the world at large two millennia later. Abraham's submission to Yahweh, to the Word come down from on high, was the primal moment of human decision between nature and history. That primal moment would be repeated some years later on behalf of Ishmael, as another young man, Muhammad, the heir of Ishmael, found himself caught between the urges of nature and history, and chose history, submission to the will of Allah, against nature.

We need to grasp the primal moment itself in order to understand its derivatives or its triplication in human consciousness, in Judaism, Christianity, and Islam. An event, which was started as a proper ritual of human sacrifice (in the goddess tradition), turned out to be Yahweh's grandstand pronouncement against human sacrifice (Gen. 22). The tale itself is too well known to require repeating. I need only draw attention to one small detail—that a ram (like the high mountain sheep/goat imaged in the zodiacal Aries) appeared as a substitute sacrifice for Isaac. Isaac was saved from the Great Mother ritual of human sacrifice under the sign of the Ram. The ram was symbolic in human consciousness of the power of the archetypal masculine, the energy exhibited in the world by Yahweh. It was a sign (or a symbol) that followed Israel down through the ages. The shofar, the great horn of the ram, had been blown to summon the twelve tribes of Israel to their first assembly as they entered the "promised land." It would be blown as a summons to the final assembly of the eschaton. Thus the nation of Israel was prefigured and given its archetypal credentials in the episode with Isaac.

Abraham received the blessing of his new god—this Johnny-come-lately to the archetypal scene—for his absolute faith. It was important since only absolute faith could sustain the new god with his new kind of consciousness against the threat of chthonic regression. Abraham, and the descendants of Abraham through Isaac, were appointed as the evolutionary leaders of all humankind. They were the patriarchs—"the fathers," not "the mothers"—of the development of human consciousness. Two millennia or so later, a man named Paul would cash in on this ancient appointment, as he opened the promises of the covenant with the god of Abraham and Isaac to the gentiles. It emphasized, if anything, the split with Ishmael. Ishmael was doubly vanquished.

Down through the ages there would be another such joke on the Great Mother—an Isaac sort of joke, as Paul recognized. Yahweh would laugh again, this time, however, at his own expense. Another son would be led to the sacrificial slaughter. Like Isaac, this son demonstrated Yahweh's fertility, his power to beget. He was an even more radical demonstration, for he had no phallic intermediary, no earthly father. He joined Abraham's progeny on the stage of history, but he was prior to Abraham's progeny. "Before Abraham was, I am," he asserted to his confused countrymen (John 8:58). This son, in himself, was the great I AM, an aspect of the inner aseity of Yahweh. He was clothed in the unique flesh and blood of Yahweh, the essence of Yahweh, fashioned through *hieros gamos*, the sacred marriage of Yahweh and the Spirit, the inner feminine of Yahweh.

Neither the word nor the concept was encompassed in Hebrew vocabulary.

One had to go dangerously close to the Greek to catch the archetypal significance of the strange birth, foreshadowed by Isaac's birth. The womb that bore this new son, however, was the womb of a virgin mother. She was a daughter of Sarah, especially chosen like Sarah, but immaculately conceived for the occasion. This was no ordinary Hebrew mother and no ordinary Hebrew wife. She was, by special appointment of Yahweh, elevated over her husband. It was not something most Hebrew husbands would have accepted, but this husband exhibited the faith of Abraham, and he stuck with his Sarah, no matter the odds. This son, the new Isaac, was also to be saved for history, but in a different way. This time no last minute ram would appear. This son was to be his own ram, a lamb without blemish. This time the sacrifice would take place, amidst a darkening of heaven, a wild sweeping wind, a shaking of the foundations of the earth. This son would be led "outside the camp," outside of the community of the chosen, like a scapegoat—this time not to Mt. Moriah, the place of the Temple, but to Golgotha, the place of the skull, the place of dishonorable death, the place of banishment (Hebrews 13:11-13). He would be crucified as a common criminal among common criminals. So far, it does not sound like a joke, and so far it was not. It was real, this strange sacrifice of Yahweh to Yahweh, this scapegoating of his own inner power of renewal, this taking upon himself of the sins of the world, his own world, his own partial creation, and thus his own sins.

Exegesis VII

The Great Mother must have held her breath, along with all the chthonic powers. Now (or so it would seem to them) they had him, and they would never let him go. This time he had overreached himself. He had trapped himself in a great mother body. As he would find, it was possible to sit in heaven and exercise power over the chthonic realm, and it was possible to work from a living body—for the power of heaven was still viable in a living body. But it was another thing entirely for the power of heaven to be trapped in a dead body—for a dead body would certainly snuff out the great Logos light. And, in one way or another, a great mother body always dies. His death, according to his own standards, was the worst way to die. To the Great Mother it made no difference. At home in bed or on Golgotha, she didn't care. However he died, he, who had promised transcendence of nature, would go down into the darkness of nature, and into oblivion. The world of humanity would recognize once and for all the falsity of this god, who claimed to be the One and Only God, who claimed to supersede nature, who had repressed the chthonic deities. They gave him three days, three days of a nonbreathing body, and then the chthonic realm—itself in captivity to Yahweh—would take Yahweh captive. It would claim the unwanted and disgraced Christ as one of its prisoners, its most illustrious, of course. He may not have been wanted in Israel, but he was wanted in Hell—the Hell of his own making, his own repression. The light of Logos would be extinguished once and for all in that Hell. It would never be seen again in the world of men. There would be no more "world of men." The balance of power would be put back to rights. Persephone would come into her own again. She (the power of the Great Mother's renewal) would no longer be repressed by the repressive powers of patriarchy. Yahweh had never acknowledged the mythic scenario which split the Great Mother and trapped part of her—the renewal part of her—in heaven's underworld, its world of dead "physis." Yahweh had never acknowledged any other diety at all. Such hubris would have to be punished for the sake of the archetypal totality. And now was the time.

So they waited down in the chthonic realm, waited for their chance to recapture the world of men by capturing its most virulent god. They waited three days, but when they went to claim the dead body as their own it was not there. The tomb was empty. The Logos had obviously not died. It had not been snuffed out. Yahweh had transcended his own law and his own first creation, his first Adam. The world of men, the world of egoic humanity, was no longer dependent on his famous Mosaic Law (which, despite all Pharisaic casuistic contortions, they could not keep). Egoic humanity would now belong to Yahweh in some other way—by grace, not by law, it would seem.

Paul, the foremost interpreter of the Christic event, put it succinctly:

> If you live according to the flesh you will die, but if by the Spirit you put to death the deeds of the body you will live. For all who are led by the Spirit of God are sons of God. (Romans 8:13–14)

The great patriarchal trick this time around was that the body of Jesus—the god man—had not been a flesh body. As the Great Mother herself might have put it, it had not been a great mother body at all. It had been composed of the Spirit of Yahweh, his own inner feminine, his own self-contained *hieros gamos*.

Exegesis VIII

She should have guessed it, but there were so many bodies, you couldn't keep track of them all. She took no personal interest. They came and they went, ashes to ashes, dust to dust, she gave, she received—why keep count? Of course, these ego bodies were peculiar, had been peculiar from the beginning. They used her stuff, but gave her no credit at all. They were always complain-

ing, at least those of the Hebrew variety. Now the Greeks were different. The Greeks knew how to appreciate a body. They had never really split off from the chthonic. Of course, the Olympian gods were deplorable. They had brought chaos into the mother world, but still their vaunted egos were much less exalted than this so-called great Lord of the Hebrews, who had named himself Yahweh. You could negotiate with Zeus. Demeter had managed to strike a straight bargain with Zeus. Zeus, unlike this Yahweh, knew where his bread was buttered. Satan still smarted over his thrice outsmarted defeat at the hands of this purely begotten son of Yahweh. "It is written, 'Man does not live by bread alone!'" he had said (Luke 4:4). Well, let him try to have his men live without it. It was small comfort—since patriarchy was patriarchy and even the Olympic version was detestable—but Yahweh was bound to lose out to the Greeks in the world of men. This latest mighty act of his had confused even his own people. Ironically, they thought it was much too Zeusian. Hardly anyone recognized its radical transcendence of her, its utter put-down of the chthonic realm. Thus it was reassuring to know that Aphrodite and Eros, among others, still lived in luxury with the Greeks. That little mother/son pair had a way of keeping things earthy and carnal. This heavenly god—he was a heavenly slob! Used earth as a footstool. But what could you do? He seemed to have some sort of pull in the archetypal totality. Still it would get him someday. She would get him someday through the Greeks. Aphrodite and Eros would see to that. Dionysus and Hermes would carry the Satanic energies into the patriarchy. The thrice greatest Hermes would turn around the thrice outsmarted defeat. The great Hebrew Lord would certainly be brought down to earth, and that inflated, airtight heaven of his, which ruined everyone's view, would be punctured.

But it would not be today. The joke was on her again. It was an Isaac-type joke alright. She now recognized the connection. Yahweh had thrown her off when he failed to substitute a ram. The Jesus body—as, of course, looking back, she should have guessed—had been a Spirit body. Jesus was not composed of her stuff, but of his stuff—his own unique materiality, his own essence. It should have dawned on her when Satan was tossed so summarily from the heaven of Yahweh (Luke 10:18). She should have seen that Yahweh had acquired a new independence from the chthonic. He needed his chthonic connections no longer. It really should have dawned on her when Jesus parried Satan so deftly. No Adam, or no son of Adam, had ever differentiated from Satan so cleanly. And certainly no Eve. But the Eves didn't count. They were such hemmed-in and watched-over creatures, almost completely subdued. The Liliths had been much better. But, of course, no one even mentioned the Liliths in Yahweh's world anymore, except to scare the poor Adams out of their sexual instincts. Lilith had been relegated to the underworld, the murky world of unbelief, the Great Mother world, her own world. No one believed anymore *that Yahweh had actually created the Lilith, scooped her out of the primordial clay, her own prima materia, and created her on a par with Adam. The Great Mother still laughed when she thought of the fabled first night of the two Eden dwellers, with Lilith, like a true great-mother daughter, insisting on top billing (Patai 1967, p. 183). That settled it, of course. There could be no Liliths in Eden. Obviously Adam wouldn't know what to do with a real woman. He had to have that secondary little Eve thing made out of his own rib, for heaven's sake. She couldn't really use the Eves. Satan had succeeded to some extent, but it just got the Eves in trouble, not the men. She had wondered, as a matter of fact, when Yahweh would bring forth his own inner feminine, his own Eve, out of his own rib, so to speak, and make his own stuff. He had tried it with manna. He had come close to a special sort of body with Isaac. Now here it was, a man for all history to see. A man for all history to proclaim. The higher truth, the truth of her own realm, the truth of the archetypal totality, was not for history. It was for the other side of history.*

Again Paul catches the connection:

> For not all who are descended from Israel belong to Israel, and not all are children of Abraham because they are his descendents; but *'Through Isaac shall your descendents be named.' This means that it is not the children of the flesh who are the children of God, but the children of the promise are reckoned as his descendents.* For this is what the promise said, 'About this time I will return and Sarah shall have a son' [italics added]. (Romans 9:6–10)

These were deadly words. They meant that not merely Israel belonged to Yahweh, with his Isaac-type joke. He was claiming the whole face of the earth, the global four corners. All peoples everywhere were to be children of the promise. The Great Mother was now totally defeated, denied her own natural rights in the world of men, imprisoned forever in her own repressed creation.

Or was she? As Jung sees, the mythic prediction would deny this. The Great Mother would begin a new creation of her own. She would bring together her own energy in a new form, more potent than the ousted Satan. There would be no more gentlemanly temptations in a wilderness. Yahweh thrived in the wilderness. This time the Great Mother would lure the enemy down into her own inner being. The egoic ilk would be pulled in over its head. Let them probe and analyze. She would pretend to be passive, inert, inanimate. Then, when they least expected it, she would spring a new confrontation on her own turf. She now knew the strength of her enemy, as she had not known before. He had played his trump card in the Christ. His Christ would now have to confront her Antichrist.

Thus we see the archetypal situation as it developed through Isaac. It is the archetypal situation against which Islam is pitted. It involves Judaism and Christianity, as descendents of Isaac, in a monotheistic tie-in—an uncomfortable tie-in perhaps, but biblically clear.

A Jungian Hermeneutic

The three quarreling sibling offspring of Abraham seem hopelessly divided in the arena of world history today. Monotheistic divisiveness, devoid of cohesiveness, seems to typify the archetypal work of ego. The archetypal wholeness which belongs to Yahweh/Christ/Allah lacks historical expression. And yet, if we are to take the monotheistic myths seriously, we must look for historical actualization. The signs of the times are that we now must look to the symbology of the eschaton. The direction of history must be plotted along the eschatological chartings of ego mythology (Judaism, Christianity, Islam). From the perspective of a Jungian hermeneutic, we can place ego eschatology against the deeper eschatology of the self. This juxtaposition avoids the dead end of biblical and koranic fundamentalism, not by dehistorizing the myths, but by finding that mysterious link between historical and transhistorical consciousness, between egoic and microcosmic being.

It is difficult not to notice the similarities between the monotheistic situation of the world today and the apocalyptic projections of the first century, as it opened the era we now close (Luke 21:23–33). And yet, in the New Testament view, the wave of violence that heralds the end of an era, heralds also the establishment of the Kingdom of Yahweh in human consciousness. It heralds the fulfillment of Yahwistic consciousness, when swords will be beaten into plowshares, and spears into pruning hooks, when nation will not lift up sword against nation, and war will be history (Isaiah 2:4).

Perhaps the fierce message of the Muslim world is that a comprehensive resolution of history must be obtained, one that reintegrates the whole of history, beginning at the beginning of its divisiveness. Only a total resolution can open the postbiblical world of the biblical god to transbiblical myth. Thus the coming of the eschaton (Paul's resurrection of the dead) depends upon the fragmented postbiblical progeny of Abraham coming home to the higher wholeness of the eschaton. The sounding of the last trumpet—the ram's horn, the ancient shofar, which calls the children of Abraham to wholeness—recalls ego to self (I Cor. 15:51–52).

From a Jungian point of view, we need not expect humanity's egoic divisiveness to be resolved at the evolutionary level of Yahwistic monotheism. The canon itself makes clear that ego finds itself, rather than loses itself, as it enters the new age of the Self. The New Testament holds forth the possibility that ego (as its god did not) will not dissolve in the dark, chthonic lower realm of nature. Inherent in the creative wilderness of the eschaton is the emergent possibility that ego is not to be reformed to the old ways of Yahweh, but transformed. Transformation creates a new *prima materia*, a new heaven and earth, a new masculine and feminine conjunction, an androgynous oneness. Singer (1976), as we have noted, refers to this new archetypal conjunction, this marriage between heaven and earth, as an androgynous monotheism, a monotheism beyond ego and the ego god, a microcosmic monotheism that embraces the monistic wholeness of the Self.

I would submit that a Jungian hermeneutic points us first in the evolutionary direction of the phragmos (fence) between this world and the world below. From a Jungian point of view, this inner move of evolution (which, as Paul saw, moves backward to heal the psychic splits of history) must move deeper still into the most basic split of all—the primal split that ruptured in human consciousness when Abraham left Ur to enter the creative wilderness of Yahweh. This is the primal split that preceded Ishmael and ruptured a wholeness prior to the wholeness of which Islam speaks, the archetypal wholeness of the primal pair before the differentiation of evolution. The inner move of evolution must go where neither Torah, nor Gospel, nor Koran can take us, down beneath the biblical genesis and into the chthonic realm it left behind. In Jungian terms, evolution must recover the shadow of the ego world. It must move downward to rediscover the serpent, the lost quality of chthonic consciousness (the nous) which the serpent symbolizes. Evolution must recoup and integrate into ego consciousness the split-off animal/vegetable soul of humankind (the *anima mundi*, or primal world soul). In the hostile situation of repression, Israel must confront its Ishmael. But, even more critically, the Christ must confront the Antichrist. The way up to androgynous monotheism is the way down into the primal split.

It is an endeavor fraught with danger. Success depends upon the strength and maturity of ego. As previously discussed, both Jungian and transpersonal psychology emphasize the crucial importance of ego stability in human consciousness. To quote Jung more fully at this point:

> We therefore need more light, more goodness and moral strength, and must wash off as much of the obnoxious blackness as possible, otherwise we shall not be able to assimilate the dark God who also wants to become man, and at the same time endure him without perishing. (1952a, par. 742)

The collapse of ego, the failure of the paradigm of history, could only negate the tenuous process of evolution. My contention is that the development of ego maturity was the canonical aim, and Paul's focus. The christic mission was to open the Hebraic covenant of ego formation to the chthonic world and to open the chthonic world to the formation of ego.

Paul's work aligns with the archetypal impetus that blossomed in a period of history Karl Jaspers (1953) has called the axial age (800–200 B.C.). Jaspers points out that this period of time saw the widespread emergence of "confessional religions," religious experience that called forth individual response. The prophets of Israel, during this time, were able to find a firm basis for such a development in Israel's covenant with Yahweh and to set forth the covenant ideal in terms that underscored both individual responsibility and covenant inclusiveness. The prophet, Jeremiah, called for a new covenant, a covenant written not on tablets of stone, but upon the heart, a covenant that affected the human constitution from the inside out. Such a covenant would be deeply personal, independent of community. The heart covenant, in the long run, would be capable of development apart from synagogue, or church, or umma. It was the covenant toward which the axial age was geared. It was this covenant that Paul took to the gentiles, recognizing, however, that the work of Christ was proleptic, and the time of fulfillment was not yet.

For the duration of the Christian era, until the Parousia, Paul planted his "people of the promise" in churches. A protective container, a kind of cocoon, beyond and yet comparable to the function of Israel itself, was necessary for the morphological development of ego in human consciousness. Judaism had pioneered the way for such a development with the rabbinic synagogue. Both synagogue and church had the capacity to function independently of nationalism. But the ecclesia of Christ (those called out by Christ) fostered a radical emphasis on the person. It lifted the individual out of all former membership ties (at its most radical, the family). Christianity demanded a second birth, the second one in Christ.

Islam, reverting to nationalism, took an antecedent position on the scale of evolution. Its umma fosters national unity, not personal distinction. Its sense of ego is thus projected onto territory, and it is caught up for now in a consuming hatred of Zionism. The emergence of Zionism out of world persecution recalls biblical eschatology, predictions of a Zionist deliverer and the great return. History today is precisely where history was at its beginning—pitting Ishmael against Isaac, Islam against Israel.

Jung speaks of a transcendent function, a dynamic that moves human consciousness beyond the pitched battles of the ego world. It is a dynamic that gives hope to the ancient, apocalyptic promise of the appearance of the Kingdom of Yahweh, absorbing Abraham's divided progeny into a final wholeness, resolving (again in Tillich's words) the ambiguities of history, healing the conflict between the Christ and the Antichrist.

The work of the Christian era (fed by the three monotheistic religions of Judaism, Christianity, and Islam) has been to develop the mental ego as a durable phylogenetic property of human consciousness, proof against biological death. Thus the era has been studded with communal enclaves for ego formation. Inescapably, however, in incubating ego the Christian era (or the monotheistic era) has also incubated the shadow of ego. Since the great god of ego, in his own aseity, is incomplete, and yet proclaims himself exclusive of other gods (the ancient earth mother, in particular), he generates the enmity of other gods. He generates a primal split between himself and the ancient earth mother with her chthonic minions. Ego must bear the brunt of a hostile archetypal situation, unwittingly of its own making.

It needs to be pointed out that while synagogue, ecclesia, and umma all represent feminine energy (the containing, incubating energy of ego), these institutionalized forms of the patriarchy do not represent the energy of the primal feminine. They represent instead the syzygistic energy of Yahweh, his inner feminine. These containing institutions of ego energy are themselves products of the primal split. Energy pertaining to the archetypal feminine and her chthonic consorts is inevitably left out of ego formation. Ego monotheism, although inclusive of the human whole, is not, as Singer has made clear, inclusive of the archetypal totality.

Paul clearly felt the mind/body split produced by Yahwism. He writes:

> I see in my members another law at war with the law of my *mind* and making me captive to the law of sin which dwells in my members. Wretched man that I am! Who will deliver me from this *body of death*? Thanks be to God through Jesus Christ our Lord! So then, I of myself serve the law of God with my *mind*, but with my *flesh* I serve the law of sin. (Rom. 7:23-25)

Paul, however, did not perceive this primal split as incompletion. He could not see an androgynous monotheism beyond Yahwistic monotheism. He could not see a microcosm beyond the christic ego. His mission was focused on global Yahwism and on a final, historic reconciliation of Jew and gentile (including the children of Ishmael). Paul simply accepted his mind/body split as an evolutionary finality. The important thing was to make sure that mind (the mind of Christ) was in control and fixed on the goal of history (the heaven of Yahweh). Here, flesh and blood could not go. There would be a new and more appropriate body for the christic ego, composed of the stuff of Christ and free at last of the stuff of Satan. In Paul's estimation, there would be no rapproachment with the stuff of Satan, no assimilation of the dark God.

I believe that the cutting edge of the christic mission today cannot be, as it was for Paul, to establish ecclesia. The formation of ego cannot be equated with the formation of church (or church surrogates) in the world. The communal cocoons of ego (synagogue, church, umma) must open into the higher consciousness emerging in transbiblical myth. The egoic institutions must learn to nurture ego without limiting the human personality to ego. If we identify the work of the biblical/koranic god with the formation of ego capacity in human consciousness, occurring within the paradigm of historical time/space, we gain insight into the ongoing requirements of history. If we recognize also, from the perspective of transbiblical myth, the formation of the shadow of ego in human unconsciousness, we gain insight into the future direction of evolution. *Translation* of the ego paradigm would seem to occur through the inculcation of ego capacity in the phylogenetic field of humanity and through the higher development of agapic concern and I/Thou relatedness. *Transformation* would seem to occur through an integration of the chthonic.

The new task of ego is to break through its own paradigm. The new task of evolution is to develop microcosmic being. The world sits on the edge of history, awaiting the last judgment of the god of history. The canon has led us to this hour, but it cannot lead us beyond. The basic canonical criteria (Hebrew, Christian, Islamic) must find new definition in the gnostic depths and heights which extracanonical accounts preserve. The canon has developed history. The extracanon must develop eschatology.

Chapter Thirteen

GNOSTICISM

*T*races of gnosticism are found in many ancient cultures, notably in Egyptian, Babylonian, Iranian, and even Indian culture (Puech 1957, p. 55). Scholars find compelling evidence today that gnostic thought arose not as an aberration of hellenistic Christianity, as widely believed, but as an independent phenomenon in its own right. Nevertheless, even though the movement of gnosticism seems to have affinities, and perhaps even historical connection, with Eastern thought, its major development has occurred in conjunction with, and in counteraction to, Western traditions—Judaism, Christianity, and Hellenism. (Sufism, as noted, is a gnostic counteraction within Islam.) Gnosticism seems, in the main, to have constituted a general protest movement against the development of the mental ego in the human psyche, opposing the primacy and the alleged ultimacy of the Logos gods.

In relation to the biblical tradition, gnosticism now appears as a pre-Christian phenomenon. It existed in reaction to the Hebrew world view before Jesus of Nazereth entered upon the scene. It appears as a movement peculiarly inimical to Yahwism, constituting a direct response to the emergence of Yahweh in human consciousness (Fuller 1962, p. 124; Perkins 1980, p. 16; Quispel 1973, p. 4; Rudolph 1983, p. 276–277). The "protest exegesis" of the "external text" (to follow Rudolph) surfaced as a critique of the Hebrew canon, but it gained impetus in early Christian times as it sought to give gnostic interpretation to christic experience. Out of this counterprocess to biblical development, a gnostic theology emerged, more developed perhaps in its opposition to orthodox Christianity than in any of its other forms. Of those now extant, only the hermetic tradition (esoteric Hellenism) shows comparable development.

Gnostic theology, like biblical theology, hinges on narrative. Gnostic myth, like the biblical myth, tells a story of archetypal energy at work in human consciousness. It employs a biblical cast of characters, but the cast is greatly expanded in gnostic myth. The characters are seen from a different angle and very differently assessed. Gnostic myth tells a story of a plurality of archetypal energies in a dynamic and often conflicted process of evolution. It devalues the god of the biblical story and points toward a god far above any gods known in the human milieu. The high god of the gnostics provides energy for the teleological pull beyond Yahwism.

Gnostic myth also rejects the milieu of history as a suitable setting for human existence. The meaning of human life is not to be found in the categories of historical time/space. It can be found only beyond the veil of history and the god of history. As we have seen, gnostic literature spells out fantastic systems of thought, involving three phylogenetic levels of humanity, or three cosmogonies (the hylic, the psychic, the pneumatic). These three cosmogonies (or strands of humanity) offer a striking correlation with the chthonic humanity of nature, the Logos humanity of history, the eschatological humanity beyond history (or the matriarchal, patriarchal, androgynous; or the prepersonal, personal, transpersonal). The least attractive cosmogony from the gnostic point of view is the one that is stuck in history. The least attractive god is the biblical god. The early gnostics, in their attempts to circumvent this god, either fell into the regressive domain of the hylic or followed an ascetic path into the pneumatic heights, ignoring in either case (as Judeo-Christian orthodoxy did not) the demands of historical time/space.

A comprehensive view of this intricate and complicated theology is far beyond the scope of this book. I will merely sketch in broad outline those general aspects of gnostic thought that are most pertinent to the development of a Jungian hermeneutic. Such a sketch should not be taken as a general consensus of opinion in regard to gnosticism. Scholars have yet to arrive at a general consensus in this regard. My intent is to show that gnostic myth provides a mythic analogue to Jung's psychological construct of the self, and that the process and counterprocess of biblical development relate in the overall process of evolution as ego relates to self.

The Gnostic Critique

A compelling ambition seems to have burned in the heart of the gnostic world. It was an aim in stark contrast to the missionary aim of the Christian world. Gnosticism was not interested in transporting the worship of Yahweh to the world at large. It was interested in transcending the worship of Yahweh from within. The gnostic movement sought to tap human personality into a sphere of consciousness that was not reducible to the singular worship of the biblical god, and it sought to disconnect the work of Christ from the work of the Hebrew god. It sought to redirect the movement of Christianity from geographical expansion to consciousness expansion. The missionary target of gnosticism was not the heathen and pagan worlds of polytheism, but the orthodox Christian world of Yahwistic, patriarchal monotheism (Rudolph 1983, p. 92).

Pagels (1979) presents evidence that gnostic Christianity was concerned primarily with the fuller development of the individual. It opposed the orthodox practice of mass conversion and baptism, which seemed to lose the individual within the church. Perkins (1980) does not find this evidence pursuasive (p. 176n) but, nevertheless, describes "the true gnostic soul as one which concentrates on its immortality and is not bogged down in passions and conflicts" (p. 192). Gnosticism, in other words, attempted to lead the individual beyond the passions and conflicts of history, which is the world of Yahweh, and beyond the ecclesia of Yahweh. It attempted to hatch the individual personality system out of the ego cocoons of Pauline Christianity. It looked for a metamorphosis into microcosmic personality.

It is important to recognize, however, that orthodoxy, at its own level, did not neglect the development of individuality. Both Judaism and Christianity brought the individual out of an impersonal and uncovenanted pagan relationship with the deities of nature and into a personal and dialogic relationship with Yahweh. Both of the canonical traditions insisted on individual responsibility to Yahweh and to the world at large. Orthodox Christianity extended the possibility of personal relationship with Yahweh beyond the confines of Judaism, claiming that through incarnation Yahweh had personally extended himself into the world beyond Judaism.

Thus the issue which presents itself in the orthodox/gnostic controversy is not between nonindividuality and individuality, but between ego-centered individuality and the higher individuality of the microcosmic personality. Orthodox individuality was centered in personal relationship with Yahweh and based on faith. It was pitted against the danger of regression into polytheism and paganism. Gnostic individuality moved the development of personality beyond the purpose of Yahweh. It moved the personality into gnosis, or into a consciousness beyond the consciousness instilled by Yahweh. It was pitted against the danger of being trapped in Yahwism, of not transcending Yahwism. Thus the orthodox/gnostic controversy, as noted, provides the mythic details of the struggle of evolution between three phases (or paradigms, or cosmogonies) of human consciousness—the matriarchal prepersonal, the patriarchal personal, the androgynous transpersonal. This general evolutionary scheme, as we have seen, is encompassed in Jungian psychology and more specifically spelled out by Singer and Wilber as the theoretical underpinning of evolutionary process.

Gnostic sensibilities were appalled at the emergence of a god in human consciousness who identified himself as the great I AM and presented himself in the human arena as the only god. In the opinion of gnostic seers, this posture represented a dangerous hubris, an overweening pride, an absurd inflation, and they called the intruder Yaldabaoth, "the child of chaos," and, therefore, "the accursed god" ("The Apocryphon of John," Robinson 1978). The gnostics sought to transcend Yaldabaoth by belittling him and by attacking the canonical claim that his world was "good." He is presented in gnostic myth as an archetypal pretender, a fraudulent creator, a mistaken maverick of a god. His boasted independence, his emergence into human consciousness seemingly out of nowhere, hid a scurrilous connection to the archetypal feminine and to a prior cosmogony. It hid also the reality of a reality higher than Yahweh, the reality of the unknown god above Yahweh, to whom Yahweh must give account.

Gnosticism, although it concentrated its ire on Yahweh, tended to survey the whole process of evolution with a jaundiced eye. From the gnostic point of view, the act of archetypal differentiation, in itself, was an act of hubris, an act of overweening pride. In Jungian terms, it courted the psychological danger of inflation (of confusing one aspect of reality—one's own—with the whole). Therefore, evolution, which begins with archetypal differentiation, could not begin without hubris. The first act of hubris (the creation of the chthonic cosmogony) was committed by the archetypal feminine herself.

The archetypal feminine was known as Sophia (or Wisdom) by the gnostics (there were other names for and many different facets of the archetypal feminine). Gnostic wisdom seems simply to imply knowledge of the pleroma, an awareness of the archetypal totality of all that is, an acceptance of one's own particular place within the whole. Wisdom, then, is the opposite of hubris. The hubris of Sophia becomes wisdom. Sophia is trapped in physis (the physicality of her own creation), but not hubris.

In the gnostic view, all deities struggle between wisdom and hubris. All deities but one, however, manage to remain in touch with wisdom. The one who did not was the Logos god, whose task was to constellate ego in human consciousness. In so doing, he rendered his connections with Wisdom (Sophia) unconscious. He repressed the archetypal feminine and her chthonic creation. The monotheism of Yahweh opposed itself not only to the polytheistic realm of nature, but also to the higher androgynous monotheism of the unknown god. Yahweh is to the gnostic pleroma as the monotheistic ego is to the monistic self.

As gnostic myth goes (I will skim it briefly, patching varied sources together), Sophia, in spite of her basic wisdom, had independent thoughts. She wanted to create on her own, without the aid of the archetypal masculine ("The Hypostasis of the Archons," Robinson 1978). This desire or passion of Sophia occurs against the wholeness of the pleroma, moving against its syzygistic nature. The pleroma then (for purposes of my own interpretation of gnostic myth) might be designated as the Higher Syzygy, akin to the taichitu model of the Tao. Jung speaks of the androgynous nature of the gnostic god in *Memories, Dreams, Reflections* (1961, p. 201). Singer recognizes the gnostic god as the ultimate source of androgynous monotheism. He/She provides the ultimate teleological pull into the monistic Self.

Out of her original hubris, as gnostic myth records it, Sophia rashly initiated the process of evolution by differentiating herself from the original totality, or pleroma. In splitting herself off from the pleroma, Sophia thereby destroyed the inner harmony of the pleroma. On her own (or, as I would argue, out of her inner syzygy), Sophia brought the material (hylic) world into existence. Her hylic cosmogony existed as a shadowy, chaotic creation. It was a chthonic (earthy) creation, which lay, like an abortion, outside "the nature of the immortals" (or outside the pleroma). This hylic cosmogony of matter was cut off and separated from the high world of the spirit (the pneumatic world). It was a deficient cosmogony, forgetful of the pleroma. The pneumatic world had no involvement in the hylic cosmogony; nevertheless, without a pneumatic deliverer or redeemer, this chthonic breeding ground was destined to exist in its own hopeless round of biological repetitiveness and decay ("On the Origin of the World," Robinson 1978).

Confronted with this situation, there is mythic evidence of a split in Sophia ("The Gospel of Philip," Robinson 1978). An aspect of Sophia—the higher, incorruptible Sophia—is able to return to the pleroma. Another aspect of Sophia is mired in the chthonic world. In this aspect she was known as the Sophia of death, or the little Sophia, known as the earth mother. The gnostics depict her in her regressive form, since they contrasted all forms and phases of evolution with the wholeness of the pleroma and a higher consciousness. The little Sophia was trapped in her own creation, unable to return into the higher fullness of herself. But, in her fallen wisdom, the little Sophia of death recognized the error of her ways and repented. She longed to return to the pleroma. She longed for a deliverer, or redeemer, from the unknown god.

Then, out of this hopeless chaos, there emerged a new god and a new cosmogony (the biblical Genesis). The new god brooded over the hopeless chaos and used it to mold his own creation. He utilized the existing *prima materia* (since he had no substance of his own), but he breathed himself (his own essence) into it. He created a new being (an egoic man) "ex nihilo," out of his own mind, in his own image. He called the man Adam (earth), since Adam was composed of the hylic stuff of the little Sophia (the earth mother), and he pronounced his work "good," since Adam carried the living image of Yahweh in his earthen form. Adam, as the image of Yahweh, not surprisingly in the light of the taichitu, turns out to possess an inner Eve (in Adam's eyes, the mother of all living). This is highly suggestive, an implicit admission that the god in whose image Adam was created possessed an inner feminine of his own. The biblical god constituted a smaller syzygy, and his work proceeded out of the smaller syzygy, apart from the Higher Syzygy. The Logos god loses touch with the pleroma. He exhibits a detestable tendency toward hubris, presenting himself as the ultimate god. This new god, seemingly complete in his own smaller syzygy, became known to the orthodox as Yahweh, but to the gnostics, as noted, he was known (among other things) as Yaldabaoth, "the child of chaos."

Thus the main problem with Yahweh/Yaldabaoth was that he had no wisdom (not in the gnostic sense). He lacked a vital sense of pleroma. He possessed a vital knowledge of himself. He thought of himself as the only god. As as emanation of the masculine principle, this controversial deity transcended the hylic creation, and thus he had the ability to usurp it, to make it his own. And so he did, in a process recorded and sanctioned in the biblical story and still sanctioned, in the higher theological echelons of the Judeo-Christian tradition. Yahweh's essential purpose (to the gnostics anathema; to the orthodox holy) was not to redeem the hylic world and bring it into the pleroma, but to dominate it, to bring it into conformity with himself.

It was obvious to the gnostics that the new god would not rescue Sophia. Instead, he severely repressed her. He not only demeaned and devalued her, but he denied his intrinsic connection to Sophia (and to the pleroma). He left the great gnostic Sophia (her corruptible half) trapped in matter (physis), and he treated physis as inaminate matter subject to his exclusive control. Through the agency of his own inner feminine, he set about recasting the hylic world into his own image. He appropriated hylic material, but he made it his own. He reanimated it with himself (his own breath) and created a world radically distinct from the chthonic world. It was a Logos world, a world where the Word was supreme, an ego world created in the image of the Logos god (Yahweh, the great I AM). The gnostics called it a psychic world. It contrasted with the hylic world below and the pneumatic world, as yet to unfold, above. Gnosticism struggled against Christian orthodoxy to assert that the Christic appearance of Yahweh (his trinitarian unfolding) derived from a pneumatic, not a psychic, source.

Sophia and Yahweh

Given Sophia and given Yahweh, a peculiar mythic situation evolves. We are faced with a primal conflict, a primal split. The biblical myth sees Yahweh's side of it. Gnostic myth takes the point of view of the pleroma.

Egoic humanity was embodied. It was clothed in the chthonic flesh and blood of the hylic world, but it was imbued with the transcendent Logos capacity to dominate the body. Ego, deriving from the masculine principle (the primal, lower manifestation of this principle), was now externalized as Adam and proceeded through Adam to dominate the new cosmogony. The archetypal feminine herself (as the Sophia of death, or the little Sophia, or the earth mother) was repressed, but the inner feminine of the masculine principle was externalized in Eve. Eve was the second attempt at providing a mate for Adam. The first mate, Lilith, as accounted for in kabbalistic tradition, had been molded like Adam, directly from the chthonic clay (Zohar I, 34b). She had proven much too unruly for Adam, however. She had assumed the prerogatives of a goddess. Eve, therefore, was a corrective. She was not molded directly from the chthonic material. She was drawn from the rib of Adam, bone of his bone, flesh of his flesh. Eve was intended as a perfect helpmate to Adam, a true reflection of the inner feminine of Yahweh. She was intended as the mother of egoic humanity, or the mother of "all living" (for, at this phase of evolution, in the emerging ascendancy of the biblical myth, only the Logos cosmogony was considered to be alive). Through the hylic flesh of Adam, however (even though once removed), Eve, too (although less intractable than Lilith), proved susceptible to the realm of the archetypal feminine (the lower Sophia, the earth mother). It soon became obvious that the chthonic world was alive, although to Logos consciousness it appeared as the realm of death, a realm that swallowed up ego.

A representative from the chthonic world was not long in approaching Eve (as the most susceptible member of the new humanity) and pointing out to her, from the point of view of the mother world (with nous, or gnosis, or wisdom), the flaws and inconsistencies in Yahweh's world. Yahweh was not appreciative of this uninvited visitor to his new creation. He preferred that his inconsistencies be ignored. He did not care to try to explain his own logic to this slithery, underworld demon. So he retreated to his monotheistic position, totally denying that there could be any other point of view, although his persons now knew better. They now knew that ego reality was not total reality. They now knew "evil," or what Yahweh had defined as evil. They now knew the snake, the serpent of chthonic instinctuality. He is sometimes called Saboath, the "lord of the powers." He is sometimes called Beelzebub, the "lord of the flies." He is sometimes called Lucifer, the "bringer of light." He is most often called Satan, the "adversary." Whatever his name, it is generally agreed that he belongs to Sophia. He worships Sophia, and, like her, he resides simultaneously in the lowest depths and highest heights of the archetypal totality ("On the Origin of the World," Robinson, 1978).

After the snake's visit, Adam and Eve are possessed of a hidden gnosis which Logos cannot destroy. What is destroyed, in the episode with the snake, is the paradise of Yahweh's world. The people of Yahweh's world are no longer in ignorance of the chthonic world. Their knowledge is no longer confined merely to ego knowledge. They are already pushing against the limits of Yahweh. Drastic punishment is inflicted upon Adam and Eve for their venture into gnosis, providing a perpetual reminder that Yahweh, and not the snake, is the god to obey. Thus Adam and Eve bring a conflicted progeny into a conflicted world, a progeny in drastic conflict with its own creator. This conflict is heightened by the dramatic tragedy of Cain and Abel (Gen. 4:1–16). Cain follows the way of the agricultural matriarchy, with its regressive callousness of the sanctity of the individual. Abel, a keeper of sheep, is a prefiguration of the canonical Christ.

The dilemma of ego is that ego, with its strange requirement of singular identity, cannot form in human consciousness if the human psyche is contaminated with other gods. The ego god cannot create in his own image if he cannot command exclusive attention. Ego is weak and prone to collapse. If it collapses, it dies, for the chthonic world does not preserve egos. The chthonic world knows nothing of egos and really nothing of death – since to die is merely to reenter the earth mother. Thus the snake was a bit misinformed when he promised a deathless life. The god of ego cannot risk such propaganda. He must expel all distracting energies and proclaim himself "the only god." Human consciousness, therefore, becomes the exclusive preserve of Yahweh – except for an indefatigable tendency (most obvious in the daughters of Eve) to "sin," to have knowledge (or gnosis) of the prior cosmogony, the chthonic world created by the already repentant Sophia.

Gnostic myth saw clearly the hypocrisy of ego. The much-vaunted good creation of the biblical god was, in gnostic opinion, but the evidence of a gigantic archetypal misadventure, an unredeemed hubris. The difference between Sophia and Yahweh lay in Sophia's recognition of the error of her ways, her repentance, her yearning to reenter the pleroma. In the opinion of the gnostics, it was now Yahweh's turn to see the error of his ways and repent. His monotheistic hubris was much deadlier than Sophia's. It is here, over the issue of Yahwistic repentance, that gnosticism takes up its voluble interchange with orthodox Christianity. Orthodox Christianity, like Yahweh, was not appreciative of this independent "other godly" point of view. It preferred to ignore the hypocritical partiality of ego. Orthodoxy took the view that Yahweh was what he claimed to be – ultimate god. *He* needed no repentance. Humanity did, especially that part of humanity who listened to the snake and to gnosticism.

In the view of orthodox Christianity, Christ had redeemed the world from the sins of a weak humanity by taking upon himself the punishment of those sins. Christ was Yahweh incarnate. He had entered the world directly from Yahweh. He was begotten by Yahweh. He was Yahweh. Orthodox Christianity was never able to explain the origin of the snake, but it asserted, nevertheless, that Christ had overcome the snake. The orthodox Christ had come, not to rescue the gnostic Sophia, but to rescue the whole of humanity from her influence. The canonical Christ had come, not to deliver the gnostic Sophia into some far off, irrelevant pleroma, but to deliver Yahweh into the world at large. The orthodox Christ had come, not to transcend Yahweh, but to establish the permanency of Yahweh's world (the durability of ego even in the face of the Sophia of death, the devouring earth mother).

In gnostic eyes, such a solution did not redeem the situation, but compounded the original error. The hubris of differentiation was not redeemed. The pleroma was not restored to its original fullness. The world of Yahweh, claiming ultimacy, stuck out like a sore thumb in the fragmented pleroma. In gnostic opinion, the redeemer could not come from Yahweh. Redemption of the false world of Yahweh could not be accomplished by the false god himself. The redeemer must be sent from a god transcendent to Yahweh, a god of higher omniscience than Yahweh, who would rescue humanity *from* Yahweh, not *for* him. The redeemer must be a pneumatic personality, not an historical person, and not composed of hylic flesh and blood.

In gnostic eyes, the incarnation was "docetic" (meaning appearance or seeming). The docetic Christ had only *seemed* to be contained in body. He had only seemed to be Adamic (earthy). He had only seemed to belong to Yahweh's cosmogony, to have suffered and died in that cosmogony and for that cosmogony, as Jesus of Nazareth. In gnostic reality, the docetic Christ was not clothed in hylic materiality. He was not interested in the conflicts and passions of history. He was pneumatic, composed of a spiritual stuff, transcending the hylic/psychic conflicts of Yahweh's world.

Pitted against the gnostic point of view, orthodoxy struggled to draw its own distinction between the physical being (and consciousness) of Jesus (as the "new Adam," or as "new being") and the physical being (and consciousness) of the "old Adam" of the biblical genesis. This complicated issue has never been resolved in Christian theology. As Rudolph points out, "Gnosis raised a problem which could not be solved with the categories of the dualism current in antiquity" (1983, p. 372).

The dualism of antiquity was the dualism of matter and spirit. Body, even psychic (or ego) body, was hylic and opposed to spirit. For the "old Adam" this had indeed been the case. Psychic humanity had been molded from hylic material, the original stuff of the gnostic Sophia, or the earth mother. New Testament theology recognized, however (in a muted way), that this was not true of the Christ. He was not of the "molded" progeny. He was born uniquely of a virgin, and his body was not susceptible to material decay. His body was immune to hylic sin and death. He could move through the gates of hylic death into psychic permanence. He gave substance to Yahweh's pure being. He was the pure stuff of mind, uniquely begotten from the essence of Yahweh himself. He closed the ontological gap between Yahweh and his own creation, inserting the reality of Yahweh, like yeast, into the on-going phylogenetic process of human evolution. The Christ represented Yahweh's victory over the hylic. He established a permanency of personality which transcended the hylic with its sting of physical death. He did not move human consciousness into the restored pleroma. He moved it into the Kingdom of Yahweh, the kingdom of the monotheistic ego.

New Testament theology hinted that the Christ was uniquely embodied, but, in the face of gnosticism, it was more concerned to assert his historical concreteness and reality. In the face of the gnostic threat, to disidentify Yahweh and Christ, New Testament theology emphasized the historical reality of the Christ, his actual death, his actual burial, his actual suffering. The essence of the gospel was that, in the Christ, Yahweh had deliberately taken human suffering upon himself. He had sinlessly and redemptively suffered the sufferings of humanity, even unto physical death. Through incarnation, he had irrevocably given himself to humanity, with the purpose of bringing all of humanity into his own covenant and into his own heaven. Christ was fully Yahweh and fully human (spelled out, amid much controversy, in the Council of Nicaea, A.D. 325, but most emphatically in the Council of Chalcedon, A.D. 451).

There is, nevertheless, a masked docetic tinge to the incarnation. The trinitarian dogma of homoousia (one god in three persons), which, as Jung points out, makes of the trinitarian unfolding a self-contained divine drama (1948, par. 226), means that the incarnation contains the unique substance of Yahweh and owes nothing to the chthonic stuff (the *prima materia*) of the Great Mother. Jung's emphasis on the homoousia is in striking and simultaneous concert with the work of his somewhat ignored countryman, Karl Barth, who prevailed upon the theological world to turn back to its patristic basics. Jung's categories, however, his spectrum of consciousness with an ultimate human potential beyond Yahweh, remains in definite contrast to Barth. The dilemma for patristic theology, which Rudolph points out, is that between the dichotomy of matter and spirit, there was no intermediate precedent by which to describe the unique substance of the incarnation of Yahweh. The nearest precedent for a nonchthonic materiality was the wilderness manna, the "bread" which had come down from heaven, not up through the earth (Ex. 16:15). The gospel of John (6:41-59) drew the comparison and the distinction. The body of Jesus had come down from heaven, like the manna. Like the manna, it fed humanity, but, unlike manna, to partake of this bread (through the eucharist) insured eternal life. The source of this bread, however, like the manna, was Yahweh. For John, as for the Christian canon as a whole, the purpose of the Christ was the fulfillment of the work of Yahweh, not a trancendence of Yahweh.

The difficult problem of the nature of the flesh and blood of Christ is not solved in the orthodox/gnostic controversy. The very intensity of the issue prevented a solution. Jung's thinking, however, suggests an orthodox/gnostic answer. It is one which Jung himself does not press, but which I shall consider in the study. We can combine his thinking at this point with the work of biblical theology to establish the trinitarian aseity of Yahweh and the establishment of the milieu of history. From this, it follows that the "begotten" flesh and blood of Jesus derives from Yahweh. (Again, in the Barthian view, it is Jewish flesh.) It is of the very essence of Yahweh—not from the hylic creation and not from the pneumatic sphere. The Christ enters and redeems the Yahwistic milieu of history—the second (psychic) cosmogony, not the first (hylic) cosmogony of nature, nor the third (pneumatic) cosmogony beyond history.

The gnostics, as we can recognize today, were ahead of their time. They lived in the time of Yahweh, but their god was the god beyond Yahweh, the Omniscience higher than Yahweh. They saw through the visible world of Yahweh and recognized the fallacies of Yahweh's creation because they belonged not to Yahweh's creation, but to a higher cosmogony. They represented a higher breed of humanity, which functioned at a more advanced level of phylogenesis. They represented Wilber's growing tip, the seeding of a new critical mass. They stood at the apex of human potentiality, the apex of human transcendence, and they recognized the androgynous potential of human transformation from lower to higher dimensions of consciousness. They considered human personality to be potentially more conscious than Yahweh and Yahweh's humanity. They considered the serpent in the Garden of Eden to be wiser than Yahweh and potentially transformative of Yahwistic consciousness. The noetic serpent worked with the gnostic redeemer to tap human personality into the wisdom, the nous, the gnosis, which was beyond the Word, the Logos, of Yahweh, and to release a petrified, rocklike consciousness from the limiting grip of Yahweh. The gnostic redeemer would open this closed, rocklike consciousness. This was in contrast to the orthodox redeemer who built on it.

In the gnostic view, the ascending soul was in danger of being entrapped in Yahweh's cosmogony, in a world embroiled in the throes of history and which sought to sustain history. The human psyche was in danger of being confined to a world that encouraged martyrdom for the sake of history, rather than a transcendence of history into higher consciousness (Rudolph 1983, pp. 94–95). Gnosticism could see the dangers of Yahwism. What gnosticism apparently could not see was the evolutionary necessity of Yahwism, the necessity of a slow tempering of ego, the 2,000 years of Pisces (or the Christian era).

Gnostic Feminism

Gnostic criticism cut against the grain of Yahwism by valuing the feminine. To the prophetic core of Yahwism, the gnostic world opposed the gnostic wisdom of Sophia. To the apostolic core of Christianity, it opposed Mary of Magdala. At immediate stake was the validation and continuation of the Hebrew patriarchy in a Christian world. Also at stake, as I will contend, was the long range development, or differentiation, of a third version of the feminine (to be distinguished from the lower and higher Sophia) and the preeminence for the time of the Christian era of the archetype of trinity.

Mary of Magdala, the enigmatic and troublesome female follower of Jesus, became the great heroine of the underside gnostic drama. The canon minimized her presence among the disciples and played down her strange relationship with Jesus. The gnostics played up the evolutionary significance of the Magdalene. In *this* Mary, as opposed to Mary of Nazareth, the gnostics detected traces of the primal feminine repressed by Yahweh. The Magdalene had inherited the credentials of the great gnostic Sophia (both lower and higher), and thus she possessed a superior gnosis, a capacity unavailable in Yahweh's world and denied to the twelve ("The Gospel of Mary," Robinson, 1978). Therefore, the Magdalene, in contrast to Mary of Nazareth, could not be contained in the canon and creeds of orthodoxy. She was easily converted from the canon to star in gnostic myth and to provide a focus for the feminist protest exegesis of gnosticism.

As I read the myths, Mary of Magdala represents the higher and lower Sophia. Mary of Nazareth represents a third strain of femininity, brought into greater prominence in Christianity, which can be characterized as the inner feminine of Yahweh.

As the gnostics saw it, stalking the patriarchal twelve into the Christian era was the problematic femininity of the Magdalene. Gnostic exegesis located the nexus of the conflict within the canon itself. The drama shadowing the canon had two protagonists. There was Peter (as the "Rock," the leader of the patriarchal twelve, the carrier of ecclesiastical authority, the prime apostle of the Christian era) and there was Mary of Magdala (as the canonical representative of the great archetypal feminine herself, the carrier of a superior gnosis, the prime apostle of the eschatological era yet to come). It was a heady situation. Canonical myth picked up the historical side of it. Gnostic myth picked up the same story, but from the extrahistorical side.

The gnostic view of this mythic/historical situation is traced (extracanonically, of course) most notably in the "Gospel of Mary," the "Gospel of Thomas" (Robinson 1978) and "Pistis Sophia" (Schmidt and MacDermot 1978). The main point of the shadow story is that the Magdalene, whom the twelve reject, is beloved by Jesus. Her gnosis, which the disciples resent, is valued by Jesus. She emerges in the gnostic tradition as a thirteenth apostle (where the apostolic tradition, itself, places Paul). The Magdalene in gnostic myth becomes not merely a canonical enigma whose time is past, but the leader of an extracanonical, feminist tradition, whose time will come. Like the great gnostic Sophia, she was devalued and repressed for the time of the Christian era, but gnostic myth skips over the Christian era. It moves to the eschaton and plays out an eschatological drama, ahead of its time. At the advent of the gnostic redeemer (the Parousia, not the first coming, of the Christ), the Magdalene (as the little

Sophia) would be rescued and returned to the pleroma. Both principles – the archetypal masculine and feminine – would enter into their own inner fullness, or wholeness, and from this they would reunite them in the Higher Syzygy of the pleroma. The unheralded love affair between the first-century pair would be consummated in the gnostic pleroma.

Despite the high drama which attends the gnostic rescue of the feminine, feminist expectations of today are sometimes disappointed in gnostic myth. Particularly in its later stages, gnostic myth seems to take a developmental point of view that accepts the evolutionary necessity of patriarchy, and by extension, the necessity of ego formation. In the final analysis, gnostic myth is posed against the ultimacy of matriarchy as well as patriarchy. It does not advocate a return to matriarchy. It insists that ultimately the feminine principle must be rescued from the lower phase of evolution and integrated into a higher phase of evolution. Gnostic myth (as does Jungian psychology) moves against feminist attempts to deontologize the masculine and feminine principles and to romanticize matriarchy.

The surprising twist of the gnostic drama, however, is not so much its tacit acceptance of patriarchy; it is rather the assertion, on the part of Jesus, that Mary herself can be made male (the Gospel of Thomas). Mary can possess the capacity of masculine leadership on a level of equality with the twelve. She is capable of uniting with an inner masculine (the Logos masculinity which Jesus provides), just as he himself, as he dramatically demonstrates to Mary, is capable of uniting with an inner feminine (a femininity which, judging from the context, she provides) (Jung 1951, par. 314, citing Epiphanes).

The joining of Mary (made whole through an inner marriage with Logos) and Jesus (made whole through inner marriage with the gnostic feminine) represents the eschatological possibility of ultimate wholeness. Jung often refers to this ultimate potentiality as (among other terms) the quarternity. Gnosticism speaks of it as the restored pleroma. The femininity of the Magdalene (which gnostic myth upholds) is different from canonical femininity. It is important to note that the canon does not touch this ultimate, quarternitarian wholeness. It does touch, however, the possibility of a trinitarian wholeness, which only recently has begun to surface, primarily in the work of biblical theology. We will return to this later, especially as we move into the conceptual field of biblical theology. The gnostic sense of both coequal sexuality and contrasexuality within the monistic polarity of the pleroma vividly parallels Jungian psychology, and it brings valuable hermeneutical insight to bear on biblical exegesis. It moves toward a clearer discrimination between trinity and quarternity. It moves toward a clearer explication of the syzygistic nature of both the archetypal feminine and the archetypal masculine. Gnostic myth sent forth an early beacon pointing us beyond both matriarchy and patriarchy, toward androgyny.

To return to the myths, "Pistis Sophia" (faithful wisdom), suggesting a certain degree of gnostic resignation, sums up the orthodox/gnostic controversy somewhat benignly. The account leaves the orthodox hero, Peter, with a hopeless lack of gnosis and emphasizes his continued opposition to women, and yet, in spite of this, it recognizes a hopeful quality of mercy in the "Rock." "Pistis Sophia" seems to be a kind of temporary gnostic farewell to the Christian era, a way of saying that the superior gnosis of the Magdalene, although blocked during the Christian era, awaits the eschaton—the culmination of the Yahweh/Christic story, the transformation of the Yahweh/Christic world.

Gnostic eschatology, it seems to me, blends at this point with biblical and koranic eschatology. We can begin with Paul as he stands at the center of the paradigm of history. The deliverer will come from Zion. That would fit the Parousia—the first coming was from Zion and the second coming will connect with the first. Zion, as the spiritual center of the paradigm of history, will bring the paradigm to a close. The deliverer will restore not only the wholeness of Israel, but the primordial wholeness of history. In this, he will fulfill the mission of Judaism, Christianity, and Islam. The three offspring of Abraham will recognize their essential oneness, their one common root. In this recognition, the fullness of the paradigm of history is actualized. Thus the paradigm of history, in its fullness, can link at the end of the Christian era (as it could not link in the first century) with the gnostic phase of evolution, whose time has come. The new deliverer (the Parousia in Zion of the Christ) will rescue Sophia and restore the wholeness of the pleroma, thus bringing together (as previously noted) the differentiated masculine and feminine, each with an inner syzygy fulfilled, into the Higher Syzygy. This is tantamount (as we will see) to the *mysterium coniunctionis*, the alchemical ultimatum of evolution to which Jung subscribed. It is tantamount also to the androgynous monotheism described by Singer. The aim of gnostic feminism, as Singer recognizes, is not feminism per se, but androgyny.

Chapter Fourteen

CONCLUSION

*I*n conclusion I would like to offer an overview capturing the essence of the hermeneutical position of this study and setting the stage for an extended study of the biblical story in the light of a Jungian hermeneutic.

A Hermeneutical Overview

About 4,000 years ago a new god emerged in human consciousness. His entry seemed unpropitious at best, incommensurate with the established order of the times, but nevertheless presaging a general transition in human affairs. Nameless at first, this new god set about separating out of the mass of humanity a people peculiar to himself, to exist in the world as a people in covenant with him and for whom there were to be "no other gods" (Exodus 20:3); a people who, according to his covenant promise, would "father. . . a multitude of nations" (Genesis 17:5). True to his promise, the god, who came to be known as Yahweh, during his approximately 4,000-year span (a moment in evolutionary time), has become indeed not merely the tribal god of an obscure people, but the monotheistic father-god of Western civilization, more powerful perhaps in his impact on human consciousness than any other deity.

The Bible presents what can be called an "official" revelation of this god. It constitutes an inspired biographical account of his distinctive, foundational work in human consciousness. The Bible conforms to a canon (a rule or standard) by which we can see the germination of Yahweh's specific energy in the phylogenetic field of human development. He heralded a consciousness so new that it required a standard of its own by which to define itself. At that disruptive moment in evolution, there was no outside reference in human consciousness by which to come to grips with the strange and innovative energy of the god. Only Yahweh himself could provide that standard. Thus the Bible, the canonical account, furnishes a definitive story of the god called Yahweh. His activity, his intent, his aseity are "revealed" in the canon and extended into history through the Judeo-Christian tradition.

The claim of the canon is that we find in Yahweh the highest and ultimate expression of deity. The claim of the canon is that Yahweh has displaced all other gods. The canon, in effect, informs us that there are "no other gods." There is "one god" who lives in heaven, and he rules the earth from his heavenly position above it. He is superior to nature. He is superior to humanity. He is ontologically distinct from nature and from humanity. He is not made of the same chthonic, earthy "stuff" of which humanity is made. Nevertheless, he has breathed his essence into the primordial stuff of nature, and out of the primordial substance he has created "persons." The persons are intended to reflect him, to actualize his aseity in the time and space of history, to do his will on earth as it is done in heaven.

The Hebrew canon is extended in the Christian tradition to include the event of the god's incarnation in the human milieu. The Christian canon asserts an essential mystery: that is, that out of his own intrinsic being, or out of his own aseity, at a particular point in the time and space of history, Yahweh, the totally transcendent god, has "begotten" himself. Out of his own substance, distinct from the primordial stuff of nature, he has presented himself concretely in the human arena; and through his own unique incarnation he revises his own creation. He creates his own humanity anew. It is a mystery which has inspired intense theological controversy and generations of creeds. It is an evolutionary riddle which is not yet understood.

Against the backdrop of this canonical enigma, the psychology of Carl Jung has provided a breakthrough in our time concerning the powers and the potentialities of divinity. Jung met these powers from a fresh empirical point of view and recognized that what seemed to impinge from without were the powers of foundational, archetypal energies at work in human consciousness. The powers of divinity are thus to be understood as innate and indigenous to human existence. They are not ontologically alien to humanity, but rather comprise a macrocosmic totality to which all of humanity is heir. Oneness, in Jungian terms, is monistic, an integration of multiple energies. True oneness is not monotheistic, the exclusion of all archetypal energies but one. All of the archetypal energies inherent in the macrocosm seek to actualize, or to distinguish themselves, in human consciousness, through a process of differentiation and reunion. It is a developmental process that expands the field of consciousness, spiralling it upward (and sometimes downward) as humanity evolves. The developmental process is both ontogenetic and phylogenetic, pertaining both to the individual and to humanity as a whole. The evolution of human consciousness is still in process. At this point in evolutionary time it has produced the individual personality system, but it has produced a personality system inherently in conflict. Evolution now moves beyond its current conflicted system toward the development of microcosmic personality, a system that transcends egoic conflict, a system that replicates the fullness of the macrocosmic totality.

Jung's psychology opens the way for an understanding of divinity inclusive of, but not limited to, the archetypal energy of the god called Yahweh. For Jung, as noted, there are other goddesses and gods, other archetypal energies at work in human consciousness. Myth records humanity's experience of them. The biblical story represents but one myth, the myth of the god called Yahweh. It is, as noted, the "official" myth of Yahweh, and thus it is our primary source of understanding Yahweh. Jung views the trinitarian unfolding of Yahweh, revealed in the canon, as a self-contained drama, involving an inner marriage, or *hieros gamos*, and a "begetting," or incarnation. His thoughts on the matter strew significant clues to the strange, unresolved riddle of the incarnation of Yahweh, the god-man called Jesus. These clues lead to a radical view of the meaning of the biblical trinity and the incarnation, but a view which is nevertheless implicit in Christian dogma.

The canonical accounts unite in viewing Yahweh as ultimate god. There are, however, extracanonical accounts of the experience of Yahweh that "see" him differently and experience his energy differently. From Jung's point of view, these sources must be considered in understanding the archetypal work of Yahweh in human consciousness.

What did and does the god called Yahweh accomplish in human consciousness? What did and does Yahwistic energy provide which otherwise would be lacking in human consciousness? What did and does Yahwistic energy not provide? What would be lacking in human consciousness if the prevailing premise of the canon (the premise of Yahwistic ultimacy) were to constitute final truth? Granted the move toward wholeness, how can a god, whose thrust it has been to displace other gods, finally come to coexist in harmony with other gods? How does a god who sought to make goddesses obsolete make peace with the goddess world? How may we interpret, reinterpret, and further illumine the canonical accounts of Yahweh? Is there inherent in Jung's psychology, in spite of its challenge to the canon, a new hermeneutic for biblical interpretation? It is my contention that such is indeed the case.

In the perspective of Jungian and transpersonal psychology, there is a spectrum of consciousness reflecting the overall evolutionary story. This spectrum unfolds in the human psyche through the powers of divinity, encompassing both pre-Yahwistic and trans-Yahwistic levels of consciousness. As previously noted, these distinctions are based on the recognition of three basic evolutionary levels of human consciousness, or three cosmogonies. The concept of the threefold stages of the evolution of consciousness, implicit in the writings of Carl Jung, is further explicated in the writings of June Singer (1976, 1983) and Ken Wilber (1980, 1981).

The three stages can be summarized as follows. The *first* is a prepersonal, or pre-ego level of consciousness, dominated by the feminine principle. It is thus matriarchal in its arrangement of human existence. The *second* is a personal, or ego level of consciousness, dominated by the masculine principle. It is thus patriarchal in its arrangement of human existence. The *third* is a transpersonal, or transego level of consciousness. This third stage opens a dialogue between ego and a higher center of consciousness which Jung called the Self. It is dominated by a reunion of the differentiated feminine and masculine principles and is thus androgynous in its arrangement of human existence.

Ego consciousness constitutes the second phase of the evolution of human consciousness. Humanity as a whole exists today in this second evolutionary phase. Ego consciousness is introduced and established in human consciousness largely through the archetypal energy of Yahweh. A reading of the biblical story in a Jungian framework suggests that the archetypal purpose of the work of Yahweh during his 4,000 years of evolution has been to "father" ego capacity in human consciousness, to differentiate the faculties of the human mind out of a prior undifferentiated embeddedness in "mother nature."

From this point of view, Yahweh represents the personal creator god, not of primal humanity, but of egoic humanity. His creative activity describes a second cosmogony in the overall evolutionary process. He moves human existence out of prepersonal fusion, both in nature and in social membership. He moves human existence into a state of personal and interpersonal awareness, with all the contingencies of existence such awareness entails: "knowledge of good and evil" (Genesis 2:17) and a consequent knowledge of mortality (Genesis 3:22); a new "dominion over" nature (Genesis 1:28); a new understanding of time. Time was stretched out in the consciousness of the people of Yahweh, bypassing the cyclical rhythms of nature, clocking instead the speeded-up process of linear history. As the primacy of historicity surpassed the primacy of nature, so patriarchy, rooted in historicity, overruled earth's ancient matriarchy, the nursery of humanity's infancy, rooted in nature and nature's redundancy. Yahweh's act of creation is the transformative thrust of Logos masculinity, and in that thrust the character of human life takes on its now familiar dimensions.

Yahweh's act of creation couples in the biblical myth with his act of redemption, his "new creation" in Christ. The egoic mode of existence cannot stand on its own merits. It begins in ruthless alienation from a prior totality, the original matrix of life. It is subject to the devouring pull of that matrix. Only its god's personal incarnation in the throes of history could secure egoic humanity against collapse into the primal, prepersonal past. Only its god's victory over primal death could secure egoic humanity for a durable future beyond primal death. Only its god's assumption of the "sin" inherent in his own creation could save egoic humanity from the god's wrath.

Jungian and transpersonal psychology imply a transbiblical hermeneutic and theology, in which the personal mode of existence finds a transcendence beyond its own transcendence of nature, a transformation beyond biblical redemption, an eschatological future beyond the biblical future. Transbiblical theology opens egoic existence (including its quick and its dead) to a re-rooting in a larger totality, a re-connection with the archetypal feminine, a re-centering of human personality beyond the centeredness of ego.

Finally, in the eschatological new age of transpersonal being, the microcosmic personality becomes the measure of all things, because in the microcosm the macrocosm finds at last its own centeredness.

BIBLIOGRAPHY

Unless otherwise indicated, biblical quotations are from the *Revised Standard Edition of the Holy Bible*, © 1946, 1952, and © 1971, 1973 by the Division of Christian Education of the National Council of Churches in the U.S.A.

The Koran is translated by R. Bell, *The Qur'an, Translated with a Critical Rearrangement of the Surahs*, 2 vols. (Edinburgh: T. and T. Clark).

Avens, R. 1984. *The New Gnosis: Heidegger, Hillman, and Angels*. Dallas: Spring Publications.

Barth, K. 1936. *Church Dogmatics*. 4 vols. G. T. Thompson, trans. New York: Charles Scribner's Sons.

Bohm, D. 1980. *Wholeness and the Implicate Order*. London: Routedge and Kegan Paul.

Boorstin, D. J. 1985. *The Discoverers: A History of Man's Search to Know His World and Himself*. New York: Vintage Books.

Buber, M. 1970. *I and Thou*. W. Kaufman, trans. New York: Charles Scribner's Sons.

Capra, F. 1982. *The Dead Sea Scrolls*. New York: Gramercy Publishing Co.

Coward, R. 1988. For and beyond the personal: a response to Andrew Samuels' "Beyond the Feminine Principle." Harvest 34:147–151.

Edinger, E. 1984. *The Creation of Consciousness: Jung's Myth for Modern Man*. Toronto: Inner City Books.

_____. 1988. The relation between personal and archetypal factors in psychological development. *Psychological Perspectives* 20, 2:263–280.

Eisler, R. 1987. *The Chalice and the Blade: Our History, Our Future*. San Francisco: Harper and Row.

Eliade, M. 1969. *The Quest: History and Meaning in Religion*. Chicago: University of Chicago Press.

Fordham, M. 1985. *Explorations into the Self*. Library of Analytical Psychology, vol. 7. London: Karnac Books.

Fuller, R. H. 1962. *The New Testament in Current Study.* New York: Charles Scribner's Sons.

Grof, S. 1985. *Beyond the Brain: Brain, Death, and Transcendence in Psychotherapy.* Albany, N.Y.: State University of New York Press.

Hall, J. 1986. *The Jungian Experience: Analysis and Individuation.* Toronto: Inner City Books.

Heisig, J. 1979. *Imago dei: A Study of C. G. Jung's Psychology of Religion.* Lewisburg, Pa.: Buchnell University Press.

Huxley, A. 1970. *The Perennial Philosophy.* New York: Harper and Row.

Jaspers, K. 1953. *The Origin and Goal of History.* M. Bullock, trans. New Haven, Conn.: Yale University Press.

Jung, C. G. 1921. *Psychological Types. CW*, vol. 6. Princeton, N.J.: Princeton University Press, 1971.

_____. 1940. Psychology and religion. In *CW* 11:3–105. Princeton, N.J.: Princeton University Press, 1969.

_____. 1944. *Psychology and Alchemy. CW*, vol. 12. Princeton, N.J.: Princeton University Press, 1953.

_____. 1948a. Foreword to Harding: *Woman's Mysteries.* In *CW* 18:518–520. Princeton, N.J.: Princeton University Press, 1950.

_____. 1948. A psychological approach to the dogma of the trinity. In *CW* 11:107–199. Princeton, N.J.: Princeton University Press, 1969.

_____. 1951. *Aion. CW*, vol. 9ii. Princeton, N.J.: Princeton University Press, 1959.

_____. 1952a. Answer to Job. In *CW* 11:355–470. Princeton, N.J.: Princeton University Press, 1969.

_____. 1952b. Forward to White's *God and the Unconscious.* In *CW* 11:299–310. Princeton, N.J.: Princeton University Press, 1969.

_____. 1954a. On the nature of the psyche. In *CW* 8:159–235. Princeton, N.J.: Princeton University Press, 1969.

_____. 1954b. Transformation symbolism in the Mass. In *CW* 11:201–296. Princeton, N.J.: Princeton University Press, 1969.

_____. 1955–1956. *Mysterium Coniunctionis. CW*, vol. 14. Princeton, N.J.: Princeton University Press, 1970.

_____. 1965. *Memories, Dreams, Reflections*. A. Jaffe, ed. R. and C. Winston, trans. New York: Vintage Books.

Kuhn, T. 1962. *The Structure of Scientific Revolutions*. Chicago: University of Chicago Press.

Litvak, S., and Senzee, A. W. 1986. *Toward a New Brain: Evolution and the Human Mind*. Englewood Cliffs, N.J.: Prentice-Hall.

Lovelock, J. E. 1979. *Gaia*. New York: Oxford University Press.

Loye, D. 1983. *The Sphinx and the Rainbow: Brain, Mind, and Future Vision*. Boulder, Colo.: Shambhala.

MacLean, P. D. 1973. *A Triune Concept of the Brain and Behavior*. T. J. Boag and D. Campbell, eds. Toronto: University of Toronto Press.

Meier, C. A. 1988. Science and synchronicity: a conversation with C. A. Meier. *Psychological Perspectives* 20, 2.

Mendenhall, G. 1973. *The Tenth Generation: The Origins of the Biblical Tradition*. Baltimore: The Johns Hopkins University Press.

Monick, E. 1987. *Phallos: Sacred Image of the Masculine*. Toronto: Inner City Books.

Moore, R. L. 1987. Ritual process, initiation, and contemporary religion. In *Jung's Challenge to Contemporary Religion*, M. Stein and R. L. Moore, eds. Wilmette, Ill.: Chiron Publications.

Neumann, E. 1954. *The Origins and History of Consciousness*. R. F. C. Hull, trans. Princeton, N.J.: Princeton University Press.

_____. 1955. *The Great Mother: An Analysis of the Archetype*. R. Manheim, trans. Princeton, N.J.: Princeton University Press.

Pagels, E. 1979. *The Gnostic Gospels*. New York: Random House.

_____. 1988. *Adam, Eve, and the Serpent*. New York: Random House.

Perkins, P. 1980. *The Gnostic Dialogue: The Early Church and the Crisis of Gnosticism*. New York: Paulist Press.

Pribram, K. 1971. *Languages of the Brain*. Englewood Cliffs, N.J.: Prentice-Hall.

Prigogine, I. 1980. *From Being to Becoming: Time and Complexity in the Physical Sciences*. San Francisco: W. H. Freeman.

Prigogine, K., and Stengers, I. 1984. *Order Out of Chaos: Man's Dialogue with Nature*. New York: Bantam Books.

Puech, H. 1957. Gnosis and time. In *Man and Time: Papers from the Eranos Yearbooks*, J. Campbell, ed. Princeton, N.J.: Princeton University Press.

Qualls-Corbett, N. 1988. *The Sacred Prostitute: Eternal Aspect of the Feminine*. Toronto: Inner City Books.

Quispel, G. 1973. The birth of the child. Some gnostic and Jewish aspects. In *Eranos Lecture 3: Jewish and Gnostic Man*. Dallas: Spring Publications.

Robinson, J. M., ed. 1978. *The Nag Hammadi Library in English*. New York: Harper and Row.

Rudolph, K. 1983. *Gnosis: The Nature and History of Gnosticism*. R. M. Wilson, trans. New York: Harper and Row.

Samuels, A. 1988. Beyond the feminine principle: a post-Jungian viewpoint. *Harvest* 34:67–76.

Schmidt, C., and MacDermot, V. 1978. *Pistis Sophia*. NHS IX. Leiden: E. J. Brill.

Sheldrake, R. 1987. *A New Science of Life: The Hypothesis of Formative Causation*. Los Angeles: Jeremy P. Tarcher.

Singer, J. 1976. *Androgyny: Toward a New Theory of Sexuality*. Garden City, N.Y.: Doubleday. Reprinted as *Androgyny: The Opposites Within* (Boston: Sigo Press, 1989).

_____. 1983. *Energies of Love: Sexuality Re-visioned*. Garden City, N.Y.: Doubleday. Reprinted as *Love's Energies* (Boston: Sigo Press, 1990).

_____. 1984. The yoga of androgyny. In *Ancient Wisdom and Modern Science*, S. Grof, ed. Albany, N.Y.: State University of New York Press.

Singer, J., and Loomis, M. (1984). *Interpretive Guide for the Singer-Loomis Inventory of Personality*. Palo Alto: Consulting Psychologists Press.

Sperry, R. W. 1988. Structure and significance of the consciousness revolution. *Re-Vision*, 11, 1:39–56.

Stein, M. 1987. Looking backward: archetypes in reconstruction. In *Archetypal Processes in Psychotherapy*, M. Stein and N. Schwartz-Salant, eds. Wilmette, Ill.: Chiron Publications.

Stevens, A. 1982. *Archetypes: A Natural History of the Self*. New York: Wm. Morrow and Co.

Terrien, S. 1985. *Till the Heart Sings: A Biblical Theology of Manhood and Womanhood*. Philadelphia: Fortress Press.

Tillich, P. 1951. *Systematic Theology.* 3 vols. Chicago: University of Chicago Press, 1964.

Toynbee, A. 1946. *A Study of History.* Abridgement of vols 1–6. D. C. Somervell, ed. London: Oxford University Press.

Ulanov, A. 1981. *Receiving Woman: Studies in the Psychology and Theology of the Feminine.* Philadelphia: Westminster Press.

Vyshelawzeff, B. 1968. Two ways of redemption : redemption as a solution of the tragic contradiction. *The Mystic Vision: Papers from the Eranos Yearbooks,* J. Campbell, ed. Princeton, N.J.: Princeton University Press.

Wehr, D. 1985. Religious and social dimensions of Jung's concept of the archetype: a feminist perspective. In *Feminist Archetypal Theory: Interdisciplinary Re-Visions of Jungian Thought,* E. Lauter and C. S. Rupprecht, eds. Knoxville, Tenn.: University of Tennessee Press.

Westman, H. 1983. *The Structure of Biblical Myths: the Ontogenesis of the Psyche.* Dallas: Spring Publications.

Whitmont, E. 1983. *Return of the Goddess.* New York: Crossroad.

Wilber, K. 1980. *The Atman Project: A Transpersonal View of Human Development.* Wheaton, Ill.: The Theosophical Publishing House.

_____. 1981. *Up from Eden: A Transpersonal View of Human Evolution.* Garden City, N.Y.: Doubleday.

_____. 1982. Physics, mysticism, and the new holographic paradigm: a critical appraisal. In *The Holographic Paradigm and Other Paradoxes: Exploring the Leading Edge of Science,* K. Wilber, ed. Boulder, Colo.: Shambhala.

_____. 1983a. *Eye to Eye: The Quest for a New Paradigm.* Garden City, N.Y.: Doubleday.

_____. 1983b. *A Sociable God: A Brief Introduction to Transcendental Sociology.* New York: McGraw-Hill.

INDEX

Abel, 176
Abram (Abraham), 16, 23, 38, 75, 83,
  90, 104, 110, 146–147, 153,
  156–160, 163–166, 182
active imagination, 40, 137
Adam, 47, 96, 126–127, 134, 150,
  161–163, 173–175, 177
  Edenic, 68, 89
Adam Kadmon, 89, 135
Adonai Elohim, 146
agape, 111, 143
Age of Bronze, 109
Age of Iron, 109
agriculture, 33
alchemy, 15, 57, 65, 69, 73, 85,
  121–125, 127–128, 131, 135
Alexander the Great, 42
Allah, 21, 156–157, 159, 164
amplification, 137
anatomy, 28, 30, 38, 51, 55, 59
androgyny, 14, 17, 26, 29, 31, 37, 58,
  63–69, 80, 88–91, 111–112, 124,
  129, 135, 145, 165, 172, 179,
  181–182, 186
anima, 51–52, 57–59, 63–64, 88
anima mundi, 165
animus, 39, 51–52, 57–59, 63–64, 81,
  88
annunciation, 157
Answer to Job (Jung), 46, 125–126,
  132–133, 135–137,
Anthropos, 89, 135
Antichrist, 37, 46, 52, 54–55, 66, 87,
  93, 123, 126–127, 148–149, 163,
  165, 167
anti-Semitism, 85
Aphrodite, 42–43, 162
apocalypse, 100
  see also eschaton
Apollo, 149
Aquarius, 91, 127, 132, 137
archetypal energy, 24, 28, 32, 52,
  65–66, 71–73, 82, 93, 95–97, 102,
  109, 111–112, 140, 154, 169,
  184–186
  see also libido
archetypal essence, 21–23

archetypal feminine, 10–11, 28–30,
  36–38, 42, 50, 52, 55, 58–59, 63,
  65–66, 73–75, 81–82, 87–89, 91,
  107, 123–126, 129, 131, 133, 140,
  142, 154, 167, 172, 174–175,
  180–181, 187
archetypal image, 21, 23–25, 110
archetypal masculine, 10–12, 28–30,
  35–37, 42, 46, 50, 52, 63, 65–66,
  72–74, 82, 87–89, 91, 124, 126,
  129, 140, 154, 159, 172, 181
archetypal totality, 7, 10, 29, 53–54, 57,
  60, 66, 73–74, 77, 86, 92, 94,
  111–113, 115, 120, 122, 126–127,
  131, 133, 143, 152, 161, 163, 167,
  172, 175
archetypes, 13, 19–20, 35, 38, 66, 73,
  103, 105, 110, 112
  ego, 16, 31, 123, 126, 131
  of trinity, 131, 135, 180
  wise old man, 64
  wise old woman, 64
Aries, 126–127, 145, 159
artist(s), 110
Assumption of Mary, 125
astrology, 64, 126, 148
atman, 78
atomic fission, 79
axial age, 166

Baal, 44, 142
Babylon, 169
baptism, 171
Barth, K., 152, 178
Beelzelbub, 175
behavior, 103
  human, 63, 107, 114
  sexual, 63
  see also sexuality
behaviorism, 71, 95, 103, 114–115
bene Yisra'el, 25, 33, 42, 47, 56, 84
Bell, J., 99–100
Bible, 8, 21, 37, 141, 156, 183
  Christian, 142
  Hebrew, 142
biblical criticism, 139
biblical myth (story), 3, 5–9, 11, 14,

MacDermot, V., 180
MacLean, P. D., 105, 112–113
macrocosm, 6
mandala, 29
manna, 178
Mark, 104
marriage, 69
  sacred, 64, 66
Mary of Magdala, 179–182
Mary of Nazareth, 124, 157, 180
masculine, 10–12, 29–30, 36–40, 46, 50,
  57–58, 63–64, 88, 112, 124, 131,
  142, 149, 158, 165, 174, 181–182,
  186
  see also archetypal masculine
  chthonic, 23, 38–39
masculinism, 39
masculinity, 67–68, 139, 146
  chthonic, 53, 81–82
  Logos, 58, 64, 72, 81, 83, 123, 140,
    181, 186
  phallic, 81
Mass, 134
materialism, philosophical, 71
mathematics, 116
matriarchal culture, 16
matriarchy, 17, 23, 26, 31–32, 38–39,
  44, 63, 81–84, 158, 176, 181, 186
matter, 88, 98–99, 122, 128, 130,
  173–174
  vs. mind, 73
  vs. spirit, 26, 177–178
Matthew, 104, 146, 150
Meier, C. A., 25
Memories, Dreams, Reflections (Jung),
  119–120, 122, 172
memory, 113
Mendenhall, G., 84
messiah, 147
microcosm, 6
Middle Ages, 46, 73–74, 122
mind, 73, 88, 96, 105, 112–114, 134,
  136, 146, 154, 157, 167, 173, 177,
  186
  of man, 139–141
Mithras, 149
Monick, E., 39
monism, 10, 30–33, 36, 39, 58, 63–64,
  68, 80, 89, 92, 126, 131, 165,
  172–173, 181, 184
monotheism, 30–31, 36, 64, 89, 92,

110–111, 121, 126, 130–131, 143,
  152, 156–157, 171–172, 183–184
  androgynous, 64, 68, 165, 167,
    172–173, 182
  Yahwistic, 89, 164, 167
moon, 108, 150
Moore, R. L., 6, 16–17, 20, 104, 143,
  153
morphic resonance, 15, 17, 20,
  103–105, 135
morphogenetic fields, 103
mortality, 186
Moses, 47, 110, 127
mother, 23, 124, 146, 158–159, 173,
  175
  -daughter relationship, 123
  -son relationship, 23
  -world, 122–123, 132, 175
Muhammad, 156–157, 159
Muslims, 157, 164
mysterium coniunctionis, 39, 44, 57–58,
  63–65, 69, 89, 91, 129–130, 134,
  182
mysticism, 146
  biblical, 87
myth, 35–36, 97, 102, 104, 109, 122,
  140, 151–152, 180, 185
  and science, 3
  function of, 27
  Muslim, 156
  transbiblical (new), 97, 101, 105,
    136, 126, 139, 148, 152, 164,
    168
  see also biblical myth
mythic membership, 32–33, 82–83, 107,
  109
mythology, 16, 37, 40, 110, 121
  Greek, 23
  primitive, 39

natural sciences, 3–4
nature, 3–5, 8–9, 16, 30–33, 36–37, 40,
  43–44, 46, 52, 54–55, 71–74, 81,
  83–84, 90, 95–96, 98–99, 107, 115,
  120, 127, 130, 132, 134, 142, 144,
  146–147, 149, 152–155, 158–159,
  165, 170, 172, 179, 184, 186–187
  physical, 81
Neumann, E., 15, 39, 81
neurology, 97, 105–113
neurosis, 11
New Androgynes, 91, 145